What You Should Know About the War Against America's Public Schools

Related Titles

The War Against America's Public Schools:
Privatizing Schools, Commercializing Education
Gerald W. Bracey
Order No. 0-321-08073-4

When Children Are Abused: A Teachers Guide to Intervention
Cynthia Crosson-Tower
Order No. 0-205-31962-9

Creating Safe Schools for All Children
Daniel L. Duke
Order No. 0-205-32018-X

Teachers and the Law, Sixth Edition
Louis Fischer, David Schimmel, and Cynthia Kelly
Order No. 0-321-08210-9

How to Get Grants and Gifts for the Public Schools
Stanley Levenson
Order No. 0-205-30887-2

Human Relations in Educational Leadership
Ronald W. Rebore
Order No. 0-205-32212-3

Instructional Leadership: A Learning-Centered Guide
Anita Woolfolk Hoy and Wayne K. Hoy
Order No. 0-205-35497-1

For further information on these and other related titles, contact:

College Division
Allyn and Bacon
75 Arlington Street
Boston, MA 02116
www.ablongman.com

What You Should Know About the War Against America's Public Schools

Gerald W. Bracey

Boston   New York   San Francisco
Mexico City   Montreal   Toronto   London   Madrid   Munich   Paris
Hong Kong   Singapore   Tokyo   Cape Town   Sydney

Senior editor: *Arnis E. Burvikovs*
Series editorial assistant: *Christine Lyons*
Manufacturing buyer: *Andrew Turso*
Executive marketing manager: *Amy Cronin Jordan*
Production coordinator: *Pat Torelli Publishing Services*
Cover designer: *Suzanne Harbison*
Editorial-production service: *Stratford Publishing Services, Inc.*
Electronic composition: *Stratford Publishing Services, Inc.*

For related titles and support materials, visit our online catalog at www.ablongman.com.

Portions of this book first appeared in *The War Against America's Public Schools: Privatizing Schools, Commercializing Education*, Gerald W. Bracey, copyright © 2002 by Allyn & Bacon.

To obtain permission(s) to use material from this work, please submit a written request to Allyn and Bacon, Permissions Department, 75 Arlington Street, Boston, MA 02116 or fax your request to 617-848-7320.

Between the time Website information is gathered and then published, it is not unusual for some sites to have closed. Also, the transcription of URLs can result in unintended typographical errors. The publisher would appreciate notification where these errors occur so that they may be corrected in subsequent editions.

Library of Congress Cataloging-in-Publication Data

Bracey, Gerald W. (Gerald Watkins)
  What you should know about the war against America's public schools /
Gerald W. Bracey.
    p. cm.
  Includes bibliographical references and index.
  ISBN 0-205-35188-3
    1. Privatization in education—United States. 2. Public schools—United States. I.
Bracey, Gerald W. (Gerald Watkins) War against America's public schools II. Title.

LB2806.36 .B72 2003
371.01—dc21   2002067580

Printed in the United States of America

10 9 8 7 6 5 4 3 2 1   06 05 04 03 02

Contents

Preface

While editing *The War Against America's Public Schools*, I realized that in aiming that book at educators—teachers, administrators, researchers, and professors—I may have missed an important audience: parents. But the issues, events, organizations, and motives mentioned in that book are vitally important for parents to understand. After all, it's their children who will reap the benefits or pay the price of experiments with the public schools.

Advocates of school vouchers and charter schools say "Give parents a choice." But if parents are to choose wisely, they must have easy access to good information about the choices that are available or possible. The experimenters and their advocates rarely provide unbiased information. After all, advertising is advertising. If it were the truth, there would be no need for watchdog agencies or *Consumer Reports*. You cannot know if your child will get a better education in, for example, Edison Schools than in public schools from reading Edison's promotional materials. Edison does not provide all of the information, and the information it does offer is presented in the best possible light. The people who run Edison schools are out to make a buck. As a publicly traded company, Edison's obligations are to its stockholders. Caveat emptor.

This book is intended to even the scales of information about public schools. *The War Against America's Public Schools* assumed that its readers knew the field of education and the various actors in the world of education research and reform. This book for parents does not. Rather, it follows the old maxim of speechifying: Tell 'em what you're gonna tell 'em, tell 'em, tell 'em what you told 'em. It provides references of works mentioned in the text so that the reader can look into the topic in more detail.

The first sections of the book set the context, examining the various philosophies that underlie different approaches to schools. They provide a historical perspective about what events have made parents concerned about public schools. They then look at the data, mostly test scores, that bear on that concern to determine if these data justify the anxiety.

Following these context-setting chapters, the book then describes a wide variety of educational experiments. It provides examples and describes the methods that dominate in each particular arena.

In 1983, "A Nation at Risk," a booklet produced by a federal commission, decried the state of the nation's public schools (National Commission on Excellence in Education, 1983). It was largely propaganda, but people accepted it and even hailed it as a "landmark study." It was propaganda because it consisted largely of statistics that its creators had selected and spun to convey their predetermined message. For instance, it claimed that "there was a steady decline in the science scores of seventeen-year-olds." This was true. But suppose one asked, "Why did they choose science and why did they choose only seventeen-year-olds?" The answer is that only science for seventeen-year-olds showed such a decline. Nine- and thirteen-year-olds had stable science scores. At all three ages tested, reading and mathematics scores were stable or increasing slightly. Thus, of nine test-score trends (three ages by three subjects), only one would support crisis rhetoric, and that was the only trend the commissioners mentioned.

The authors of "A Nation at Risk" wrote in an arch, cold-warrior style: They claimed that "If an unfriendly foreign power had attempted to impose on America the mediocre educational performance that exists today, we might well have viewed it as an act of war." The message, though, was meeker: To make schools work, we needed only "more"—more hours in the school day, more days in the school year, more courses, more rigorous courses, more computers in the schools, more credits for both students and teachers, more training for teachers, and so on.

Soon after "A Nation at Risk" appeared, though, some school critics called not for "more" but for "different." First, people said we had to "restructure" the public schools. But soon people began to say we had to abandon the public schools for other structures altogether. Former assistant secretary of education, Chester E. Finn, claimed that the public school system was so "ossified" it could not possibly undergo meaningful reform from within (Finn, 1998).

I don't know if Finn has ever been in a public school (he attended private schools). Like many reformers, Finn peers at public schools from afar. But he symbolizes a group of reformers who feel that if we could just get those recalcitrant educators—those *educrats*—out of the schools, then achievement would soar, kids would love to go to school, and our future would be assured.

Education reform has a long history of searching for magic bullets. After the Russians launched Sputnik in 1957, people blamed the schools and reformers called for massive curriculum reform. After Charles Silberman's 1970 tome, *Crisis in the Classroom*, people called for the "open education" that Silberman had championed. Currently, charter schools, vouchers, tuition tax credits, education management organizations, and other experiments are all being touted as quick-fix panaceas.

Those who wage war on the public schools come from many quarters. Some are mere opportunists who look at the $800 billion that America spends annually on education and want a piece of the pie. "We made a bundle privatizing the prisons and the hospitals," they say, "The only big, juicy market left is the schools." Others truly believe that a market-driven, privatized system would mean a better education for all. Still others would like to teach religion in publicly supported schools without having to worry about the separation of church and state. Liberals and researchers at universities often decry the problems of education in order to obtain more resources and grants. And others, especially those starting charter schools, have a "vision" of what education should look like.

No one has summarized in one place these various types of experiments, and that is the purpose of this book. I will not, though, leave any doubt about where I stand on some of these experiments. Indeed, one of the pleasures of writing this book for consumers has been to take the gloves off a bit, after the more polite treatise of *The War Against America's Public Schools*. The context-setting opening sections of this book should also make it clear that no one can justify the various experiments by claiming that the public school system is in crisis. It is not.

All schools can be improved and we should improve them because we can. Many schools do not teach mathematics or science very well. Many poor urban and rural schools *are* in critical condition. The much talked-about "achievement gap" between white and black and Hispanic students is real. The average black high school senior scores the same on National Assessments of reading and mathematics as the average white eighth-grader. In science, black seniors lag substantially behind white eighth-graders.

But many American schools compare well with the highest-scoring nations in the world. Secretary of Education Rod Paige often mentions "islands of excellence" in public education, as if to say these islands are few and surrounded by vast seas of incompetence. In this book I hope to show that, in fact, these "islands" make up most of the continent.

—Gerald W. Bracey

Acknowledgments

I would like to thank Susan Ohanian and George Schmidt for reviewing this manuscript. I would also like to thank those who reviewed *The War Against America's Public Schools* from which this book is derived: Bonnie Fisher of the College of St. Catherine, Anthony A. Koyzis of the University of Wisconsin-Oshkosh, Claire Sibold of Biola University, Angela Spaulding of West Texas A&M University, and Sandra M. Stokes of the University of Wisconsin.

As with earlier publications my wife, Iris, made many useful comments. She comes out of a theater and dance background, a perfect complement to my scientific thinking.

Part

I

The War on America's Public Schools

1

Prologue

A war is being waged on America's public schools. They are under siege. Many entrepreneurs and some former U.S. Department of Education officials are out to destroy them. Former Secretary of Education William J. Bennett has said, "In America today, the longer you stay in school, the dumber you get relative to your peers in other industrialized nations" (Bennett, 2000a). He also said, "Nationally, over half of high school graduates have not mastered seventh grade arithmetic" (Bennett, 2000b). If Bill Bennett were a former secretary of defense, rather than former secretary of education, and if he had uttered as many falsehoods about the Pentagon as he has about public schools, he would risk being charged with treason. As it is, he is developing a for-profit company to deliver curriculum aimed at home-schoolers via the Internet.

Chester E. Finn, Jr., former assistant secretary of education, is little better. On the op-ed page of the *Wall Street Journal* Finn wrote, "The public school system as we know it has proved it cannot reform itself. It is an ossified government monopoly that functions largely for the benefit of its employees and interest groups rather than that of children and taxpayers" (1998, p. A22).

A few bomb-throwers like Bennett and Finn garner media attention, but generally the war doesn't look like a war because it is one waged mostly in the polite language of academic debates. Indeed, the polite language is so important that when some of us have called it a war, we have been shunned. In 1993, Michael Usdan, then executive director of the Institute for Educational Leadership, and Lowell Rose, then executive director of Phi Delta Kappa International, proposed an education conference to be called Common Ground. The conference would bring together school critics and school defenders. I learned that some critics from the right (Finn and Denis Doyle among them) told Usdan and Rose that if I were invited, they wouldn't come. I pointed out to Usdan and Rose that we would find little "common ground" if one side was allowed to set the rules. Still, I received an invitation only on condition that I not be a speaker.

The conference was a bust—a very polite bust, but a bust nonetheless. The various antagonists danced around the issues for two days and nothing came of it. The right has no interest in common ground—it has an agenda.

It is not that schools, even "good" schools, don't need to change. Too many schools still bore too many students. Indeed, they probably bore more students today in spite of being much more exciting than in the past: Today's students' knowledge and sophistication certainly outstrips my generation. The advent of niche magazines, targeted television, computers, CDs, DVDs, and the Internet permit students to amass vast amounts of specialized knowledge at very early ages. A lone teacher cannot keep up with all of the different directions that students can go.

Eric Harris and Dylan Klebold, students at Columbine High School, killed twelve other students, a teacher, and finally themselves in a 1999 shooting spree. Some reports said they were "high ability" students. In our need to view the Columbine tragedy as just that, no one to my knowledge has observed that Harris and Klebold were also amazingly knowledgeable, resourceful, and thorough (fortunately, they were not infallible and some of their most devastating devices did not explode). Other students demonstrate these qualities in more socially benign ways, but the Columbine killers demonstrate them nonetheless, posing powerful challenges to teachers. (Harris's suicide note, incidentally, blamed parents for not instilling the right values in the students who rejected him. It did not mention teachers or school administrators.)

The war on schools is being waged by multiple enemies. We can spot some of them by observing the research they fund. "Follow the money" was the advice given to Watergate investigators Bob Woodward and Carl Bernstein by their informant, "Deep Throat." It's good advice. For instance, in August 2000, a report appeared finding that black students using vouchers apparently scored higher than a matched sample remaining in public schools (Howell, Wolf, Peterson, and Campbell, 2000). The authors credit a virtual who's who of conservative foundations for funding the study: The Achelis Foundation, Bodman Foundation, Lynde and Harry Bradley Foundation, William Donner Foundation, David and Lucille Packard Foundation, Smith-Richardson Foundation, Spencer Foundation, and Walton Family Foundation.

The National Committee for Responsive Philanthropy has pointed out that these foundations do not operate as neutral organizations advancing the free debate of ideas. Over the past forty years, while mainstream foundations such as Carnegie, Rockefeller, Ford, and MacArthur followed pragmatic, issues-oriented programs of funding, conservative foundations poured money into a single idea: triumphing over "liberal big-governmentism." Conservatives often refer to public schools as "government schools." Getting the government out of schools is part of the conservative agenda (National Committee for Responsive Philanthropy, 1998).

One person who wants the government out of schools is Milton Friedman, the man most responsible for popularizing the idea of school vouchers. He and his wife Rose Friedman created their foundation precisely and solely to promote vouchers, an idea he put forward in 1955 and elaborated in his 1962 book, *Capitalism and Freedom* (Friedman, 1962). On their website, the Friedmans had this to say (the material has since been removed):

> Since then [1955] we have been involved in many attempts to introduce educational vouchers—the term that has come to designate the arrangement we proposed. There is a distressing similarity to attempts made over three decades and from coast to coast. In each case, a dedicated group of citizens makes a well-thought through proposal. It initially garners widespread public support. The educational establishment—administrators and teachers' unions—then launches an attack that is notable for its mendacity but is backed by much larger financial resources than the proponents can command and succeeds in killing the proposals. (Friedman and Friedman, 2000, www.friedmanfoundation.org)

Interestingly, in the November 2000 election, voucher proposals in California and Michigan went down in flames with 70 percent of the voters in both states voting "No." In these instances, the proponents of vouchers had outspent opponents—the "educational establishment"—by two to one. When I asked Friedman how he interpreted this debacle, he said that the "defeats are highly relevant to the question of political tactics," but not to his faith in the efficacy of vouchers (Friedman, 2001).

New enemies appear from time to time. On October 3, 2000, the day of the first debate between presidential candidates Al Gore and George W. Bush, a full-page ad appeared in the *Washington Post* comparing American students to those in other nations and declaring the school system a failure: "Every year we pump more money into our public education system, and every year the system gets worse. . . . Only when schools are forced to compete for students will they be motivated to improve. Only then will the system open up, new options emerge, and education look like the rest of America. Meanwhile, nearly 90 percent of American children are stuck in a failing system."

The Campaign for America's Children sponsored the ad. Billionaire industrialist Theodore J. Forstmann and the ubiquitous William J. Bennett lead this group. Part of this book will discuss how our system is not only *not* failing, it is improving. It will also raise questions about whether education *should* look like "the rest of America" (whatever that may mean).

Higher Education: Biting the Hand That Feeds

Some of the schools' enemies do not perceive themselves as such. Large research universities often abet the more open enemies of public schools. To extract money from foundations and governments, they emphasize the negative. Susan Fuhrman, at the time a professor at Rutgers and now dean of the school of education at the University of Pennsylvania, once declared "If you want money, ya gotta say the schools are lousy. So what else is new?" She said this in a room full of other professors. For all the reaction her remark caused, she might as well have said "The sky is blue."

The commission that produced "A Nation At Risk" commissioned virtually all of its forty-odd research and policy papers from professors at large research universities; a few commissions went to think tanks, which are essentially universities without students. Think tank denizens debate issues and conduct research just like professors, but they have no students to teach. Only one paper was written by a public-school employee: A teacher in San Diego wrote to criticize one of the commission's symposia. And even that contribution was aided by chance: The president of the San Diego Board of Education was vice-chair of the commission and invited the teacher's response. The teacher said that people who don't know anything about education should stop trying to tell educators what to do (Harvey Prokop, personal communication, December 2001).

Although "the commission was impressed during the course of its activities by the diversity of opinion it received regarding the condition of American education," no such diversity was apparent in the papers or in the final report. Given this loading of the critical dice, the schools never had a chance.

The antischool position of university professors is not new. University of Illinois historian Arthur Bestor's influential 1993 book *Educational Wastelands: The Retreat from Education in America's Public Schools* laid waste to the schools and, especially, to the schools of education that prepared teachers. For some reason, professors at colleges of arts and sciences rarely acknowledge the link between themselves and schools of education: Schools of education teach those who will teach the students who will later show up in the classrooms taught by professors of arts and sciences. Public school teachers groom the future students of the arts and sciences professors. The good professors of arts and sciences should help, not attack, schools of education.

In some cases, the enemy is found within. I cannot speak to the motives of all the governors, boards, and legislators who have sponsored "standards" and "high-stakes tests." It is clear, though, that the Virginia State Board of Education established ludicrously high standards: Ninety-eight percent of the schools failed the tests the first time around. After four years of standard testing, some high schools have pass rates on tests such as Algebra I that remain below 10 percent. Several board members favored vouchers and reasoned that in light of such massive failure, nervous parents would be more willing to accept voucher legislation and/or tuition tax credit laws that would use taxpayer dollars to subsidize private schools.

Business and Industry: A Workforce at Risk?

Business and industry have not always been antischool, although they have certainly tried to direct the curriculum for over a century. Business and industry see students as "products" and have prodded schools to turn out "products" that will more readily suit business's needs for a docile yet energetic workforce and voracious consumers who will spend and spend.

Some who wish to do away with the public schools simply want to make a profit. The investment firm Lehman Brothers reportedly sent brochures to their clients saying, essentially, "We've taken over the health system; we've taken over the prison system; our next big target is the education system. We will privatize it and make a lot of money" (Chomsky, 2000). Virtually no firms have made any money starting or managing schools, yet many articles have reported that investors remain bullish on privatization (the companies have not made a buck, but officers of the companies have made fortunes).

The various corporate efforts have been coupled with deliberate attempts to mislead Americans about the nature of the future job market. The National Commission on Excellence in Education, Bill Clinton, Al Gore, Senator John Glenn, IBM CEO Lou Gerstner, and a host of others have made bogus arguments and cited nonexistent "facts" in this effort. "We have to prepare students for the jobs of the future," goes the refrain.

Before the 2001–2002 recession, each month brought news of a further decline in manufacturing jobs and a continuing explosion in the low-skill service sector. Still, reformers scream that "new technology" will make jobs in the future more complicated and difficult than they are today. The goal is simple: If you can make people anxious about their future, you can control them. People who worry about the future are less able to see their neighbors as fellow citizens working toward common goals and more likely to perceive them as competitors for what good jobs there are.

The National Commission on Excellence in Education was assembled by then–secretary of education Terrel Bell in 1981 to document all the terrible stories Bell had heard about schools. It made Americans nervous by putting forth an absurd theory about what makes a country economically healthy and competitive in a global marketplace. The commissioners said, "If only to keep and improve on the slim competitive edge we still retain in world markets, we must dedicate ourselves to the reform of our educational system. . . ." (p. 7). The commission thus tightly yoked the economic health of the nation to the standardized test scores of children aged five to eighteen.

Wise observers recognized this as the nonsense it was and responded with statements such as this from education historian Lawrence Cremin:

American economic competitiveness with Japan and other nations is to a considerable degree a function of monetary, trade, and industrial policy, and of decisions made by the President and Congress, the Federal Reserve Board, and the Federal Departments of the Treasury, Commerce, and Labor. Therefore, to conclude that problems of international competitiveness can be solved by educational reform, especially educational reform defined solely as school reform, is not merely utopian and millennialist, it is at best a foolish and at worst a crass effort to direct attention away from those truly responsible for doing something about competitiveness and to lay the burden instead on the schools. It is a device that has been used repeatedly in the history of American education. (1989, pp. 102–103)

Alas, only a few educators, and not the general public, saw Cremin's remarks. His sensible comments never caught the media's attention. As the nation slipped into a recession during 1989–1990, the Commission's theory gained widespread popularity. Many commentators uttered variations on "Lousy schools are producing a lousy workforce and that is killing us in the global marketplace." But then a funny thing happened: The economy came roaring back. The headline "The American Economy, Back on Top" appeared in the *New York Times* in early 1994, and many other publications ran similarly enthusiastic banners. *Times* reporter Sylvia Nasar painted not only a positive picture of the present, but also a glowing portrait of the future:

> A three percent economic growth rate, a gain of two million jobs in the past year, and an inflation rate reminiscent of the 1960s make America the envy of the industrialized world. The amount the average American worker can produce, already the highest in the world, is growing faster than in other wealthy countries, including Japan. The United States has become the world's low-cost provider of many sophisticated products and services, from plastics to software to financial services.
>
> For the most part, these advantages will continue even after countries like Japan and Germany snap out of their recessions. It is the United States, not Japan that is the master of the next generation of commercially important computer and communications technologies and also of leading-edge services from medicine to movie making. (Nasar, 1994)

While the *Times* gushed about a three-percent growth rate, the economy was edging up to a four-percent growth rate per year.[1] Unemployment dipped to 4 percent, a level considered theoretically impossible—until it happened. America's workers became even more productive. And the increase in productivity allowed gains in growth without any significant inflation. Even when recession struck, productivity continued to rise.

From 1993 to 2001, America enjoyed the longest sustained economic boom in its history. Not even when the world reindustrialized after World War II did we see such spectacular growth. One might think that, in such good times, school bashing would be considered bad form. Yet three months after the *New York Times* article appeared, IBM CEO Louis V. Gerstner, Jr., in the midst of firing 90,000 employees, took to the op-ed page of the *Times* to declare "Our Schools Are Failing" (Gerstner, 1994). They are broken, wrote Gerstner, because they do not prepare students who can compete with their international peers.

In the 1980s reformers waxed enthusiastic about the high test scores of Asian students and credited those scores with producing the economic miracle of

---

1. The earlier estimates that it actually attained 5 percent were revised in light of later figures. Calculating the growth rate of the economy is not an exact science.

the "Asian Tiger." Some declared we should adopt the Asian model as our own. Then the Asian economies tanked. Japan has endured a recession for more than an entire decade and pundit William Safire worried in the *New York Times* that it might be in for *another* ten years of economic stagnation (Safire, 2001). So far, Safire seems to be correct.

In the "benchmarking" phase of the Third International Mathematics and Science Study, Japanese students finished fifth among 38 nations in mathematics and fourth in science (other top spots went to other Asian nations). Yet Japan's economy continues to contract. Singapore finished first in this study, well ahead of even the other high-scoring Asian countries. On July 10, 2001, Singapore declared itself in recession. So much for the relationship between test scores and the economy.

Being wrong hasn't fazed Gerstner. At the 1998 "education summit," which he organized and hosted, he convened a group of governors and business-people with a speech outlining "the good, the bad, and the ugly of American education." It began:

> The good: Our kids have the potential to be the best in the world. In science and math, our fourth-graders are right up there with the very best.
> The bad: By 8th grade, we rank 28th, behind, among others, Russia, Thailand, and Bulgaria.
> The ugly: By 12th grade we trail every developed nation in the world. In fact, we're doing better than only Cyprus and South Africa. (Gerstner, 1998)

As we shall see, the data do not support Gerstner's claim.

For their part, Bill Clinton and Al Gore contributed to the ongoing debate of the schools' effect on the economy with a letter to the editor of *USA Today*. In it, they declared that "By the year 2000, 60 percent of all jobs will require advanced technological skills" (Clinton and Gore, 1995). My research on education reform has taught me to be wary of undocumented claims—you should be, too. I wrote Clinton and Gore and asked for a citation for their 60 percent figure and for a definition of "advanced technological skills." I also sent copies to Richard Riley and Robert Reich, then secretaries of education and labor, respectively. My four inquiries elicited one reply: Someone in Riley's office wrote to say that she was certain that someone in Reich's office could answer my queries. No one ever did.

As noted, many speakers state, or strongly imply, that advancing technology will make jobs more complex, sophisticated, and difficult. In fact, advances in technology often make work easier. Who, reading this book, would trade their current word-processing program for one from fifteen years ago? An analogy can be drawn with the development of single-lens reflex cameras with built-in light meters, which greatly simplified photography. Yet those SLRs now seem cumbersome, unwieldy, and difficult to use compared to today's digitals and point-and-shoots. The first computer I ever used extensively was housed in its own building and those graduate students who were qualified to use it could get permission to run it only after 2 A.M. No one at the time, 1963, ever imagined a desktop computer, much less one you could hold on your lap or in your palm, or one that virtually anyone could learn quickly to use. But twenty-five years later, I replaced my secretary's IBM Selectric III typewriter with a personal computer. She thought she had died and gone to heaven: Imagine, being able to revise a document with a few keystrokes instead of having to retype the whole thing.

The Bureau of Labor Statistics has a different idea about what the jobs of the future will look like. The most recent projections are given in Table 1.1.

Occupations in the computer and health fields dominate the list. As the population group known as the baby boomers gets closer to retirement—the oldest are less than a decade away—health occupations are expected to become more numerous. Yet only five of these fast-growing jobs require "advanced technological skills," if one assumes that phrase means something more than sitting in front of a computer and using a word processor or a spread sheet.

However, we often see a different picture when we look at *rates* than we do when we look at *numbers*. When we say something is the "fastest growing" we are talking about a rate. But a rate might double and still produce small numbers. If I make a dollar today, two dollars tomorrow, and four dollars the next day, my rate is increasing rapidly, but I'm still not making much money. Table 1.2 shows the projections for the ten occupations with the largest increase in *numbers*.

Only three occupations make both lists. Two require sophisticated use of information technology (systems analysts and computer support specialists), and one does not (personal and home-care aides). Most of the occupations in this second list have traditionally provided large numbers of jobs. Retail sales, for

TABLE 1.1   *The 10 Fastest Growing Occupations, 1998–2008 (In Thousands)*

		Employment		Change	
		1998	2008	Number	Percentage
1.	Computer engineers	299	622	323	108
2.	Computer support	429	869	439	102
3.	Systems analysts	617	1194	577	94
4.	Database administrators	87	155	67	77
5.	Desktop-publishing specialists	22	44	19	73
6.	Paralegals and assistants	136	220	84	62
7.	Personal and home-care aides	746	1179	433	58
8.	Medical assistants	252	398	146	58
9.	Social service assistants	268	410	141	53
10.	Physicians' assistants	66	98	32	48

Source: Bureau of Labor Statistics, *Occupational Outlook Handbook* (Washington, DC: Bureau of Labor Statistics, 2000).

TABLE 1.2 *The 10 Occupations with the Largest Job Growth, 1998–2008 (In Thousands)*

	Employment		Change	
	1998	2008	Number	Percentage
1. Systems analysts	617	1194	577	94
2. Retail salespersons	4056	4620	563	14
3. Cashiers	3198	3754	556	17
4. Managers and executives	3362	3913	551	16
5. Truck drivers	2970	3463	493	17
6. Office clerks	3021	3484	463	15
7. Registered nurses	2079	2530	451	22
8. Computer support specialists	429	869	439	102
9. Personal and home-care aides	746	1179	433	58
10. Teacher assistants	1192	1567	375	31

Source: Bureau of Labor Statistics, *Occupational Outlook Handbook* (Washington, DC: Bureau of Labor Statistics, 2000).

example, provide only 570,000 fewer jobs than the top 10 fastest-growing jobs combined, 4,620,000 versus 5,189,000. High-tech jobs might be growing fast, but growth in the low-tech, low-pay service sector swamps them.

Christian Conservatives

Attacks on public schools also come from the Christian right movement. Some Christian educators promote vouchers and tax credits in the hope of funding schools that can teach religion with taxpayer dollars and not worry about the First Amendment. Others, though, oppose vouchers on the grounds that taking public money will inevitably result in government regulation and loss of independence.

Catholic school officials have for the most part discreetly refrained from public comment on the war. It is hardly a secret, though, that many would like to see vouchers provide money to their financially ailing schools. An article by Joanna Massey noted an "exodus" of teachers from Catholic schools because of low pay. Some Catholics, she reported, "point to the growing national voucher movement, which would allow parochial and private schools to receive taxpayer funding in the form of student vouchers—perhaps freeing additional money for teacher salaries" (Massey, 2000). In 1960, Catholic schools accounted for 12.6 percent of all schoolchildren. In 2000, they accounted for only 4.7 percent (Brimelow, 2000). Certainly these schools would welcome vouchers as a means to fill empty desks, if they could get past the problem of the separation of church and state. Indeed, one reason a federal court ruled Cleveland's voucher program unconstitutional was that of the 4,000 students using vouchers, 96 percent attended Catholic schools.

In September 2001, the United States Supreme Court agreed to hear the Cleveland case. In December 2001, People for the American Way, among other organizations, filed a "friend of the court" brief pointing out that not only did 96 percent of the students attend Catholic schools but that those schools had no restrictions on using the money the students brought. They could buy prayer books or religious icons, or fund activities directly promoting the school's religion.

Although the various camps wage their war in polite terms, the attackers do not fight honestly. The critics of public schools often present distorted, selected, or spun statistics to make their case. We have already seen such distortion in the speech presented at the Education Summit by Gerstner. William Bennett drew from the same study for his own spin: As noted, in a speech celebrating the twenty-fifth anniversary of The Heritage Foundation, Bennett declared flatly that "In America today, the longer you stay in school, the dumber you get relative to kids from other industrialized nations." To make this statement, Bennett had to uncritically accept results from one of the worst studies, methodologically speaking, ever conducted: the Third International Mathematics and Science Study's Final Year Study. I have discussed the many problems with this study elsewhere (Bracey, 2000b). Bennett's interpretation of the data is a political statement, not an intellectual or scientific analysis of the facts.

The spectacle of a former secretary of education—and author of *The Book of Virtues*—skewing the facts to support his criticism of our public schools is appalling, but there is apparently no limit to the depths to which Bennett can sink. In a September 4, 2000, op-ed essay in the *Washington Post*, Bennett wrote, "About half of high school graduates have not mastered seventh-grade arithmetic" (2000b, A25). I offer some advice to readers: If an article alleges some flaw in schools, but doesn't back up the charge with data, track down the data. "Show me the money!" cried Cuba Gooding Jr. at Tom Cruise in *Jerry McGuire*. "Show me the data!" should be your cry.

Bennett's statement struck me as peculiar on several counts. First, we don't test "high school graduates." Second, Bennett offered no definition of "mastery." Third, he offered no definition of "seventh-grade arithmetic," a phrase without consensual meaning among educators or parents today. Fourth, he provided no data and no citation of data to back up his claim.

I called Bennett's office. His assistants told me that the figure came from *The Book of Knowledge*, which in this instance is not the familiar childhood encyclopedia, but a 1996 book on how to invest in the "education industry" by Michael Moe and Kathleen Bailey. Moe is a former director of Global Growth Research at Merrill Lynch who now runs his own consulting firm (Moe and Bailey, 1999).

I called Moe's office and was told that the statistic was "an interpretation of 1996 National Assessment of Educational Progress (NAEP) mathematics test results." Rest assured, dear reader, that there is no *possible* way to go from the

NAEP data to the "interpretation" that Moe spun from them. Bennett uncritically accepted *The Book of Knowledge* as correct without the least questioning of the veracity of its interpretations. Bennett, the author of *The Book of Virtues*, would do better to pay more attention to two of them: truth and honesty.

These examples could be multiplied many times over by statements from Bennett, the Heritage Foundation, the Hoover Institution, and the Hudson Institute, to name but a few of the more well-known right-wing think tanks. (I am being kind here. In the *Washington Post*, Michael Kinsley, former editor of *The New Republic* and *Slate Magazine*, called the Heritage Foundation a "right-wing propaganda machine that masquerades as a tax-exempt nonpolitical research institution [Kinsley, 2002].) They would all show, though, that most of the critics of public schools have no interest in what the facts really say, but only in what their ideology demands that the facts say. It's a war, and all's fair.

2

Dueling Visions

People have different opinions on what purpose education is meant to serve. Some see it primarily as preparing students for the workplace. Others see it as liberating humans from the stale routine of the workaday world and opening the mind to intellectual, social, and cultural richness. Still others see it simply as another commercial transaction.

If we are to evaluate the public schools, we need to know what people think the schools *ought* to be doing. What is the purpose of education? Aristotle said it's about the "good life." Because people will always differ over what constitutes the good life, people will also always argue about the purpose of education. At this moment in American history, however, much of this debate has been muted, overwhelmed by a recent shift to a single-minded view about education: that education is about jobs. It is about acquiring skills to get a good job in the information society. *A Nation at Risk*, published in 1983, emphasized jobs. Bill Clinton pointed to the 22 million jobs created during his administration as his leading achievement. Education is about acquiring skills to keep the United States competitive in the global marketplace, a contention that thrived even as the "Asian Tiger" nations turned into pussycats and the economies of Japan, South Korea, Singapore, Malaysia, Indonesia, and Thailand sank into the Pacific.

The myth has been perpetuated that new jobs are high-skill and high-tech. As we saw in Chapter 1, the overwhelming majority of jobs are not. Despite the glowing rhetoric about prosperity and record low unemployment in the United States, there are currently 15 million more families in this country than there are jobs that will support them comfortably (Finnegan, 1999). If you think the working poor can live comfortably, spend a little time with Barbara Ehrenreich's *Nickel and Dimed: On (Not) Getting By in America* (2001). Ehrenreich, a well-regarded writer in her fifties with a Ph.D. in biology, spent two years working at a variety of minimum-wage jobs. It ain't easy. Early on she reports being astonished by the realization that in her present condition "trailer trash is a demographic category to aspire to."

Given all this emphasis on jobs, jobs, jobs, it should come as no surprise that many people have stopped viewing education as a public good or as something that liberates the human spirit from the grind of everyday life, something that enriches life culturally, intellectually, and emotionally, and started viewing it simply as another market to be exploited. Peter Cookson of Columbia University has framed the issues nicely:

> Two competing metaphors will shape the public education system of the future. The first is that of democracy. At the heart of the democratic relationship is the implicit or explicit covenant: important human interactions are essentially communal. Democratic metaphors lead to a belief in the primacy and efficacy of citizenship as a way of life. The second metaphor is that of the market. At the heart of the market relationship is the implicit or explicit contract: human interactions are essentially exchanges. Market metaphors lead to a belief in the primacy and efficacy of consumership as a way of life. (1994, p. 99)

For Cookson the development of the child into a consumer is a betrayal.

> We are challenged to choose between the fragmented consciousness of the modern materialistic mind and the humanistic vision of the whole empathetic and productive mind. We need a transcendent view of education, the elements of which include individual responsibility, the centrality of individual worth, equality, peace, and the primacy of the child's physical, intellectual, and spiritual rights. (1994, p. 121)

It is a measure of how far the discourse has changed that Cookson's words, which would have struck most people as vital thirty years ago, now seem soft, almost sappy, in light of today's conversations about how the world works.

Jeffrey Henig of George Washington University makes the same points as Cookson, but adds an important extra dimension: When public schools are public, discussion about what they should teach and how occurs in public discussion. The discussion about schools is important. If the private sector takes over schools, it will terminate that discussion. Schools that are operated as for-profit businesses under the market metaphor are not open. If they become the dominant mode for providing instruction as "service-delivery mechanisms," they also constitute a threat to democracy (Henig, 1994). As Carol Ascher and her colleagues put it, "We will not survive as a republic, nor move toward a genuine democracy unless we can narrow the gap between rich and poor, reduce our racial and ethnic divides, and create a deeper sense of a common purpose" (Ascher, Fruchter, and Berne, 1996, p. 112). Privatization will not help attain these goals. Some privatizers have claimed that a market-driven school system can accomplish the first two of these goals, but evidence points to the contrary.

Certainly, no privatization advocate, to the best of my knowledge, has ever said that a market-driven school system would lead to "a deeper sense of common purpose."

In a slightly different vein, Benjamin Barber of Rutgers University proposed that "If schools are the vessels of our future, they are also the workshops of our democracy . . . Public schools are not merely schools for the public, they are schools in publicness: institutions where we learn what it means to *be* a public" (Barber, 1995). Who will volunteer in a community? Who will vote? What kind of communities do we want? Market-driven schools are not likely to entertain, much less answer these questions.

Some food for thought: Would private, for-profit schools increase the amount of crime in education? Consider these opening sentences of news reports that occurred over a two-week period:

> Providian National Bank, the nation's sixth-largest issuer of credit cards, has agreed to reimburse customers at least $300 million to settle allegations that it unfairly charged and deceived customers. (Chea, June 29, 2000)
>
> About 240 criminal investigations into possible mortgage fraud are underway in 38 states. . . . (Fleischman, July 1, 2000)
>
> The former head of a company that runs group homes for mentally retarded Washington, D.C., residents was accused yesterday of stealing more than $800,000 from the firm and using the money for luxury vacations, furs, and other extravagances. (Miller, July 11, 2000)
>
> One of the world's largest makers of generic drugs tentatively agreed to pay $147 million to settle accusations that it improperly cornered the market on raw materials for two widely prescribed drugs and then raised the price of those drugs, in some instances more than 3,000 percent. (Labaton, July 13, 2000)

These were not an exceptional two weeks in the world of corporate crime. With one exception the papers didn't even put the stories on page one (the *Washington Post* fronted one report because it was a local story), but in the business section. People take crime in the private sector for granted. Profit increases the chance that greed will cause people to engage in criminal acts. And even where there might not be criminal actions, neglect of standards and quality in pursuit of profits is the order of the day, as, for instance, the Bridgestone/Firestone incident revealed—surely both corporations knew that the tires were defective long before they were forced to admit it.

The two-week period mentioned above occurred in 2000. I decided to update these examples and checked more recent (July 4, 2001) issues of the *Washington Post* and *New York Times*. I didn't find articles about corporate crime, but I did find a review of a book about corporate crime; specifically, how to *manage* the scandal of corporate crime to the benefit of the corporation:

> The corporate landscape is littered with companies that were destroyed or transformed by fighting scandal the wrong way. Drexel-Burnham Lambert, Inc., was

done in by securities crimes in its junk bond division, for example. E. F. Hutton & Company was destroyed by wire and mail fraud; Perrier was tainted by efforts to minimize the extent of contamination of its bottled water; and Columbia/HCA Healthcare Corporation was disgraced by a massive health care fraud. . . . Faced with such a bleak history of corporate wrongdoing . . . managers should actively prepare for trouble. (Eichenwald, 2001)

The message is not "Don't do it," the message is "Get ready for it 'cause it's bound to happen." Doesn't that make you feel warm and secure about the invasion of corporate America into the public schools?

Recent debacles in the private sector indicate that the deceits just keep on coming. In fall 2001, Enron Corporation collapsed, the largest bankruptcy ever seen in the United States. It was followed shortly by Global Crossing, the fourth largest. The events of September 11, 2001, were so dominant in people's minds that the media and Congress were slow to gather the import of the story, but once they did, stories filled the papers and the Justice Department, Labor Department, and the Securities and Exchange Commission launched investigations as did some eleven congressional subcommittees.

Shortly before the debacle, while Enron's head officers were telling employees to buy Enron stock and forbidding those employees from acting on stock options, those officers were selling $275 million of their own holdings. CEO Ken Lay alone sold shares worth $101.3 million (Behr, 2001). As Enron's stock dropped from $85 a share to18 cents a share (as of May 15, 2002), thousands of employees whose retirement plans consisted mostly of Enron stock found themselves with no nest eggs. Many of them were also out of a job.

Enron went from being the darling of both Texas and Washington to being "radioactive." The City of Houston bought back the naming rights of its brand-new Enron stadium. Enron had been President Bush's leading campaign contributor, and Bush had attended baseball games with CEO Ken Lay whom he, with his penchant for giving people nicknames, called "Kenny Boy." After the collapse Bush acted as if he had no knowledge of Lay and claimed that Enron had supported rival Ann Richards in Bush's campaign for governor of Texas. In fact, Enron had given some money to Richards, but gave three times as much to Bush.

Early on, suits against Enron named the accounting firm Arthur Anderson as a codefendant, claiming that Anderson knew that Enron's bookkeeping techniques were phony, but signed off on them anyway. After it came to light that Anderson had shredded many Enron documents, some even after the SEC had launched an investigation, Anderson was indicted by the Justice Department for obstruction of justice.

Enron's most common deceptive activity, it appears, was to form spurious partnerships with other corporations that kept huge debts off the books. During the initial phases of the Enron story, Bloomberg Financial observed that the books of Edison Schools, Inc., the nation's largest for-profit manager of schools, inflated its earnings by some $96 million a year. Edison claimed that amount as income when, in fact, it was the money for teacher salaries paid for by the districts while Edison never saw a penny (Bloomberg, 2002).

Spectacular cases such as Enron's appear all too often; the most common word used to describe American corporations is "amoral." They are not interested in morality. The most glaring example of this came to light in the 2001 book *IBM and the Holocaust: The Strategic Alliance between Nazi Germany and America's Most Powerful Corporation* (Black, 2001). The next time you see a Holocaust movie and notice those blue numbers tattooed on death camp prisoners, remember that those numbers were generated by machines made by Big Blue—IBM. Although reviewers of the book concluded that the death camps would have operated in any case, they also concluded that the IBM Hollerith punchcard machines—the forerunners of computers—greatly improved the Third Reich's efficiency in keeping track of the prisoners and moving them around. In 1937, Hitler awarded IBM president Thomas B. Watson his country's highest civilian award. Accounts differ as to whether Watson returned it when the United States entered the war or when the Nazis bombed Paris.

I present this extended discussion of corporate criminality in order to lead up to a question: Do you want your children's schools to become just another big business? If so, convicted felon Michael Milken might be your new Dean of Education, and his $4 billion company, Knowledge Universe, might be the place to educate your children. Knowledge Universe is described and discussed on pages 128 to 134.

In contrast to the amorality of industry, taxpayers take the honesty and basic moral grounding of most public school for granted: The books are public records, and the occasional scandal makes big news simply because it so rarely occurs. And the numbers involved pale in light of the billions involved in cases such as Enron. However, in numerous instances, private school management companies have refused to show their books or to report student test scores even when a state's Freedom of Information Act required such a release. Edison Schools, for example, refused to specify how it spent a $2.7 million grant from the state of Pennsylvania, even though the money was taxpayer dollars.

People form private companies to make money. If they become publicly traded companies, such as Edison Schools, Inc., or Nobel Learning Communities, Inc., their first responsibility is to the shareholders, not to the parents of the children who attend their schools. The operators face many pressures to make sure that the bottom line is written in black ink with the largest possible numbers.

Public school principals receive praise and pats on the back if their athletic teams win or their students get academic recognition. In Flint, Michigan, Edison School principals have received Ford Mustangs for meeting attendance and test-score–gain performance goals. It costs Flint taxpayers $600 more per child in the Edison schools than in the public schools, but Edison officials report they have yet to turn a profit in Flint (Bach, 2001). Nor have they turned a profit nationally. So where is the money for those sports cars coming from? Edison is discussed on pages 104 to 117.

In private, closed settings, the temptations to cheat, deceive, and scheme that do not exist—cannot exist—in public schools become great. One Arizona company, for instance, charged the state $1.95 a mile to ferry students to its charter schools. Can you imagine a public school trying that?

3

The Master Myth:
Money Doesn't Matter

In this chapter we examine the evidence that has been put forward to claim that spending on schools is unrelated to the performance of schools. We find that evidence badly flawed. We then look at other evidence that money, does, in fact, make a difference in students' achievement.

A central assumption underpins most criticism of public education: the master myth that money doesn't matter. Without this assumption, many of the privatization efforts would collapse of their own inconsistencies and contradictions. Several forces sustain the myth: studies that apparently show no correlation between spending and achievement; studies that apparently show that increases in spending over time do not produce increases in achievement; and accusations that the United States spends more money on its schools than any other nation, yet realizes less achievement in its students. We treat each type of study in turn.

The Correlations between Spending and Outcomes in Schools

State Spending

The myth can be sustained at the state level because, within a given state, the amounts that schools spend fall within a fairly restricted range. To be sure, in most states, the districts that spend the most money spend three to four times more than those that spend the least. If money doesn't matter, someone should inform the high-spending districts. Wealthy districts have more, and more current, books, more computers, and more enrichment activities. And if a school in a wealthy district lacks money, the parents might fill the void: For instance, when parents were concerned about the renovations in a Montgomery County, Maryland, elementary school, forty of them kicked in $200,000 of their own money to make sure the renovations were done right. "Done right" means so that they would "fit in with the upscale surrounding community" (Schulte, 2001).

Wealthy districts also have higher test scores, but it is hard to know if the high scores come from quality schools or high income families. Probably both are factors—wealthy families pressure the schools for quality education and, as shown in the preceding paragraph, they also contribute resources beyond the means of poor parents (contributions which do not get counted in official tallies of per-pupil expenditures).

Aside from the extremes, most districts in a state have quite similar expenditures. When spending is mostly within a narrow band, its relationship to achievement is affected by a statistical phenomenon known as *restriction of range*. Restriction of range reduces the possible size of the correlation between money and spending.

This might sound like a complicated concept at first, but it isn't. We can understand restriction of range with a concrete example. Suppose we wished to investigate how important height is to success at basketball. To do that, we calculate the correlation between height and basketball prowess defined by one or more criteria: dribbling acumen, percentage of field goals made, rebounds, and so on. But suppose everyone we measure is 6′6″ tall. Our correlation *must* be zero because everyone looks the same. Similarly, suppose we give a test to predict college success and everyone scores 100 percent correct. We cannot make predictions about who would do well in college because everyone has identical scores.

School districts don't spend exactly alike, but most districts spend similar amounts and this limits the size of the possible correlation between money and achievement and also increases the importance of other variables. For instance, if two districts spend the same amount and one of them contains a university, all other factors being equal, that district will have higher test scores. Academics are people who did quite well on tests, and their children usually fare well, also. Similarly, if one of two equal-spending districts contained the corporate headquarters of an industry that employed large numbers of highly educated workers, it would have higher test scores.

We can show the limits of the money-doesn't-matter myth by imagining a wider range of spending. Suppose school spending fell to $0 per student. Surely achievement would plummet, as it did in Prince Edward County, Virginia, in 1959 when the schools were closed rather than face racial integration. And, just as surely, if spending rose to $40,000 per student, achievement would soar. Forty thousand dollars is the average annual teacher salary nationwide. For this amount, we could provide each child with a tutor. One-on-one tutoring is an effective way to raise achievement, but is exorbitantly expensive.

The SATs and State Participation Rates

Some claims that money doesn't matter come from flawed, ideologically driven studies. For instance, William Bennett conducted a "study" that purported to show that money doesn't matter (Bennett, 1993). Bennett claimed that there was no relationship between state-level spending and state-level achievement as measured by state-level SAT averages. He did not actually perform any statistical analyses on the data, but merely pointed out that some high-spending states had low SAT scores and some low-spending states had high SAT scores.

Now, a lot of people would argue, rightly, that SAT scores are no measure of state-level achievement because the proportion of high school seniors who take the test varies from state to state. Only 4 percent of Utah's seniors take the SAT while nearly 80 percent of seniors in Connecticut and other northeastern states do so. Nevertheless, pundit and fellow conservative George Will anointed Bennett's "study" in one of his columns. Will echoed Bennett's observation that some of the top-scoring states spent little, but that New Jersey, which spent more money per student per year than any other state, finished thirty-ninth in the Great SAT Race (Will, 1993).

Neither Will nor Bennett made any adjustments for the different costs of living in different states. More important, neither Will nor Bennett pointed out that in the top-scoring states very few students take the SAT. Most students in these states take the ACT college admissions battery. In the year of the study, in high-flying Iowa, only 5 percent of the seniors sat for the SAT, while in New Jersey, 76 percent did so. No Iowa public colleges or universities require the SAT (or even the ACT if students' grade point averages place them in the upper 50 percent of their class). This elite group was students applying to Stanford or Harvard or other schools on the coasts that require SAT scores for admissions consideration.

One might want to say "OK NJ!" for encouraging three-quarters of its students to apply to colleges that require the SAT, but when three-quarters of New Jersey's senior class are compared to a 5 percent elite group from Iowa, there can be no doubt about the outcome.

Since 1993, Bennett's annual "report card" has come to include a number of additional indicators other than SAT scores: ACT scores, NAEP, and so on. By 2000, Bennett was no longer the author and the new authors included some statistical analyses. The message, though, remains unchanged:

> The story they [analyses in this report] write will describe a 20-year period of declining academic achievement accompanied by unprecedented increases in public spending. The characters in this story will include an education bureaucracy that continued to ask for more while delivering less. A generation of children growing up in the world's lone superpower at the end of the millennium . . . lag behind students in dozens of other, less-developed nations [sic] . . . What this *Report Card*

proves is that the current path is not good enough, and that throwing money at the problem is not the answer. (Haynes, in Barry and Hederman, 2000, p. 1)

Someone should ask Ray Haynes, a California state senator, where he found the "dozens" of less-developed nations that have higher educational achievement. The largest international comparison in math and science scores ranked forty-one mostly developed countries and American students fell in the middle (Beaton et al., 1996a, 1996b). In the largest international comparison of reading skills, American students ranked second among twenty-seven nations (Elley, 1992).

Bennett's "analysis" puzzled researchers Brian Powell and Lala Carr Steelman. They asked how much of the differences among states could be accounted for by the differences in participation rates that we discussed above. Their analysis found that these differences in student participation rates accounted for 83 percent of the differences in scores. They then asked, "If the states all had the same SAT participation rates, would differences in spending make any differences in scores?" Adjusting participation rates can be accomplished with a simple statistical procedure. When they carried it out, they found that for every increase of $1,000 above the national average for spending, total SAT scores rose by 15 points (Powell and Steelman, 1996). Therefore, even on a test that does not directly measure what happens in the classroom, money has a significant impact.

Studying the Studies:
A Closer Look at Methodology

Some have studied the relationship between money and school achievement by studying the studies. That is, they have examined the studies that have investigated the relationship, to see if they could find any consistency in the results. In 1989 University of Rochester economist Eric Hanushek conducted such an analysis and wrote, "there is no strong or systematic relationship between money and achievement" (Hanushek, 1989). This statement has become the bedrock, the mantra, for those who would undo public education. It is the conclusion that California Senator Haynes used in the above quote when stating that "throwing money at the problem is not the answer."

Although Hanushek's work is not well known to the general public, he has affected many public schools by testifying in numerous court cases involving school finance laws. It is worth a short digression to note that by offering his testimony, Hanushek has shifted from being a researcher to being an advocate. Researchers are supposed to be disinterested and willing to change their minds if new data contradict earlier studies. (We have seen the influence of such data on the changing medical positions on salt, cholesterol, eggs, and mother's milk.) Remaining open to new data often makes a researcher's public statements appear tentative, even mealy-mouthed, to the lay public. But that is how it must be if one is a researcher because results are, usually, tentative. An advocate, however, especially one who has testified often in court, has taken a position. To change that position would jeopardize both any unresolved court cases and the advocate's credibility as a witness.

Researcher Keith Baker has pointed out that Hanushek (1) did not explain how he reached his conclusion; (2) suffered an egregious lapse in logic; and (3) was contradicted by his own data (Baker, 1991). In his 1989 article, Hanushek merely presented his collection of studies and then baldly drew his conclusion without providing any rationale for it. Hanushek placed each study he looked at in a certain category depending upon the study's results. His final tally looked like this:

	Number of Studies
Positive and significant:	13
Negative and significant:	3
Positive and insignificant:	25
Negative and insignificant:	13
Unknown outcome:	11

Significant and *insignificant* here are statistical terms that are unrelated to *important* and *unimportant*. Results are statistically significant if the outcomes are unlikely to have occurred by chance. Statistical methods can determine the likelihood of an outcome being due to chance.

Hanushek's data above clearly show more positive studies (thirty-eight) than negative studies (sixteen). If the relationship between money and achievement did not exist, the results would not be so skewed toward the positive side.

Hanushek has not acknowledged any of the studies that show a positive relationship. In the summer 1997 issue of *Educational Evaluation and Policy Analysis*, he updated his own research and wrote that "there is no strong or consistent relationship between variations in school resources and student performance." There is only a strong and consistent relationship between what Hanushek says from time to time, which is often quite independent of anything the data might indicate.

Indeed, many of the studies Hanushek included in his analysis seem inappropriate to the issue. Many titles of studies suggest that they have nothing to do with achievement and imply that money is a variable of, at most, minor interest: "Student Perceptions, IQ, and Achievement"; "Instructor Effects in Economics in Elementary and Junior High Schools"; "Selectivity Bias and the Determinants of SAT Scores"; "Children Who Do Exceptionally Well in First Grade"; "Merits of a Longer School Day"; "School District Leave Policies, Teacher Absenteeism, and Student Achievement"; "Do Additional Expenditures Increase Achievement in the High School Economics Class?" (Hanushek, 1997).

Obviously, these studies did not set out to directly test the money-achievement relationship or to examine the master myth. Some don't even include what most educators typically have in mind when they speak of measuring "achievement"—for example, SAT scores. In addition, studies using tests such as the SAT cannot be generalized to the whole realm of education. The SAT involves only a single class, high school seniors,[1] and those who take the SAT do not represent high school seniors in general. Currently, 45 percent of the nation's high school seniors choose to take the SAT because they are applying to colleges that require it. As discussed earlier, however, the rates of SAT takers vary from state to state, from 4 percent to 80 percent.

Does Spending Equal Achievement?

Master myth proponents claim that while spending for public schools has "soared" over the years, achievement (test scores) has been "flat" or even, as Senator Haynes claimed, falling. Much of the increased spending since the late 1960s, though, has funded special education services, and many students in special education receive exemptions from testing. New federal regulations require that more special education students be tested, which may raise or lower test scores in the future.

Hanushek has claimed that scores from the National Assessment of Education Process (NAEP) are "flat." He can make this claim only by looking at some scores for seventeen-year-olds and by not separating the scores by ethnic group. Table 2.1 shows the changes in NAEP scores over time for all seventeen-year-old students, for three ethnic groups, for three grade levels, and for three performance levels (until the 1996 assessment NAEP sampled too few Asian students to report them separately). Looking at Table 3.1 for all students at the seventeen-year-old level, we do see that the average score (fiftieth percentile) has not moved much over time. For reading, scores have stayed at 288; for math, scores increased from 301 to 308; and for science, scores rose from 291 to 298. Low-performing students, those at the fifth percentile, show improvement across the board. The only group showing truly "stagnant" scores are high-performing seventeen-year-olds.

Hanushek, and others, have not acknowledged the NAEP changes, or have ignored trends shown by other tests that refute the claim that increased spending has not produced increased achievement. The trends in question come from the Iowa Tests of Basic Skills and are shown in Figure 3.1. These test score trends cannot be *directly* linked to money, but they have been anything but "flat." The Iowas, as they are known, have been around since the late 1920s and are constructed to reflect what happens in classrooms. Looking at the trendlines, we see

---

1. Juniors and some sophomores also take the SATs, but the scores that the College Board releases each summer are for seniors only and these are the scores that the media report.

TABLE 3.1 *National Assessment Trends for Seventeen-Year-Olds*

	Percentile							
	All		*White*		*Black*		*Hispanic*	
Reading								
	1971	*1996*	*1971*	*1996*	*1971*	*1996*	*1975**	*1996*
5th	206	213	219	225	165	200	184	198
50th	288	288	293	296	239	266	253	264
95th	356	354	359	358	310	330	321	329
Mathematics								
	1978	*1996*	*1978*	*1996*	*1978*	*1996*	*1978*	*1996*
5th	241	256	252	266	217	241	224	243
50th	301	308	307	315	268	286	275	293
95th	356	355	358	358	321	333	332	341
Science								
	1977	*1996*	*1977*	*1996*	*1977*	*1996*	*1977*	*1996*
5th	212	217	231	237	172	192	194	196
50th	291	298	298	309	240	259	262	270
95th	362	365	365	371	310	327	331	340

*Before 1975, Hispanics were too small a group to produce a reliable estimate in the NAEP sampling procedure.

Source: Adapted from *NAEP 1995 Trends in Academic Progress*, National Center for Education Statistics (Washington, DC: Office of Educational Research and Improvement, U.S. Department of Education, 1997).

scores rising from 1955 to 1965, falling from 1965 to roughly 1975 (the length of the decline varies a little by grade, as does the severity), then rising again to attain record levels by the mid- to late-1980s. The scores remained at these record highs until the mid-1990s but have since declined a little.

If you remember the sixties, goes the saying, you weren't there. The decade of 1965 to 1975 was one of the most tumultuous periods in U.S. history, beginning in 1965 with the Watts riots in Los Angeles, which spread to virtually every urban area in the nation. The decade also included anti–Vietnam War protests and Watergate. Black Panthers, Students for a Democratic Society, and the Student Nonviolent Coordinating Committee took to the streets demonstrating for civil rights. During the decade television penetrated virtually all households and the recreational use of drugs increased dramatically, leading, in part, to the Summer of Love, Woodstock, and Altamont. Antiwar protests became violent at the Democratic National Convention in Chicago in 1968, and deadly at Kent State

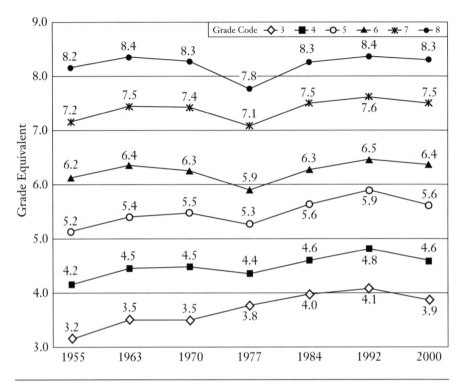

FIGURE 3.1   *Trends in ITBS Achievement: Composite Scores Grades 3–8, 1955 to 2000*

Source: Data provided by H. D. Hoover, Iowa Testing Program (Iowa City: University of Iowa, 2001).

in 1970. This period of time began 13 months after the assassination of President John F. Kennedy and included the assassinations of Robert F. Kennedy, Jr., Martin Luther King, Jr., and Malcolm X. Little wonder, then, that test scores and other indicators of educational outcomes declined. But they later recovered and climbed to record highs.

Education Spending in the United States

Another way that critics try to show that money doesn't matter is to claim that America spends more money on its public schools than any other nation and yet students don't perform as well on tests. If this is true, then it follows that America's schools are inefficient. But it is not true. There are a variety of ways of calculating how much money countries spend on their schools. The United States never finishes first in any of the calculations.

If spending is defined as the number of dollars spent per pupil, the United States is a big spender, but it is not the highest spender (Organization for

Economic Cooperation and Development [OECD], 1997). If spending is defined as the percentage of per capita gross domestic product spent on education, the United States is about average for the twenty industrialized nations for which this calculation was made (OECD, 1997). And if spending is defined as a percentage of per capita income, the United States ranks near the bottom (Rasell and Mishel, 1990).

Which statistic should one use? My preference is for percentage of per capita GDP.[2] To me, this figure best represents how much of its wealth a nation is willing to invest in its future, namely, its children.

In addition, schools in the United States provide many services that other nations do not. Many nations do not serve meals, provide transportation, or offer the services that in this country fall into the category of "special education." Nationally, about 12 percent of students receive special education services and the average special education service costs about two and a half times what regular instruction costs.

Other Justifications for the "Master Myth"

Critics also contend that public schools constitute a "monopoly," which makes them unresponsive to pressures for accountability. Because the monopolistic schools don't have to answer to investors, they can be inefficient and wasteful without consequences. One study, though, indicates that compared to various private sectors of the economy, school spending is quite lean (Robinson and Brandon, 1992). Public schools have very few administrators in relation to the number of "frontline" workers (teachers).

The master myth also justifies making a profit: If a company can provide "the same" education for less, why shouldn't it be entitled to some of what it saves? Since money doesn't matter, the money that is left over is superfluous to a high-quality education.

To be sure, money per se is not the issue. I don't know of anyone who ever said it was. But money is an important resource. Money per se does not win wars or put men on the moon, but it is the critical facilitator of both activities.

Of course, it is possible to spend money in ways that do not affect outcomes. Consider the spending debacle of Kansas City, Missouri, a school district that has become the poster child of the political right, which claims it as the definitive case proving that more money makes no difference. When a federal judge forbade a forced merger of Kansas City schools with surrounding suburban districts, a lawyer for the plaintiff, working with Kansas City schools, developed a plan to lure affluent white students back from the suburbs to the largely black city schools. The district built palatial schools and Olympic-size swimming

---

2. Using the percentage of GDP produces the same result, but some of the nations involved have large GDPs and some have small GDPs. Using the per capita GDP removes these inequalities.

pools. They offered courses in garment design, ceramics, violin, ballet, drama, and Greco-Roman wrestling, and even hired a former Russian Olympic fencing coach. The programs cost a fortune and the district hoped to attract 10,000 sub-urban students back to city schools, but it managed to draw only about 2,000. Those students who did come seldom stayed for more than a year (Ciotti, 1998).

On the face of it, the program had dubious chances of success, but political problems assured catastrophe. The district had chewed up ten superintendents in nine years. Many leading candidates for the post had taken themselves out of contention once they actually met with the school board. Unable to fire incom-petent teachers because of the black community's concern about job loss, the dis-trict raised all salaries, cementing the incompetents in place. While the new schools were built, old, nearly empty schools stayed open, causing a huge finan-cial drain.

From Kansas City, we certainly can extract a clear lesson about school spend-ing and achievement: Do not throw money at politically dysfunctional schools with incompetent teachers, administrators, and board members, who are operating under a plan that has little to do with learning and has been constructed by a peda-gogically and politically naïve lawyer and approved by an equally naïve judge.

What Spending Can Achieve

So far, we have analyzed flaws in studies that claim that money is unrelated to achievement. We can also find studies that clearly indicate that money *does* make a difference (none of which Hanushek has ever acknowledged). For instance, the SAT is only tangential to day-to-day instruction in schools.[3] Yet money can affect the outcomes on even such a remote test, as we saw earlier in the Powell and Steelman analysis (1996).

Howard Wainer of Educational Testing Service objected to William Ben-nett's claim that state SAT scores are not related to money. In addition to the dif-ferences in participation rates among states, Wainer also noted that the SAT does not measure achievement directly. NAEP, on the other hand, while not directly measuring a specific curriculum, does measure achievement using a rep-resentative sample of students from each state. Wainer found a definite relation-ship between state-level spending and state-level NAEP scores (Wainer, 1993). Another study reported that school districts that spent more money on instruc-tional materials had higher test scores than those that spent less (Lockwood and McLean, 1993).

Ronald Ferguson of Harvard found that districts that used money to lure more experienced teachers and districts that used money to reduce class sizes had

---

3. But it is becoming less so as school people increasingly choose instruction and assessment that resembles SAT skills. Thus, the Gwinnett County, Georgia, fourth-grade language arts test presents some reading passages after which come questions in the form of analogies: X:Y and Z:?.

rising test scores (Ferguson, 1991). An elaborate test of money and outcomes came from Harold Wenglinsky at Educational Testing Service (Wenglinsky, 1998). In his monograph, *How Educational Expenditures Improve Student Performance and How They Don't*, Wenglinsky found that neither teachers' level of education nor spending on administration at the building level made much difference. Spending on administration at the district level, however, paid off. This may be because the proportion of administrators in districts has dropped from 2.6 percent in 1950 to 1.7 percent in 1995, possibly leaving districts short-staffed in this area (National Center for Education Statistics, 1977). Smaller class sizes also paid off handsomely.

Small class sizes consistently increase achievement, and poor and minority students reap a greater benefit from smaller classes than middle-class students. It is important to review the research on class size, because we shall see that most students in charter schools or using vouchers attend small classes in small schools. Therefore, even if these students score higher on tests, the results might well be not because of some inherent qualities of "charterness" or "voucherness," but simply because the students sit in small classes in small schools. Using money to create small classes matters. Small schools also increase achievement (Wasley et al., 2000; Smith, 2000).

Project STAR

We've learned most about small classes from a large-scale experiment: Tennessee's Project STAR (Student Teacher Achievement Ratio). Project STAR reduced class size in kindergarten through grade 3 to an average of sixteen students. The state also appropriated money to give some regular classes a full-time teacher's aide. And some classes were untouched (Finn, 1999; Finn and Achilles, 1990; many issues concerning class size and Project STAR are discussed in the Summer 1999 issue of *Educational Evaluation and Policy Analysis*, the entirety of which is given over to the topic).

What makes Project STAR so important is that classes were randomly assigned to each condition *within each school*. This random assignment is crucial because it eliminates the possibility of selection bias. Without random assignment within buildings, principals who favored small classes could have chosen that option and worked hard to get the results they wanted. Similarly, a principal who liked to use aides could bias the outcomes in that direction. Conversely, if a principal chose a condition not favored by the teachers, they could undermine the experiment. Or, again, without random assignment within each building, it's possible that the students in the different groups would differ on some important variables such as family income or parental education. Random assignment of conditions within each building eliminates these potential problems.

Classes with teachers' aides produced a small improvement in achievement. Those with fewer pupils produced a larger one (Finn, 1999; Finn and

Achilles, 1990). Moreover, the effects were sustained through high school. Princeton University economist Alan Krueger has noted that more students who attended small elementary classes in Project STAR took college admissions tests (Krueger, 1999). Krueger even conducted an analysis of STAR data comparing different-sized regular classrooms. Students in small regular classrooms (twenty-two students on average) had higher achievement than students in large regular classrooms (twenty-five students).

More recently Krueger (2000) has issued what might be the definitive assessment of class size, even though it does not include Project STAR in its analysis. He reanalyzed the set of studies that Hanushek used to prove that class size does *not* matter. Krueger pointed to some invalid techniques Hanushek had used. When he corrected for these, Krueger found that the data overwhelmingly support the contention that using money to reduce class size does indeed matter . . . a lot.

It is important to note that, as with money, it is not small classes per se that are important. Small classes take some pressure off teachers and allow them to give individual students more attention.

Project SAGE

A smaller program in Wisconsin called Project SAGE (Student Achievement Guarantee in Education) has found similar results over three years. Most SAGE classes contain fifteen or fewer students. SAGE students consistently have outperformed their counterparts in regular classrooms (Molnar, Smith, and Zahorik, 2000).

In an interesting wrinkle, some SAGE classrooms contain thirty students, but two teachers. These classes perform almost as well as the small classes. This could be an important finding. The U.S. currently has a record number of students. The cost of building enough new schools to give all of them small classes would be huge. In urban areas, new classrooms would be nearly impossible to build because open space is rare. If students in regular existing classrooms score higher with two teachers, we don't need nearly as many new buildings.

In the small SAGE classes, the students participated more, allowing teachers to see if the students fully understood the subject being discussed. Instruction was still teacher-centered but, according to the report, "the use of hands-on activities is growing in frequency" (Molnar et al., 2000). As a consequence, students show more independence and take on more responsibility.

Mandating Small Classes

When serving as president, Bill Clinton thought small classes were so important that he proposed funds to accomplish it on a national scale. California has mandated small classes for grades K–3, and other states were preparing to do the same when the recession of 2001 forced budget cuts to even already-existing programs. Certainly Clinton's proposal was sounder than President Bush's insistence that we test all children every year in reading and math in grades 3 through 8. As proposed, this is a recipe for chaos (as discussed more fully later on).

So many problems were created by California's class-size reduction that people wondered if achievement would really rise. Horror stories abounded as California schools scurried to meet the mandate: Schools that lengthened school days, held classes in closets and restrooms, and so forth. Those are the anecdotes. What was documented was that hundreds of teachers in low-income schools have left to fill new openings in affluent, attractive, high-paying districts. Thus the small class mandate might have a negative impact on those who could most benefit from it: In Project STAR, low-income and minority students responded more to small classes than did their middle-class peers. In California, however, low-income schools were forced to hire hundreds of teachers who had only emergency credentials, not regular state certification.

In spite of all this, the first formal evaluation of the class-size initiative found positive effects (Class Size Consortium, 1999). The second evaluation noted that teacher qualifications continued to decline. It also found that teachers did, in fact, spend more time with individual students. Finally, as in the first evaluation, small positive effects on test scores showed up. In addition, students who had moved from small third-grade classrooms to regular-sized fourth-grade classrooms sustained the advantage they had gained in their small classes (Class Size Consortium, 2000).

The use of the master myth has served to distract people from the fact that many American students attend public school under terrible conditions. Jonathan Kozol documents some of these conditions in *Savage Inequalities* (Kozol, 1991). Other sources have turned them up as well. Consider these vignettes:

- Young children picking up beer bottles, condoms, and bullets on school grounds. School officials take them out of reading instruction for this "beautification work."
- Rats scurrying about on cafeteria bread racks, some with fruit in their mouths.
- Chemistry labs with no chemicals. Literature classes with no books. Computer classes where "we sit there and talk about what we would be doing if we had computers."
- Classes with no teachers. A parade of substitutes shows movies.
- Students forced to stand against the walls or sit on window sills—until enough students leave that there are chairs for all.

These scenes come to us not from the impoverished Deep South of a century ago but from California today (Cooper, 2001).

As long as such conditions exist, how dare people say "Don't throw money at the schools"? Until poor students attend schools under conditions that middle-class students take for granted, such statements represent sheer and despicable hypocrisy.

Right-wing critics have spread both the master myth and the myth that we spend more than any other country widely through the popular culture. While both of these assumptions are false, neither is likely to disappear from the discourse about the quality of schools anytime soon. Indeed, in late 2001, the *Richmond Times-Dispatch* editorialized against a plan to raise more money for Virginia public schools. Virginia ranks fifteenth in the nation in terms of wealth, and forty-fifth in terms of spending on schools. The editors said that "The premise underlying the Virginia Education Association's 'Brighter Futures' campaign is simple: more spending equals better schools. . . . Time and again, the figures have shown that spending and performance simply do not correlate" (*Richmond Times-Dispatch*, 2001). This quote illustrates that not only will the myths not disappear, but that those who have bought into the myths will continue to present them to the public in simplistic and misleading ways.

4

The Historical Context

In this chapter we examine some of the events after World War II that have led some Americans to become concerned about the quality of public schools. We will see that critics, the media, and others often make public schools the scapegoat for events over which the schools have no control—for instance, the launch of Sputnik in 1957 and the economic recession of the late 1980s through early 1990s.

In 2002, most parents still favor public education and the 2001 Gallup/Phi Delta Kappa poll indicates that their opinion of schools is on the rise (Rose and Gallup, 2001). Still, what they read in the press about standards, test scores, and how American students stack up against students in other countries makes them nervous. They're confused about school vouchers, charter schools, EMOs (Educational Management Organizations), and other incursions of private groups into the public domain.

How did we get here? Fifty years ago critics were also pummeling the public schools, but the assumption then was that we would work to improve them. Now some critics want to remake public schools as one system among several alternatives or do away with them entirely. We can understand the present condition only by discussing how it developed over the years.

The Factory Model of Schooling

Criticism of public schools is hardly new. In his historical survey of public education in the United States, Arthur Newman noted "the always abundant criticism" (Newman, 1978) and provided examples from the nineteenth as well as the twentieth centuries. Over the years, the caviling has had a certain sameness to it: schools are inefficient; schools are not preparing students for the jobs of tomorrow; schools aren't what they used to be (and never were, as Will Rogers sagely observed). Indeed, without the constant carping of business and industry, and to some extent, universities, one wonders if criticism of schools would even exist.

Serious faultfinding began early in the twentieth century. In 1912 Frederick Taylor presented to Congress his plan for "scientific management" that would make factories more efficient. Taylor's timing was impeccable: It came in a decade when the Muckrakers, as the crusading social reformers came to be called, had denounced not only corporations but also virtually every social institution as inefficient or corrupt or both. Taylor's management system, when applied to public schools, affixed an onerous—no, disastrous—analogy to them: the factory model of schooling. In 1913 Stanford University's Elwood Cubberly, the most influential educator in the nation at the time, declared:

> Every manufacturing establishment that turns out a standard product or series of products of any kind maintains a force of efficiency experts to study methods of procedure and to measure and test the output of its works. . . . Our schools are, in a sense, factories in which the raw products (children) are to be shaped and fashioned into products to meet the various demands of life. The specifications for manufacturing come from the demands of the twentieth century civilization, and it is the business of schools to build its pupils to the specifications laid down. This demands good tools, specialized machinery, continuous measurement of production to see it is according to specifications, the elimination of waste in manufacture, and a large variety in the output. (1919, p. 338)

To be sure, the dehumanizing notion of students as a "standard product" was not a sudden break with some more romantic past. Schools had not been seen as caring, nurturing, loving places. In addition, business early on had tried to steer schools in certain directions. In 1897 Jane Addams noted:

> The business man has, of course, not said to himself, "I will have the public school train office boys and clerks for me, so that I may have them cheap," but he has thought, and sometimes said, "Teach the children to write legibly, to figure accurately and quickly, to acquire habits of punctuality and order; to be prompt to obey, and not question why; and you will fit them to make their way in the world as I have made mine." (in Curti, 1961, p. 203)

Addams certainly knew quite well that *some* businessmen had indeed said "Schools, train the clerks so I can get them cheap." They still do. She was just being polite.

Not all educators bought Taylor's claims for "scientific management." John Dewey, for instance, opposed the efficiency movement. He viewed children as complex and idiosyncratic beings for whom standardization was inappropriate. Dewey urged educators to focus on this individual complexity: "It is a change, a revolution, not unlike that introduced by Copernicus when the astronomical center shifted from the earth to the sun. In this case the child becomes the sun about which the appliances of education revolve; he is the center about which they are organized" (Tyack, Thomas, and Benevot, 1987, pp. 109–110).

When the National Association of Manufacturers called for a reorganization of schools that would better prepare children for jobs, New York City school superintendent William Maxwell asked "Why?" Why did manufacturers feel it to be their right to make a recommendation? He found their motives suspect. Maxwell pointed out that manufacturers had abandoned their apprenticeship system as too costly and, as a consequence, now lacked an adequate supply of skilled workers. Apparently they wanted the schools to do for free what they earlier had paid for (as companies still try today):

> Out of this dilemma the exit was obvious—persuade the State to assume the burden. . . . And as a first step to secure their ends, they and their agents in unmeasured terms denounced the public school as behind the age, as inefficient, as lacking in public spirit. . . . The arrogance of the manufacturers was two-fold—first in condemning the schools for not doing what thinking men had never before considered it the duty of the schools to do and what the traditions of thousands of years laid it upon the manufacturers to do; and, second, in demanding that the state should then proceed to pay the bills for training their workmen. (Maxwell, 1914, pp. 175–176)

Unfortunately for the schools, the Deweys and the Maxwells did not carry the day. The "arrogance of the manufacturers" prevailed. Labor, for its part, was no match for the capitalists. Said economist Roger Babson in 1914, "However successful organized labor has been in many ways, it has never succeeded in directing the education of its children. Capital still prepares the school books and practically controls the school systems" (in Gelberg, 1997, p. 47). As a consequence, noted another influential educator of the time, William Bagley, "One can see in the mechanical routine of the classroom the education forces that are slowly transforming the child from a little savage into a creature of law and order, fit for the life of civilized society" (in Tyack, 1974, pp. 132–133). In calling children "little savages," Bagley was merely voicing a common concept of the time.

Many educators, especially superintendents, embraced the new efficiency model with a vengeance, leading to what Raymond Callahan referred to as a "descent into trivia" (Callahan, 1962, p. 241). The new model changed superintendents from scholars into managers and nothing was too trivial for their attention. In 1933 U.S. Commissioner of Education William J. Cooper wrote *Economy in Education*, offering hints on how to save money on paper fasteners, theme paper, colored pencils, and coal. Don't purchase ink as a liquid, advised another superintendent, make it from a powder.

> On the matter of school paper there is always some waste. A sheet may be larger than needed. The best remedy for this is to supply two sizes, one the regular 8½" by 11", the other 8½" by 5½". If the superintendent will study his paper and its uses he will be able to eliminate odd sizes and buy more standard sizes. Toilet paper is frequently a source of waste. I have seen school toilets in which the ceiling and

walls were literally coated with paper which had been dipped in water and thrown. As for paper towels. . . . (in Bracey, 1995a, p. 191)

Every time I look at this last quote, I wonder why, instead of studying toilet paper, the superintendents didn't study why their charges dipped it in water and slung it on the walls. In any case, the academic and social growth of children seemed distant from these men's thoughts and concerns.

Again, some people battled this totalitarian approach to school. During the 1930s, in addition to studying toilet paper, some educators, especially those in the Progressive Education Association (PEA), studied how to make schools more exciting. At their 1932 meeting PEA members criticized traditional high schools and generated ideas for reform. They also voiced an oft-heard lament: "Yes, that should be done in our high schools, but it can't be done without risking students' chances of being admitted to college" (Aikin, 1942; reprinted in Raubinger et al., 1969, pp. 164–169). Reform ideas died because public school educators feared that colleges would reject graduates from a nontraditional school.

Since the formation of the College Entrance Examination Board in 1900, college entrance requirements emphasized a traditional college-prep course of study—math, languages, literature, history, and, later, natural sciences—in spite of the fact that in 1900 only 2 percent of high school graduates continued on to higher education. In a bold move, the PEA persuaded colleges to waive their usual admissions criteria for thirty-two high schools for a period of eight years. Using a control group of similar traditional high schools, the PEA conducted what came to be known as the Eight Year Study, from 1932 to 1940. Generally, students from what the first President Bush would have called "break-the-mold" schools outperformed their traditional peers both in the college classroom and in their involvement with social and political activities on campus. "The guinea pigs wrote more, talked more, took a livelier interest in politics and social problems, went to more dances, had more dates. Especially concerned with campus affairs were graduates of the six most experimental schools. There were more dynamos than grinds among them," wrote educator Edgar Knight in retrospect (1952, pp. 114–115). One can only wonder what changes in education the Eight Year Study might have wrought but for the onset of World War II.

The Cold War Era in Public School Reform

The press for efficiency in the early years of the twentieth century had its reprise in calls for higher standards and higher skills in the century's last two decades. The foundation for the current upheaval was laid in the early 1950s when politicians and the military came to see the schools for the first time as integral to national defense and as important weapons in the Cold War. Admiral Hyman Rickover crossed the country declaring that the schools were producing insufficient quantities of scientists, engineers, mathematicians, and foreign language speakers, based on numbers supplied by CIA chief Allen Dulles. "Let us remember," said Rickover, "that there can be no second place in a race with the Russians. And there will be no second chance if we lose" (Rickover, 1959).

Students who were ordered to "duck-and-cover" will never forget how tense the world was in those days, and what an absurd exercise it was: as if students would be protected from the force of an atomic bomb by ducking under their desks and covering their heads with their hands.

The idea that the schools were not making the grade was also accompanied for the first time by a nostalgia for some undefined earlier era when things were better. History professor Arthur Bestor penned an influential 1953 book panning schools and schools of education called *Educational Wastelands* and subtitled *The Retreat from Learning in Our Public Schools* (emphasis added). This nostalgia for old-fashioned schooldays persists today and is as misbegotten and erroneous now as it was then (Bracey, 1997).[1]

The critics felt vindicated when, in October 1957, the Russians launched Sputnik, the first man-made satellite to orbit the earth. They had been right all along: The failure of the schools to get an American into space first threatened our entire nation with a Communist takeover or even annihilation of all life on earth (no one seemed to notice that American space-flight experts had long since graduated high school).

For its impact on American schools, the softball-sized Sputnik could have been an atomic bomb. Popular novelist and education reformer Sloan Wilson (*The Man in the Gray Flannel Suit*) penned a two-page essay that could have appeared in 1998 rather than 1958 with no loss of modernity:

> The facts of the school crisis are all out and in plain sight—and pretty dreadful to look at. First of all, it has been shown that a surprisingly small percentage of high school students is studying what used to be considered basic subjects. . . . People are complaining that the diploma has been devalued to the point of meaninglessness. It would be difficult to deny that few diplomas stand for a fixed level of accomplishment. . . . It is hard to deny that America's schools which were supposed to reflect one of history's noblest dreams and to cultivate the nation's youthful minds, have degenerated into a system for coddling and entertaining the mediocre. (Wilson, 1958, pp. 36–37)

In early 1958 *Life* magazine launched a five-part series on education's woes. Under the headline "Crisis in Education," the March 24 cover shows a stern-faced Alexei Kutzkov staring out at the reader from Moscow, while easy-smiling Stephen Lapekas grins from Chicago. Curiously, Lapekas is smiling in virtually all photographs, but Kutzkov smiles in only one of eleven—at least, he *appears* to be smiling while he and two girls read an English phrase-book on the subway.

---

1. When I've had the opportunity to ask nostalgics about when they imagine the Golden Age of American education took place, it almost invariably turns out to be the time period when they themselves were in high school.

Photos show Kutzkov performing complicated experiments in physics and chemistry and reading aloud from *Sister Carrie* in his English class. "A purpose in fun, too," says the text near pictures of Kutzhov at a science museum and a concert, and gazing intently at the pieces on a chessboard.

Lapekas, by contrast, is shown walking his girlfriend home hand-in-hand and dancing at a rehearsal for the school musical. One large picture catches him retreating, laughing, from a geometry problem on the blackboard. "Stephen amused his classmates with wisecracks about his ineptitude," says the text. As perhaps final proof of the intellectual vacuousness of American education, one picture shows Lapekas learning to type. It quotes him as saying, "I type about one word a minute." One comes away from the series knowing that without immediate and massive education reform, we are doomed.

Looking at the *Life* cover one day, it occurred to me that it might be informative—and fun—to find Lapekas and Kutzkov today. Lapekas joined the Air Force and is currently a commercial pilot. The Russian embassy was not very cooperative about my search for Kutzhov. National Public Radio Moscow reporter Anne Garrels returned my call to say that she could not find any evidence that Kutzkov ever existed. "There is no way that an American journalist and photographer could have gotten into a typical Moscow high school in 1957," she said. More likely, she suggested, the article might have been a payoff to Kutzkov's father for some extraordinary service to the Communist party. I searched for Howard Sochurek, the photographer for the article, but unfortunately what I found was a death notice. Sochurek often worked in Eastern Europe, and therefore it seems plausible that *Life* did not construct the story out of whole cloth. At the time of the story, however, publisher Henry Luce's reputation for slanting news would not rule out this possibility. As teenagers in the 1950s (I was a senior when Sputnik was launched), my friends and I had a saying about Luce publications: "*Time* for people who can't think, *Life* for people who can't even read."

The reputation of America's public schools never recovered from Sputnik. As years went by people accused the schools of many other failings, as well. In 1970 Charles Silberman observed that 176 of 186 studies of tests given at two points in time had favored the more recent time. But, even though 95 percent of the studies showed progress, Silberman, a journalist and *Fortune* magazine editor, still called his influential book *Crisis in the Classroom* (1970).

The "Paper Sputnik"

Eleven years later, in 1981, Secretary of Education Terrel Bell went looking for what he called "a Sputnik-like event" that would startle America into doing something about the low state of its schools. Unable to find such an event, Bell assembled the National Commission on Excellence in Education. In 1983, the commissioners launched the study that many have referred to as "the paper

Sputnik": "A Nation at Risk." By 1983, the threat had changed from the worry that Russian soldiers would overrun us to a different region:

> The risk is not only that the Japanese make automobiles more efficiently than Americans and have government subsidies for development and export. It is not just that the South Koreans recently built the world's most efficient steelmill, or that American machine tools, once the pride of the world, are being displaced by German products. It is also that these developments signify a redistribution of trained capability throughout the globe. . . . If only to keep and improve on the slim competitive edge that we still retain in world markets, we must dedicate ourselves to the reform of our educational system. . . . (National Commission on Excellence in Education, 1983, p. 7)

When the country slipped into recession around 1990, the schools again became a very convenient target. We have noted earlier that some corporate leaders such as IBM's Gerstner *still* mouth the criticism that America's schools do not educate our children to compete in a global marketplace. And while some people saw this foolishness for what it was from the beginning, they were in the minority and not favored by the media.

Even when the U.S. economy recovered in the first half of the 1990s, no one seemed to notice the contradiction between the rhetoric of failure and the reality of success. Indeed, it is a common pattern: When something is wrong in society, let's blame the schools. But when the bad something disappears or gets better, the schools get no credit. For instance, twelve years after Sputnik, America landed a man on the moon, a heavenly object that the Russians, despite their alleged technological superiority, never even managed to *hit*. No one attributed this triumph to the schools. Similarly, when the economy rebounded in the 1990s, no one attributed the revival to improved schools.

In 1998 the Final Year results from the Third International Mathematics and Science Study appeared to show that American high-school seniors lagged behind in comparison with seniors in other nations (something the study did not in fact show; the operative word in the preceding sentence is "appeared"; Bracey 2000b, 1998a, 1998b). My phone rang off the hook with inquiries from reporters, all asking some variant of the question "If our kids are so dumb, how can the economy be so good?"

The economy can be so good because, as James J. Gallagher put it in the title of an article, "Education Alone Is a Weak Treatment" (Gallagher, 2000). It can be so good because the link between schooling and the economic health of a developed nation is also weak. It can be so good because from birth to age eighteen, a child only spends 9 percent of his or her life in school. It can be so good because the things that determine success on the job and economic productivity are not measured by standardized tests (a list of such unmeasured qualities appears on page 48; a quick glance at this list will show why tests in the long run have no importance). It can be so good because the forces identified by Cremin (see pages 7–8) can overwhelm any connection between schools and a nation's economic health.[2] In the week after the September 11, 2001, attacks on the World Trade Center and the Pentagon, $1.4 *trillion* in wealth disappeared from Wall Street. Hotels emptied, tourism sagged, air travel plummeted, and over 100,000 people became unemployed. Yes, this was an extreme and unprecedented event, but it can demonstrate the negligible effect that schools have on the economy compared with other factors. In fact, the correlation between achievement, as measured by test scores, and competitiveness, as indicated by the ranking of the high-powered World Economic Forum, is nearly zero (Bracey, 2002).

Those very government subsidies that *A Nation at Risk* admired in Japan turned out to be not an asset but part of the problem. Japan's "miracle" was fueled on the assumption that, with a finite amount of land and a high population, property values would appreciate forever. At one point, the Imperial Palace and its surrounding parks were estimated to be more valuable than the entire state of California. "It was . . . insane," said a Japanese commentator on National Public Radio's "All Things Considered" on August 18, 1998. However, the Japanese government continued to subsidize unproductive industries and Japanese banks extend many bad loans (perhaps a trillion-dollars' worth), based on the belief of ever-increasing land values. No one knows the actual amount because Japanese banks lack the technology to calculate their plight. In 2001, citing a shortage of manpower in the Financial Services Agency, Japan again showed its unwillingness to assess its losses, by refusing to let the International Monetary Fund try to figure it out (Blustein, 2001).

Schooling in the New Millennium

The U.S. economy in 2001 started to slow. By September 2001, even before the September 11 terrorist attacks, economists were arguing about whether the slowdown would tip over into recession. Following September 11, the argument shifted as to when the economy would begin to climb out of recession. Optimists saw it as early as the end of the first quarter of 2002 and according to the Federal Reserve Board chief, Alan Greenspan, the optimists won. Greenspan declared the recession over in March 2002, although he said the economy remained vulnerable (Berry, 2002).

Japan, on the other hand, remains mired in recession. New prime minister Junichiro Koizumi has promised to do something, but so have a host of his predecessors. On August 10, 2001, Japan's cabinet office announced that the economy had deteriorated further (Associated Press, 2001b). Koizumi announced huge budget cuts and an attempt to privatize or abolish seventy-seven large public-sector corporations, a plan that was greeted by both praise and criticism

---

2. This statement would not be as true of a developing nation, and it would not be true if the schools were producing generation after generation of idiots, but they are not.

(Chandler and Kashiwagi, 2001). Koizumi is the most popular prime minister since World War II, but his popularity won't last long, he said, as soon as the Japanese people start feeling the effects of his reforms. In fall 2001, Moody's Investor Services, a credit-rating organization, lowered its rating of Japanese government bonds, and the nation's two largest banks announced losses because they had decided to set aside twice as much money as previously planned against the risk of unrecoverable loans (Chandler, 2001; Kashiwagi, 2001).

In a 1999 international comparison of mathematics and science scores among thirty-eight nations, Japan, three other Asian nations, and one Asian city took the top five spots.[3] Japanese students continue to ace tests, but their scores can't raise Japan's credit rating. And, actually, it's not the schools' job to save the economy.

Yet American businesses and industries continue to act as they always have: They push schools to alter the curricula to make students better fit their needs, and they call for increases in skill levels even though most jobs do not require highly skilled workers. The Hudson Institute's *Workforce 2020* rightly notes that the proportion of skilled jobs is increasing, but its own tables show that the great majority of jobs do not require highly skilled or highly educated workers (Judy and D'Amico, 1998).

Researcher John Smith III of Michigan State University delved into what skills it takes to be a competent worker in the automobile assembly industry. He found that an eighth-grade mathematics education was sufficient. He also found that some needed math skills were not taught in school and some math concepts were not used on the job in the same way that they had been taught (Smith, 2000).

The call for more and more education, and higher and higher skills, may be viewed as an attempt to hold down the wages of skilled workers. While the Bureau of Labor Statistics projections clearly show an increase in the proportion of skilled jobs between now and 2020, they also show just as clearly that the overwhelming majority of jobs will require an associate's degree or less. Increasing the supply of skilled people will only make them less valuable.

In the 1970s and 1980s, American industry grew complacent and lost its competitive edge. Given the task of renewing competitiveness in the global economy, America's corporate elite responded admirably in one sense—they accomplished it. But at a terrible cost. They relentlessly applied technology to replace people. They modified managerial functions under the phrase "re-engineering." They internationalized economic interests and investments, and ownership, talent, and ideas.

Jane Addams' hypothetical "business man" is mighty busy today. The Business Roundtable, the National Alliance of Business, and various other commercial interests work actively to push schools to provide them with "adequate" employees. Adequate employees are those who arrive on the job capable of functioning,

---

3. Singapore, Hong Kong, Taipei, and South Korea.

thereby saving the employer any on-the-job training. In 2001, the Business Roundtable, a strong supporter of mandatory testing, issued a monograph advising businessmen on how to cope with "testing backlash"—the resistance to such testing (Business Roundtable, 2001).

As indicative of the commercial approach to schools, consider this from Alan Wurtzel, president of the Board of Directors of Circuit City, a large Richmond, Virginia-based discount electronics retailer: "In hiring new employees for our stores, warehouses, and offices, Circuit City is looking for people who are able to provide very high levels of customer service, who are honest, and who have a positive, enthusiastic, achievement-oriented work ethic" (Wurtzel, 1993). Few high-school graduates show up with these attitudes, Wurtzel claimed, so they had to turn to students with some college education. After reading Wurtzel's essay on the op-ed page of the *Washington Post*, I called Circuit City's personnel office to find out what kinds of reward the firm offered for all these positive traits. The answer was: minimum wage for most, and straight commission for the sales force.

5

The Condition of American Public Education

So, there's a war on the schools. Maybe it's justified. Can fifty years of constant criticism be wholly without merit? We have already seen a lot of evidence concerning the condition of public education. This chapter completes our examination of just how well American schools are doing, at least in those areas of performance that can be measured by test scores.

It is possible, of course, that the war being waged against the schools is justified. Perhaps William J. Bennett is *right* when he claims that the longer students suffer through American schools the dumber they become relative to their international counterparts. Perhaps it is true that test scores are still falling, as we often hear. Perhaps most students are leaving school unable to read, do basic arithmetic or even, as almost everyone seems to think, make change.[1] In this chapter we examine the rightness or wrongness of these charges by looking at the data, mostly test scores, that bear on them.

Even before looking at the facts, though, we should know enough to take these assertions with a grain of salt, because, as we have already seen, whenever the United States faces a social crisis, the public schools are usually the scapegoat of choice. They took the hit for letting the Russians get into space first. When it appeared that all of *Brown v. Board* had not been realized, they were faulted for not integrating the nation ethnically. They were held responsible for the temporary decline in international competitiveness in the 1980s. And they have been faulted for not preparing students for the workplaces of the future. We earlier noted that the October 3, 2000, edition of the *Washington Post* carried a full-page ad in Section A decrying the apparent poor finish in the final-year portion of

---

1. I do a lot of traveling and most of the family shopping. In airports, hotel shops, grocery stores, and various retail stores, I have taken to deliberately over- or underpaying. I have yet to see anyone fumble over what I should pay in addition or what I should get back.

TIMSS. This ad appeared to be some vague appeal to patriotism: America must be number one in everything.

The end of the Cold War meant that school critics could no longer cite the threat of the "Red Menace" or "Evil Empire" as reasons to change the schools. Now the Soviet Union has been replaced by a new enemy, the "Rogue State." The rogues were sufficient reason for increased spending for the military, a missile defense system, and continued reform of schools. After using this phrase for a while, the Clinton administration judged it as too crass and undiplomatic and abandoned it in favor of "nations of concern." After the terrorist attacks on the World Trade Center and Pentagon, though, the term *rogue nations* regained favor with Bush and his cabinet and the media as well. Even more recently, Bush coined the phrase "Axis of Evil," but the countries named don't have the power to scare the way the old USSR did.

Currently, those who comprise what I call "The Education Scare Industry"[2] attempt to create fear by arguing that schools are not, somehow, equipping students to cope with some unspecified "future." Scaremongers can always use the future for scare tactics because no one knows what the future will look like. Thus, we find IBM CEO Gerstner and Secretary of Health and Human Services Tommy G. Thompson declaring "What's at stake is not today's economy but tomorrow's" (Gerstner and Thompson, 2001).

A commission on math and science teaching headed by former senator and astronaut John Glenn could not stop itself from choosing a hysterical title for its report: *Before It's Too Late* (National Commission on Mathematics and Science Teaching, 2000). I'm amazed they had enough restraint not to tack an exclamation point on at the end. The report claims that if the Commission's recommendations are ignored, "our children and our nation will soon pay the high price." In support of the report, Gerry Wheeler, executive director of the National Science Teachers Association, weighed in with the statement that "while less-than-stellar science and math scores may not affect the economy today, we will ultimately pay a price." The president of the NSTA said, "We cannot afford to ignore yet another warning" (Wheeler, 2000). Neither the Glenn Commission nor Wheeler specified what the price would be.

America would do well to ignore these "warnings." We've been hearing this stuff for over fifty years now. We should work to improve science and mathematics instruction because we don't teach either subject particularly well in the early grades. Beyond that, the statements linking our performance, especially the performance of nine- and thirteen-year-olds on multiple-choice tests, to some future economic debacle are so much hokum and snake oil.

One can't fault Glenn and Wheeler too much—it is dangerous to predict the future specifically. For examples of the difficulties, read *The Experts Speak: The Definitive Compendium of Authoritative Misinformation* compiled by Christo-

---

2. William J. Bennett, Chester E. Finn, Jr., Diane Ravitch, Lamar Alexander, Denis Doyle, William Sowell, Louis V. Gerstner, Jr., and others.

pher Cerf and Victor Navasky. Cerf and Navasky present thousands of failed predictions from people who, one would think, should have known better (Cerf and Navasky, 1998). Thus, IBM President Thomas J. Watson says "I think there is a world market for about five computers"; Secretary of the Navy Newton Baker promises to stand on the bridge of a battleship while General Billy Mitchell tries to sink it with airplanes; and Manet tells Monet to tell his friend Renoir to find another line of work since he obviously has no talent for painting. In a program for an Army-Navy football game, a caption under a photo of the U.S.S. *Arizona* says no plane has ever sunk a battleship. Tragically, the game was played November 29, 1941, only eight days before Japanese planes turned the *Arizona* into an underwater memorial at Pearl Harbor.

Who in the 1950s, the Eisenhower years of "togetherness," could have predicted the social turmoil of the 1960s?[3] The hugely popular 1982 futurist book *Megatrends* does not even mention what some think is the most revolutionary invention since the automobile: the Internet (Naisbitt, 1982). Naisbitt's omission is easy to understand: In 1982 the Internet didn't exist. Right now, over half of all Americans have access. And some people are blaming the schools today for somehow not anticipating this trend—which no one else foresaw—and educating sufficient numbers of information technologists to cope with the explosive demand. Congress wants to change immigration laws so that we can bring over thousands of software engineers from India. This situation proves once again that education by itself does not produce jobs. If it did, all those thousands of Indian software engineers would be happily employed at home, not standing in line for visas to the United States.

Before looking at the data that bear on the condition of public education, let us consider a statement by the National Academy of Education.

> [Many of] those personal qualities that we hold dear—resilience and courage in the face of stress, a sense of craft in our work, a commitment to justice and caring in our social relationships, a dedication to advancing the public good in our communal life—are exceedingly difficult to assess. And so, unfortunately, we are apt to measure what we can, and eventually come to value what is measured over what is left unmeasured. The shift is subtle and occurs gradually. (Glaser, 1987)

In the years since Glaser penned those words, the shift has occurred and there is nothing subtle about it anymore. Tests dominate the talk about schools. Indeed, when the Virginia State Board of Education came under pressure to permit criteria other than just their tests to be used to determine high school graduation eligibility, the board said "Okay," and added more tests—the SAT, ACT, and tests given in the program leading to the International Baccalaureate. No grades and no teacher recommendations were considered—these criteria are regarded

---

3. Pundit George Will claims that they were foreseen in *Catcher in the Rye, Rebel Without A Cause,* and *The Wild Ones* (Will, 2001). I think that's a stretch.

as too squishy, too subjective. But let us consider a few things that tests don't measure:

Creativity	Self-Awareness
Critical Thinking	Self-Discipline
Resilience	Empathy
Motivation	Leadership
Ambition	Compassion
Persistence/Perseverance	Courage
Humor	Cowardice
Attitude	Endurance
Reliability	Confidence
Politeness	Focus
Enthusiasm	Teamwork
Civic-Mindedness	

Given the importance of these qualities, it is little wonder that when one examines the success people enjoy or don't enjoy in real life, tests play virtually no role.

High-Stakes Testing in the United States and Abroad

In the new millennium terrible things are being done in the name of high-stakes testing. The Massachusetts Department of Education threatened to yank funding for a 2001 conference if Alfie Kohn, a test critic, were permitted to speak. The Gwinnett County (Georgia) Public Schools sent policemen to Vermont to threaten Susan Ohanian with five years in prison and a million-dollar fine because she had received a copy of their "secure" test. Chicago Public Schools fired teacher and publisher George Schmidt because he published Chicago's tests in his monthly newspaper. The tests were so poorly prepared (I testified on Schmidt's behalf) that CPS should have sacked its testing department instead. Steve Orel, a teacher in Birmingham, Alabama, pointed out that 522 of Birmingham's lowest-scoring students were expelled just before the state's tests were administered. Orel was fired. Details of these events are provided in "The Eleventh Bracey Report on the Condition of Public Education" (Bracey, 2001). Even more examples of the suppression of criticism can be found in Susan Ohanian's "News from the Test Resistance Trail" (Ohanian, 2001).

Unfortunately, tests are about all we have to measure performance at national and international levels. Test scores come in two basic forms: trends on tests administered from time to time in this country, and snapshots from one-time administrations to students in the United States and various other nations.

The Third International Mathematics and Science Study (TIMSS), conducted in 1995, is the source of the myth that American students become dumber than their international counterparts the longer they stay in school. American fourth-graders scored above average in both subjects while eighth-graders were average in both, and American twelfth-graders finished, apparently, near the bottom. The operative word in the last clause is "apparently." I will address this a little later.

American children probably do not learn as much math and science between fourth grade and eighth grade as children in other developed nations. There are several reasons why this should be so. For one thing, American students are burdened by gigantic textbooks. One survey in Florida found elementary-school shoulders bearing as much as 19 pounds while a similar survey in Pennsylvania found secondary students carrying as much as 28 pounds (Maraghy 2000; Oshrat, 2000). Some younger students have resorted to the kind of wheeled luggage usually seen in airports to avoid these spine-deforming weights; older students resist this as "uncool." Even when weighed individually, these are gigantic tomes compared to those of other nations—often three times as thick. Textbooks in most countries come in reasonable 100–150 page sizes.

We have no national curriculum (many nations do) and therefore we have no national textbooks. In the United States, for-profit publishers construct textbooks. Their desire to sell to the widest possible market leads to a "kitchen sink" approach to topic inclusion, and, as a result, the books are huge.

American teachers try to cover every side of every subject. Ironically, one reason American children learn less is that their teachers teach too much. As a consequence, they often spend too little time on any given topic. Coverage is often brief and shallow. Topics taught one year have to be repeated the next because the instruction didn't "take." In other nations, teachers teach fewer topics and spend more time on each.

The textbook fiasco[4] is sufficient by itself to lower achievement, but there is another reason why American performance might trail off between grades four and eight. American educators have traditionally considered the middle-school years as the culmination of primary education. For most students, these grades are intended to reinforce what was taught in the first six grades and to prepare students for the more intense study of high school. Our middle grades look back and review.

Other nations look forward and introduce challenging new material. They treat these middle years as the start of the intense academic study that terminates in graduation from high school. Thus, Japan teaches seventh-grade students substantial amounts of algebra while eighth-graders get a hefty dose of plane geometry. Most American students must wait for grades 9 and 10, respectively,

---

4. To read more about America's "textbook fiasco," see Helen Tyson-Bernstein's *A Conspiracy of Good Intentions*, 1988.

for these subjects. American educators need to rethink once again what we should teach in the middle-school grades. There are problems here, but they are hardly the stuff of crisis.

Tables 5.1, 5.2, 5.3, and 5.4 show countries ranked by the percentage of correct answers that their students attained on the TIMSS tests at grades 4 and 8 (middle school). There are different numbers of nations at the two grades because the rules of the differed. Any nation that wanted to participate in TIMSS had to test at grade 8; grade 4 and the final year of secondary school were optional.

Note that most of the nations look very much alike in terms of their percentage correct. The proximity of most nations has been obscured for two reasons. First, official TIMSS reports present the data on a 600-point scale identical to that of the Scholastic Assessment Test (SAT). Small differences in percentage correct can look large when transposed to such a scale. Second, some of the reports gave only ranks, not scores. But you can't tell anything about performance from ranks. When they run the 100-meter dash in the Olympics, someone *must* rank last. He is still the eighth-fastest human being on the planet that day and not likely to be known to his peers as "Pokey." The percentage correct tables show that small differences in scores can make large differences in ranks. For instance, if American fourth-graders had gotten 6 percent fewer items correct on the science test, they would have fallen from fourth place to a tie for fifteenth. If American eighth graders had gotten 4 percent more items correct on the science test, they would have vaulted from nineteenth place to a tie for fifth.

TABLE 5.1   *TIMSS Fourth-Grade Mathematics Results (1996)*

Rank	Nation	Percentage Correct	Rank	Nation	Percentage Correct
1.5	**KOREA**	76	14.5	Latvia	59
1.5	**SINGAPORE**	76	16	Scotland	58
3	Japan	74	17	England	57
4	Hong Kong	73	18	Cyprus	54
5	Netherlands	69	19.5	Norway	53
6	Czech Republic	66	19.5	New Zealand	53
7	Austria	65	21	Greece	51
8.5	Slovenia	64	22.5	Iceland	50
8.5	Hungary	64	22.5	Thailand	50
11	Ireland	63	24	Portugal	48
11	**UNITED STATES**	63	25	Iran	38
11	Australia	63	26	Kuwait	32
13	Canada	60			
14.5	Israel	59		International Average: 59	

Source: Adapted from *Mathematics Achievement in the Primary School Years*, TIMSS International Study Center (Boston: Boston College, 1996).

TABLE 5.2 *TIMMS Fourth-Grade Science Results (1996)*

Rank	Nation	Percentage Correct	Rank	Nation	Percentage Correct
1	**KOREA**	**74**	16	Norway	60
2	Japan	70	16	New Zealand	60
3	Netherlands	67	16	Scotland	60
5	**UNITED STATES**	**66**	18	Israel	57
5	Australia	66	19	Latvia	56
5	Austria	66	20	Iceland	55
7.5	Czech Republic	65	21	Greece	54
7.5	Singapore	65	22	Cyprus	51
9.5	Canada	64	23	Portugal	50
9.5	Slovenia	64	24	Thailand	49
11	England	63	25	Kuwait	39
12.5	Hong Kong	62	26	Iran	30
12.5	Hungary	62			
14	Ireland	61		International Average: 59	

Source: Adapted from *Science Achievement in the Primary School Years,* TIMSS International Study Center (Boston: Boston College, 1996).

TABLE 5.3 *TIMSS Middle School Mathematics Results (1996)*

Rank	Nation	Percentage Correct	Rank	Nation	Percentage Correct
1	**SINGAPORE**	**79**	22	Sweden	56
2	Japan	73	25	England	54
3	Korea	72	25	Norway	54
4	Hong Kong	70	25	Germany	54
5.5	Belgium (Fl)	66	25	New Zealand	54
5.5	Czech Republic	66	27.5	**UNITED STATES**	**53**
8.5	Slovak Republic	62	27.5	England	53
8.5	Switzerland	62	29.5	Scotland	52
8.5	Hungary	62	29.5	Denmark	52
8.5	Austria	62	31.5	Latvia	51
11.5	France	61	31.5	Spain	51
11.5	Slovenia	61	33	Iceland	50
14	Russian Federation	60	34.5	Greece	49
14	Bulgaria	60	34.5	Romania	49
14	Netherlands	60	36.5	Lithuania	48
17	Canada	59	36.5	Cyprus	48
17	Ireland	59	38	Portugal	43
17	Belgium (Fr.)	59	39	Iran	38
19	Australia	58	40	Colombia	29
20.5	Thailand	57	41	South Africa	24
20.5	Israel	57		International Average: 55	

Source: Adapted from *Mathematics Achievement in the Middle School Years,* TIMSS International Study Center (Boston: Boston College, 1996).

TABLE 5.4   *TIMSS Middle School Science Results (1996)*

Rank	Nation	Percentage Correct	Rank	Nation	Percentage Correct
1	**SINGAPORE**	**70**	19	Germany	58
2	Korea	66	23.5	Thailand	57
3	Japan	65	23.5	Israel	57
4	Czech Republic	64	25.5	Switzerland	56
6	Bulgaria	62	25.5	Spain	56
6	Netherlands	62	27	Scotland	55
6	Slovenia	62	28	France	54
9	England	61	29.5	Greece	52
9	Hungary	61	29.5	Iceland	52
9	Austria	61	31	Denmark	51
11.5	Belgium (Fl.)	60	33.5	Latvia	50
11.5	Australia	60	33.5	Portugal	50
14	Slovak Republic	59	33.5	Belgium (Fr.)	50
14	Sweden	59	33.5	Romania	50
14	Canada	59	36	Lithuania	49
19	Ireland	58	37.5	Iran	47
19	**UNITED STATES**	**58**	37.5	Cyprus	47
19	Russian Federation	58	39	Kuwait	43
19	New Zealand	58	40	Colombia	39
19	Norway	58	41	South Africa	27
19	Hong Kong	58		International Average: 56	

Source: Adapted from *Science Achievement in the Middle School Years*, TIMSS International Study Center (Boston: Boston College, 1996).

In the eighth-grade science results, there are twenty-six nations within plus or minus 6 percent of the U.S. score.

The coverage of the TIMSS eighth-grade results indicates the media's negative bias toward schools. Only two newspapers, *Education Week* and the *New York Times*, reported the American finish as "average." All of the rest deemed our performance "mediocre." However, "average" is a statistic whereas "mediocre" is a judgment. The runners who finish fourth and fifth in the final heat of the 100-meter dash in the Olympics are average but hardly mediocre. One newspaper's story occupied fifteen paragraphs. Fourteen of them were devoted to the below-average math score. One acknowledged that the science score was above average.

To make the TIMSS data more relevant to American educators, the U.S. Department of Education commissioned ETS to statistically link the TIMSS results to our NAEP data (Johnson, 1998). The link puts both studies on a common scale. It's like translating a set of temperatures measured in Fahrenheit into Celsius. ETS translated the TIMSS scale to the scale the United States uses for

NAEP. This permits us to directly compare how the forty-one nations in TIMSS stacked up against the 40 states that take part in the NAEP state-by-state analyses.[5]

Six of the 41 nations outscored the highest scoring states in math, and only *one* outscored the highest states in science,[6] but only three scored lower than the lowest-scoring state. Only one nation, South Africa, scored lower than the District of Columbia in both subjects.

These results are dramatic. They illustrate the enormous variability of academic achievement in this nation. They also reveal which schools really need help. Experts consider the District of Columbia's schools to be about average among big-city systems. We don't need President Bush's comprehensive testing program to know where additional resources should go—the TIMSS data has clearly indicated where we should begin.

Interpreting international comparisons is difficult because of the number of variables that can't be measured but which likely affect test scores (more about this later). Still, at grade 4 and grade 8, most developed countries have virtually all of their students in school and receiving the same curriculum.

Once you pass eighth grade, though, comparisons become extremely difficult. American students, although often tracked in different curricula, proceed from eighth grade to comprehensive high schools. But other nations offer students differentiated and focused curricula. In some countries, over 50 percent of students enter vocational schools. Other students will attend schools focused on science and technology, or liberal arts schools that will prepare them for crucial college-entrance examinations, such as the French *baccalaureat* or the German *abitur.* Some countries have high dropout rates, and some now have high-school completion rates that exceed ours. All of these differences make end-of-secondary-school comparisons extremely iffy.

But TIMSS tried. It administered a test of math–science literacy to students in their final year of secondary school. Keep this phrase, "final year of secondary school," in mind, because it is not always the same thing as "twelfth grade" in the United States. Countries were asked to test a representative sample of final-year students. TIMSS also administered a test of advanced mathematics and a test of physics. Since not everyone takes advanced math or physics, countries were allowed to choose which students they felt would be appropriate to test. These choices made a difference.

For instance, Sweden and Norway had the highest scores in physics. The students they tested had taken physics for three years. Most American students

---

5. When the United States conducts a NAEP assessment, all states participate with a representative sample. Some states also want to test enough additional students to provide a result for the state alone. Not all states participate. Some don't think it is worth the additional money and some are satisfied with the testing data they already have.

6. The six nations with higher math scores were Singapore, Japan, Korea, Hong Kong, the Czech Republic, and the Flemish-speaking part of Belgium (which was treated as a separate country from the French-speaking part). Only Singapore had a higher science score.

study physics for only one year. It would be astonishing if Sweden and Norway *didn't* score higher than the United States in physics. These results might lead us to ask "Should United States high schools offer three years of physics, as some other nations do?" That would be a legitimate question. But to compare the physics scores of American students to Norwegian and Swedish students is not legitimate.

The inherent iffiness of final-year comparisons was compounded when the U.S. Department of Education made a monumental mistake of releasing the final-year results without emphasizing that secondary schools in different countries vary wildly in which students attend and what they are taught. The media reported the results as showing that our seniors went up against seniors in other countries and got trounced, and that our best seniors went up against their best seniors and got trounced:

> American high school seniors have scored far below their *peers* from many other countries on a rigorous new international exam in math and science.
> —Kenneth Cooper, *Washington Post*, p. 1, emphasis added

> American high school seniors—even the best and brightest among them—score well below the average for their *peers* participating in TIMSS.
> —Debra Viadero, *Education Week*, p. 1, emphasis added

> U.S. twelfth graders rank poorly in math and science study.
> —Ethan Bronner, *New York Times*, p. 1

> American 12th-graders scored at the very bottom of the rankings.
> —William Raspberry, *Washington Post*, A25

> Hey! We're No. 19!
> —John Leo, *U.S. News and World Report*, p. 14

One wonders how Cooper of the *Washington Post* knew that the test was rigorous, since he had not seen it. The media treated the study as if it were an apples-to-apples comparison. The study, though, did not compare apples to apples. It didn't even compare apples to oranges—it was more like apples to aardvarks.

In addition, the TIMSS Final-Year Study has so many methodological flaws that few conclusions can be drawn with any certainty. Although all countries were supposed to test a representative sample in a math–science literacy test, many did not. Similarly, not all tested appropriate samples in the specialized advanced mathematics and physics tests.

Most nations do not have the culture of public self-criticism that the United States does. Indeed, in some countries, such criticism can get you jailed, tortured, or even executed. If the countries were invited to pick the students to be tested, many would simply choose students who would make their country look good. TIMSS authorities tried to prevent this outcome tendency by obtaining lists of all schools in all nations, along with some demographic information about each school. They provided each nation with a list of the representative schools that they should test.

However, the TIMSS authorities could not, of course, force the participating nations to accept the lists and many of them did not. Russia, a nation of hundreds of languages, tested only Russian-speaking schools. Italy lopped off whole provinces. Some chosen schools refused to participate (typically, schools that refuse to participate have demographic characteristics that lead you to predict lower test scores than those who accept).

The TIMSS directors established criteria for participation rates and exclusions based upon how many of the designated schools refused to participate and what proportion of the eligible population was excluded. If the countries fell below these criteria, their data could be considered questionable. Only five nations met the criteria. One can wonder, then, why the study was published in the first place. It likely has to do with the enormous bundle that U.S. taxpayers coughed up for it: $53 million overall.

Many other problems afflict the data. I asked a TIMSS official why we had administered the advanced mathematics test to American students in pre-calculus classes. He said, rather nonchalantly, "just to see how they'd do." Well, they did poorly, scoring 100 points lower than American students who actually had some calculus under their belts. Students who had taken calculus scored at the international average. But, of course, neither the TIMSS officials nor the U.S. Department of Education staff said anything about this in the press release or at the press conference.

This event reflects the generally cavalier attitude of testers toward the testees. The testers have no interest in how the tests affect students. It is hard for testers (whom some call "Testocrats") to imagine children throwing up on the answer sheet, losing bladder control, or even, in rare instances, committing suicide over tests.

The poor performance of the pre-calculus students hardly came as a surprise: Twenty-three percent of the problems in the advanced mathematics test presumed that the test taker had already *finished* a course in calculus. If we convert from scores to percentile ranks, American students who had taken calculus finished average, in the fiftieth percentile. American students kids in the pre-calculus classes scored at only the sixteenth percentile rank. That's what happens when you test students on material they haven't studied yet.

Those of us who have lived abroad will never have any confidence in the international comparisons. There are also many cultural variables that can affect scores but cannot be quantified. Do other nations experience a "senior slump" as severe as that in the United States? American secondary schools generally don't give low-stakes tests to seniors. Indeed, some schools have abandoned the traditional second semester of senior year altogether, replacing it with various projects, trips, and other experiences to engage students—most of whom already know where they're going to college, if college-bound, or already have made other post–secondary plans (Mathews, 2001). Yet, American high-school seniors took the TIMSS Final-Year tests in May.

Most cultural variables that produce differences are hard to identify, much less quantify. For instance, some of my friends whose children live abroad have grandchildren in French schools. It appalls them that French teachers use shame as a motivational technique. Teachers might put an assignment's worst paper on the bulletin board and make fun of it. What are the side effects of this strategy—is it responsible for the French capacity for wicked repartee or planting the seed for future neuroses? How can you quantify the amount of shame doled out?

TIMSS did find one variable that the study could measure and that made a huge difference in scores. TIMSS asked students how many hours they worked at paid jobs. In most countries, a person is either a student or a worker, not both. The United States culture encourages teenagers to work. Our vision of the teen years also includes dates, cars, malls, and extracurricular activities. It has never been seen as a period of nose-to-the-grindstone study. We save that for college. This may work fine for the two-thirds of high-school graduates that do go to college, but is a disaster for the rest.

Does working affect achievement? Yes. Furthermore, research on the topic produces interesting findings: Students who work up to 20 hours a week achieve better in school than those who work longer hours and those who do not work at all (D'Amico, 1984; Gottfredson, 1985b; Schulenberg and Bachman, 1993). But working over 20 hours begins to eat into students' school performance.

Table 5.5 shows the profile of a typical nation, Sweden, and for the United States. The percentages in parentheses are the percent of students working the number of hours shown at the top. Fully 55 percent of American seniors taking the TIMSS tests said they worked more than 21 hours a week at a paid job. Twenty-eight percent said they worked more than 35 hours a week. Students who worked 21–35 hours a week scored well below average and those who worked more than 35 hours a week dropped almost off the chart. American students who worked a moderate amount scored at the international average.

Thus when we look at the American students who most resemble their foreign counterparts, their scores are just above average among the nations. However, the TIMSS Final-Year data are so flawed that they are best not considered at all.

TABLE 5.5   *Hours Per Week at a Paid Job and Math/Science Literacy Scores*

Hours Worked	< 7	7–14	21–35	> 35
United States	484 (39%)	506 (7%)	474 (27%)	448 (28%)
Sweden	563 (84%)	541 (5%)	511 (5%)	497 (3%)
International Average:	500			

Overall, Sweden had the second-highest score among the twenty-one nations in this part of the study, and the United States had the sixteenth.

Source: Data adapted from *Mathematics and Science Achievement in the Final Year of Secondary School,* TIMSS International Study Center (Boston: Boston College, 1996).

I have taken some time with the TIMSS study partly because of the attention it has received in the popular press, partly because that attention has been
misleading. As the reader can see from this discussion about TIMSS, international comparisons are complicated operations full of subtleties and complexities. But the media reduce them to simplistic sound bites such as, "Hey! We're
Number 19!"

In 1999, TIMSS authorities administered the TIMSS math and science
tests to eighth-graders in thirty-eight nations. American students scored slightly
better than the international average. In its analysis of the TIMSS-R ("R" for
"Repeat") data, the U.S. Department of Education produced what I like to refer
to as "microcosmic" data—a small set of data that represent the state of education as a whole.

The TIMSS-R microcosmic data show how our various ethnic groups
fared. In the TIMSS sampling system, Asian Americans and Native Americans
were too few to generate a reliable score and no reports are available. But scores
are available for the three largest groups: whites, blacks, and Hispanics, as shown
in Table 5.6.

It is unfortunate that TIMSS-R had no direct measure of poverty. Over half
of black students and nearly half of Hispanic students live below the poverty line.
Poor students score much lower than middle-class students. But the table shows
clearly that we don't need to test all American students in grades 3 through 8, as
President Bush now proposes. We already know where extra resources are
needed, but lack the political will to put them there. The master myth—money
doesn't matter—comes in handy for avoiding facing our weaknesses.

In December 2001 another international study yielded results that, again,
ranked American students favorably in comparison with overseas peers. The
PISA (Program for International Student Assessment) study was conducted by
the Organization for Economic Cooperation and Development (OECD) in

TABLE 5.6   *Ranks of U.S. Ethnic Groups in*
TIMSS-R (out of 39—38 nations plus the group)

	Mathematics	Science
Whites	13	6
Blacks	31	31
Hispanics	29	28

White students, about 65 percent of all students, ranked in the
upper third in math and near the top in science. So, about two-
thirds of America's students score quite well stacked up against
students in thirty-eight other nations.

Source: U.S. Department of Education (1999). Table of ranks
constructed by author.

TABLE 5.7   *Ranks of U.S. Students in PISA (out of 28/32 nations)*

	Reading	Mathematics	Science
White students	2nd	7th	4th
Black students	26th/29th	27th/30th	27th/30th
Hispanic students	26th/29th	27th/30th	27th/30th

For black and Hispanic students, the first rank is the rank among the twenty-eight OECD nations and the second is the rank with the addition of the four nonmember nations.

Source: U.S. Department of Education (2001). Table of ranks constructed by author.

twenty-eight OECD member countries and four nonmembers (Latvia, Liechtenstein, Brazil, and the Russian Federation). OECD administered tests designed to see how well fifteen-year-old students could apply school knowledge to solve "real world" problems in reading, mathematics, and science.

The results were remarkably similar to TIMSS. American fifteen-year-olds were average across the board. Again, most countries differed from one another only by small amounts. The disparities shown among ethnic groups—a proxy for poverty—are, if anything, even starker than those of TIMSS, as seen in Table 5.7.

Our Leaders—Accentuating the Negative

It's bad enough that researchers and the media mishandle data such as TIMSS, but, far worse, our leaders have often tried to promote their own education agendas at the expense of our public schools. Both the Reagan and the George H.W. Bush administrations deliberately hyped any negative findings about American public schools and suppressed positive findings whenever they could. They did so in order to promote the privatization of American education through school vouchers and tuition tax credits.

In 1989 Secretary of Energy James Watkins gave a speech at the Sandia National Laboratories in Albuquerque, an institution funded by the Department of Energy. He stated that education would be a priority at Sandia. This puzzled the audience of engineers, but, being engineers, they set out to systematically analyze the education system. They produced a 156-page report dealing with achievement-test scores, SATs, dropout rates, market forces, and a host of other statistics bearing on the condition of public education. Their general conclusion was that "there are many serious problems in American public education but there is no system-wide crisis.[7] The political appointees of the U.S. Department

---

7. This sentence did not appear in the published version.

of Education deemed the report too positive and killed it (Carson, Huelskamp, and Woodall, 1990). The report was finally published after the 1992 election put the Clinton administration in the White House (Carson, Huelskamp, and Woodall, 1993).

When the Sandia engineers came to Washington to present their findings to the Department of Energy, the Department of Education, and some congressional staffers, they did not receive a warm welcome. According to Sandia engineer Robert Huelskamp, David Kearns, former CEO of Xerox and then–Deputy Secretary of Education, told them, "You bury this or I'll bury you" (personal communication, February 1992). An *Education Week* article on the meeting states only that "Administration officials, particularly Mr. Kearns, reacted angrily at the meeting" (Miller, 1991). Secretary of Energy Watkins called the report "dead wrong" in a letter to the *Albuquerque Journal* (Miller, 1991). Watkins offered no specific refutations of any facts the report contained. He couldn't. The Sandia engineers made a few mistakes on minor matters, but mostly they got their data right.

The *Education Week* article also quoted a source saying that the Sandia researchers "were told that it [their report] would never see the light of day, that they had better be quiet. I fear for their careers" (Miller, 1991). Although none of them actually lost their jobs, at one point they were forbidden to leave the state of New Mexico to talk about their study.

The "official story" from Assistant Secretary of Education Diane Ravitch was that the report was not yet sufficiently professional for publication and was undergoing "peer review." This was an outrage. "Peer review" of a federal agency report by another federal agency is unheard of. The Bush administration never cleared the report. Compiled in late 1990, the "peer review" never approved it for publication. It did appear after Clinton became president, comprising the entire May/June 1993 issue of the *Journal of Educational Research* (Carson, Huelskamp, Woodall, 1993).

The fate of the Sandia Report (officially titled *Perspectives on Education in America*) was not an isolated event. One study commissioned by the U.S. Department of Education in 1983 sought to prove that people who become teachers are not very bright. Unfortunately for the ideologues, they hired researchers with integrity. The study examined the grade-point averages of future teachers and those who had other career plans at the end of the sophomore year in college, before the teachers-to-be started taking the allegedly easy education-school courses. The future teachers had GPAs as high as other majors.[8] The administration buried the study, and I uncovered it only through a chance remark by David Imig of the American Association of Colleges of Teacher Education. One wonders how many other similar reports from this era lie buried in the files of the U.S. Department of Education.

---

8. One imagines that the courses taken by teachers-to-be were not as rigorous as those taken by, say, math majors or pre-engineering students, but at the time of the study many freshmen and sophomores took a number of courses in common.

If positive reports have been deep-sixed, negative reports have been emphasized. Thus, in February 1992, when an international comparison in mathematics and science found American ranks mostly (but not entirely) low, the Department of Education held a well-attended press conference. The study received wide coverage in both print and electronic media: "An 'F' in World Competition" was the headline over the story in *Newsweek*.[9]

Five months later, in July 1992, an international study of reading skills appeared. It showed American students among the best in the world. The Department of Education called no press conference. No media reported the study. Over two months elapsed before *Education Week* found out about it—by accident. A friend of then–*Education Week* reporter Robert Rothman sent him a copy from Germany.

As we would expect, *Education Week*, which bills itself as "American Education's Newspaper of Record," carried the story on page 1 (Rothman, 1992). *USA Today* played off the *Education Week* article with its own front-page story (Manning, 1992). The *USA Today* story, though, had a curious aspect to it. It contained a quote from Deputy Assistant Secretary of Education Francie Alexander dismissing the study as irrelevant.

The study faded so completely from view that four years later, in 1996, then–Secretary of Education Richard Riley re-released the results. *USA Today* again heralded them. The only other notable coverage, though, came from the Washington Bureau of the *Los Angeles Times*. I inquired of *Times* reporter, Josh Greenberg, why his paper was interested in four-year-old data. He said that he and others had been suspicious when Riley had called them over to discuss the results. But, Greenberg said, when he checked around, he found that no one knew about the study, and therefore it was still news.

By that criterion, it still is. In speeches, I always ask for a show of hands of those who know of the international reading-skills study of 1992. Even in a room full of other researchers, I seldom see more than three or four hands in the air. In audiences of teachers or administrators or school-board members, I never see a single one.

The media handling of this story suggests something else about our perceptions of the condition of public education: Americans have a neurotic need to believe the worst of our schools. I have already mentioned the translation of "average" in the TIMSS results to "mediocre." As for the reading study, conducted by the same organization that conducted TIMSS, the story ran in the *American School Boards Journal* under the headline "Good News: Our 9-Year-Olds Read Well; Bad News: Our 14-Year-Olds Don't."

The "good" news about the study was that American nine-year-olds finished second among twenty-seven nations, outscored only by Finland. The "bad"

---

9. *Newsweek* seems constitutionally incapable of saying anything positive about schools. When the eighth-grade TIMSS data arrived, *Newsweek*'s headline was "The Sum of Mediocrity" (Wingert, 1996). American ninth-graders were average. When the TIMSS fourth-grade data showed American students near the top, *Newsweek* carried no story.

news was that American fourteen-year-olds had finished eighth among thirty-one nations. I wrote a letter to the editor of *ASBJ* asking how, in a study of thirty-one nations, where sixteenth place would be average, eighth place could be bad news.

More important, if one examines the actual test scores, one finds that the eighth-place American fourteen-year-olds are as close to first place as the second-place nine-year-olds. On a 600-point scale, the nine-year-olds were 22 points out of first place, and the fourteen-year-olds, 25 points. Once again, it is Finland, a small, homogeneous country with huge taxes and virtually no worries about teaching Finnish-as-a-second-language that significantly outscores the United States, where my school district has to cope with 105 languages.

These results are shown in Tables 5.8 and 5.9. It is important constantly to keep in mind the distinction made earlier between ranks and scores. From ranks alone, one can know nothing about performance. If we look away from the average scores, which are most-widely reported, and look at the best readers, we find that America's best readers outscored all other countries, including Finland. The scores for the United States—ninetieth, ninety-fifth, and ninety-ninth percentiles—were the highest in the world.

The good-news-is-no-news and believe-the-worst attitudes toward the reading-study story apply to more than the media. Conservatives advocate school vouchers and privatization. To further their goal, they emphasize the negative about schools. Liberals want to preserve and improve public schools. Many

TABLE 5.8 *How in the World Do Students Read? Results for Nine-Year-Olds*

Rank	Nation	Score	Rank	Nation	Score
1	Finland	569	14.5	Spain	504
2	**United States**	**547**	16	Germany (W)*	503
3	Sweden	539	17	Canada (BC)	500
4	France	531	18.5	Germany (E)*	499
5	Italy	529	18.5	Hungary	499
6	New Zealand	528	20	Slovenia	498
7	Norway	524	21	Netherlands	485
8	Iceland	518	22	Cyprus	481
9	Hong Kong	517	23	Portugal	478
10	Singapore	515	24	Denmark	475
11	Switzerland	511	25	Trinidad/Tobago	451
12	Ireland	509	26	Indonesia	394
13	Belgium (Fr.)	507	27	Venezuela	383
14.5	Greece	504			

*Germany not unified at the time of the study

Source: Data adapted from International Association for the Evaluation of Educational Achievement (1992).

TABLE 5.9   *How in the World Do Students Read? Results for Fourteen-Year-Olds*

Rank	Country	Score	Rank	Country	Score
1	Finland	560			
	Countries above this line significantly higher than the United States				
2	France	549	17	Norway	516
3	Sweden	546	18	Italy	515
4	New Zealand	545	19	Netherlands	514
6	Hungary	536	20	Ireland	511
6	Iceland	536	21	Greece	509
6	Switzerland	536	22	Cyprus	497
8.5	**United States**	**535**	23	Spain	490
8.5	Hong Kong	535	24	Belgium (Fr.)	481
10	Singapore	534	25	Trinidad/Tobago	479
11	Slovenia	532	26	Thailand	477
12	Germany (E)	526	27	Phillipines	430
13	Denmark	525	28	Venezuela	417
14	Portugal	523	29	Nigeria	401
15.5	Canada/BC	522	30	Zimbabwe	372
15.5	Germany (W)	522	31	Botswana	330

Source: Data adapted from International Association for the Evaluation of Educational Achievement (1992).

times, however, their improvement efforts take the form of pointing to problems in the schools and, therefore, to the need for more money to solve them.

Thus we have heard President Clinton repeatedly saying that only 40 percent of American third-graders could read independently, a refrain also sung by President George W. Bush and his Secretary of Education, Rod Paige. This is not actually a valid claim, but only a misinterpretation of NAEP data. More important, these are the same third-graders who, in 1992, ranked second in the world in reading.

The research universities also accentuate the negative in order to pry money from governments and foundations. As noted earlier, in a roomful of academics, Susan Fuhrman, Dean of the School of Education at the University of Pennsylvania, drew no reaction when she said, "If you want money, ya gotta say the schools are lousy. So what else is new?" What, indeed?

We can examine the reactions to the international studies from the perspective of what purpose a group wants the data to serve. Conservatives want school vouchers and tuition tax credits. Liberals want more money. The religious right wants schools where they can teach religion free of first-amendment constraints. Business and industry want docile, job-ready employees and good little consumers. Good news about America's public schools serves none of these groups' education-reform agendas.

Domestic Data on the Condition of Education

We have already looked at a variety of domestic test score data in Chapter 3. We saw that some achievement test scores rose to all-time highs and that NAEP scores have been rising, especially when examined by ethnicity. SAT scores have also risen and, again, the changes are obscured by demographic changes in who is taking the SAT—more minorities, more poor students, more women, and more students with mediocre high-school records. The Sandia Report, for instance, found that SAT scores would have risen in the period between 1975 and 1990 if just the students' rank in class had stayed the same. Instead, more and more students in the bottom 40 percent and bottom 20 percent of their classes aspired to colleges that required the SAT, and their entrance into the pool of SAT test-takers lowered the scores.

Critics have pointed to the decline of the SAT "elite"—usually defined as those scoring above 650 on each test—as reflecting declining school quality and rigor. This statistic has become so much a part of popular beliefs about education that it augments the believe-the-worst tendencies even in institutions that should know better and should be more careful—*Education Week*, for instance.

In late 1992 *Education Week*, noting that April 1993 would mark the tenth anniversary of *A Nation at Risk*, decided to look at what the reforms of the previous decade had accomplished. In an opening essay, the editors asked, in general, what had happened in ten years, and their answer was, essentially, not much.

> The proportion of American youngsters performing at high levels remains infinitesimally small. In the past 10 years, for instance, the number and proportion of those scoring at or above 650 on the verbal or math section of the Scholastic Aptitude Test[10] has actually declined. (February 10, 1993)

In a table in the margin near the text, *Education Week* provided the figures shown in Table 5.10. The figures in parentheses are the proportions of students represented by the numbers and it certainly appears as though both numbers and proportions fell during the 1982–1992 period. For some reason, these numbers looked suspicious to me and I checked the figures in my collection of "Profiles of College Bound Seniors," an annual booklet that the College Board publishes when it releases the latest SAT scores.

I determined that the figures for 1982 were correct. So were the figures for 1992—as far as they went. But the figures for 1992 were incomplete. SAT scores range from 200 to 800. The College Board arranges these scores in a table divided into 40-point intervals. The 1992 table is shown in Table 5.11.

Education Week's numbers for 1982 included all of the high-scorers—everyone who scored from 650 to 800. But its numbers for 1992 were only for the students scoring from 650 to 690. Perhaps some copying error led to the

10. Now called the Scholastic Assessment Test.

TABLE 5.10   *Number of Students Scoring between 700 and 800 on the Scholastic Aptitude Test (SAT)*

	Verbal	*Mathematics*
1982	29,921 (3)	70,352 (7)
1992	22,754 (2)	58,662 (6)

Source: Adapted from data supplied by the College Board (1982, 1995).

TABLE 5.11   *Number of Students in Selected SAT Score Intervals, 1992*

Verbal Number	*Score*	*Math Number*
1,371	750–800	14,132
8,758	700–740	33,387
22,754	650–690	56,882
—	—	—
—	—	—
—	—	—
54,786	200–240	13,414

Source: Adapted from data supplied by the College Board (1992).

omission of the students who scored 700 or better. When we add the results for students scoring between 700 and 800 to the 1992 results, *Education Week*'s table takes on a quite different appearance, as shown in Table 5.12. Over the decade the proportion of students scoring above 650 on the verbal section remained steady at 3 percent. This is less than half of what it once was, and is no cause for joy, but the proportion did not decline during the decade.

For the math section, however, the proportion rises from 7 percent to 10 percent. I wrote *Education Week*'s editors and asked for a front page correction. The editors printed only my letter in the usual letters section. They also affixed an editorial note to my letter that said in essence, yes, but it's still a tiny proportion.

I wrote a second letter, pointing out that when the SAT took its modern form in 1941, its developers imposed on it a normal, bell-shaped distribution and that it is inherent in bell curves that few people score at the extremes (an SAT score of 650 corresponds to the ninety-third percentile). More important, the standardization of the SAT test that took place in 1941 remained in place until 1996 when the test was "recentered."

TABLE 5.12   *Proportion of Students Scoring above 650 on the Scholastic Aptitude Test (SAT)*

	Verbal	*Mathematics*
1982	29,921 (3)	70,352 (7)
1992 (*Ed Week*)	22,754 (2)	58,662 (6)
1992 (Actual)	32,903 (3)	104,401 (10)

Source: Adapted from data supplied by the College Board (1982, 1992).

This raises the question: Who were the students who set the standards on the SAT in the period from 1941 to 1996? The standard-setting group consisted of 10,654 students living mostly in the northeast. They were 98 percent white and 61 percent male, and 41 percent attended private college preparatory high schools. By all measures, they were an elite. It was to this elite's average raw score (number correct) that the College Board affixed the average scaled score of 500 (Donlon and Angoff, 1971).

You can compare a standard-setting group to another group only if the other group has the same characteristics as the standard setters (or if you adjust for differences). However, the 1992 students were substantially different: They were 71 percent white and 48 percent male and a total of 18 percent attended private schools of some kind (including Catholic schools, other sectarian schools, segregation academies, and nonsectarian private schools). The parents of 42 percent of the 1992 test-takers held a high-school diploma or less. Some 30 percent reported annual family incomes of $30,000 or less. Between 1941 and 1992 the SAT test-taking group was greatly democratized, but all of the changes are associated with lower scores.

It is worth repeating that the average score of 500 was given to the average raw score (number correct) obtained by an elite group of students consisting mostly of white male New Englanders and New Yorkers—a group whose socio-economic status and educational experience in no way compares to the SAT takers of 1992 and later.

Given the statistical properties of the normal curve, we know that 6.68 percent of the standard-setting group scored 650 or better. In 1992, the verbal proportion had fallen to only 3 percent, but the mathematics proportion had grown to 10 percent. I included this statistic as one of many in a *Washington Post* op-ed essay in late 1995 (Bracey, 1995b). As an example of how our culture cannot accept good news about schools, conservative school critic Denis Doyle told readers of a Heritage Foundation publication that "[Bracey] does not tell the reader who is pushing the SAT scores higher: mostly Asian and Asian-American students" (Doyle, 1996).

Doyle's comment is typical of school critics when confronted with positive data about the schools: Let's get rid of these numbers and if we can't, let's point out some special or unusual circumstance behind the statistics. In this case, the special circumstance is imagined to be the higher proportion of students with an alleged "math gene." Doyle presented no evidence to back up the claim, meaning that, at best, he had formulated a hypothesis. I tested Doyle's hypothesis by obtaining SAT scores by ethnicity from the College Board. Over the period from 1981 to 1995, the latest year for scores at the time of the analysis, the results for all students are as shown in Table 5.13. Doyle's hypothesis holds that Asian students are pushing the scores higher. Therefore, if we remove Asian students from the sample, the 74.6 percent figure should disappear or become small. When Asian students are removed, the growth does decline, but it remains substantial, as shown in Table 5.14.[11]

In 1981, students reporting their ethnicity as Asian represented 3.0 percent of the total pool of SAT test-takers, and in 1995 they constituted 7.5 percent. From this alone, one would predict a higher proportion of high scorers, because Asian students do score much better on the SAT-Math than any other ethnic group. However, with Asian students removed from the sample at both years, we still find a 57 percent increase for black, white, Hispanic, and Native American students.

With the recentering of the scale in 1996, individual researchers cannot calculate these proportions on the old scale.[12] However, the Educational Testing Service and the College Board were considerate enough to do this for me. In 1997, the proportion remained at 12.4 percent, but by 2000 it had climbed to 13.2 percent and in 2001 it jumped to 13.5 percent.

Interestingly, the SAT's verbal scores have also crept up. In one essay, I predicted a further decline in SAT-V scores because of the emerging "iconic" culture in which pictures and graphic images played a larger role (Bracey, 1992). That prediction has also failed. The proportion of students scoring above 650 on the SAT-V bottomed out in 1983 at 2.9 percent, but had climbed back to 4 percent by 1997 and was at 3.8 percent for 2001.

The National Assessment of Educational Progress (NAEP) avoids the selection problems of using SAT and ACT scores because it draws a national probability sample of students. A "national probability sample" means that at the grades NAEP tests, every student in the nation has an equal chance of being included in the sample that gets tested.

11. These figures are not based on precisely the same numbers as those for all students. Some 99,000 students reported their ethnicity as "other" or did not report it at all.

12. If one is working only with SAT math scores and only with the proportion scoring 650 or higher, it does not matter whether one uses the original scale or the recentered one. The proportion is the same on both. Some students get slightly higher scores with the recentered scale and some actually get lower scores than they would on the original. The difference is no more than 10 points on any part of the scale, but is nonexistent at the threshold point of 650.

TABLE 5.13 *Students Scoring above 650 on the SAT-M (All Students)*

	1981		1995
Number	70,307		132,898
Percentage	7.1		12.4
Change		74.6%	

Source: Adapted from data supplied by the College Board (1982, 1995).

TABLE 5.14 *Students Scoring above 650 on the SAT-M (Excluding Asian American Students)*

	1981		1995
Number	65,672		118,879
Percentage	6.8		10.7
Change		57.3%	

Source: Adapted from data supplied by the College Board (1982, 1995).

NAEP has its own difficulties as a national barometer, though. We observed earlier that it is not tied to any specific curriculum. Until recently, it had no consequences for the test-takers, their teachers, parents, or anyone else. Now, a few states have begun to use NAEP scores or changes in NAEP scores for "bragging rights," eliciting worries that NAEP's integrity might be at risk and calling to mind "Bracey's Paradox." Bracey's Paradox, formulated around 1979, states that test scores are only significant when you don't pay any attention to them. Once you begin giving them importance, you unleash all kinds of corrupting influences. This might be happening with NAEP: States that have shown sizable gains on NAEP have also shown sizable gains in the percentage of students excluded from testing.

The No Child Left Behind Act of 2001

A great deal has been made of President George W. Bush's No Child Left Behind program. As initially planned, it was a draconian plan that would have labeled almost all schools as failures. One of its strangest proposals was that of "Adequate Yearly Progress" (AYP). A staff analysis showed that, depending on the level of test-score aggregation, between 89 percent and 98 percent of all schools in North Carolina and Texas would have failed. These two states have received much media attention for their rising test scores. If they didn't come up to snuff for AYP, who would?

The plan was opposed in its initial form by the National Council of State Legislatures and the American Association of School Administrators. Other organizations, such as the National Education Association, did not actively oppose it but said that neither could they support it. Even its author, Bush adviser Sandy Kress, called it "Rube Goldbergesque." The bill was passed by comfortable margins in both houses, but educators hoped that the conference committee called to resolve differences between the House and Senate versions would require that the program be redefined from scratch.

The committee, however, did reach agreement. In its final version, No Child Left Behind allows each state to set its own standards, choose whatever tests it wants to measure progress and define what constitutes "Adequate Yearly Progress." States have twelve years to ensure that all their students reach the "proficient" level on whatever standards they set. No one knows yet what "proficient" means. There have been hints that it refers to the proficient level on NAEP. If so, this will be an impossibly high standard to reach. Consider that in the 1998 NAEP 4th-grade reading assessment, 42 percent of white students were proficient or better. For African Americans, Hispanics, and Asian Americans, the figures were 12 percent, 16 percent, and 39 percent, respectively. For the 1996 mathematics assessment the numbers were more chilling. Eighteen percent of whites were proficient or better. For African Americans, Hispanics, and Asian Americans, the figures were 1 percent, 5 percent, and 26 percent. The definition of AYP must be "statistically reliable and valid and result in continuous and substantial academic progress for all students." States must report separate results for economically disadvantaged students, the major racial and ethnic groups, students with disabilities, and students with limited English proficiency. States must administer NAEP tests in reading and math at grades 4 to 8 every two years, but only if the secretary of education agrees to pay for it.

The concept of AYP is brand-new and no one has yet developed any meaningful manner of calculating it, much less "statistically reliable and valid" techniques. Indeed, there is research indicating that year-to-year changes in achievement are inherently unreliable and, therefore, invalid. But, given that states have twelve years to improve all students' achievement, many of the politicians who agreed to this program won't be in office when it finally begins to have an impact.

The requirement to raise all students to a "proficient" level involves perhaps fifty different definitions of "proficient"—one for each state. This encourages states to show gains by setting low standards. Texas did this with its Texas Assessment of Academic Skills. In the beginning some tests had passing scores close to the level of chance. This meant that small increases in scores could bring large increases in the percentage of students meeting the standards and Texas could point to great progress.

States must report their test results to local agencies, schools, and teachers "in a manner that is clear and easy to understand" and that can "be used by those local educational agencies, schools, and teachers to improve the educational achievement of individual students." But no tests generate such information. Tests do not tell teachers or administrators what they need to do next to improve instruction and achievement. They provide information only on whether the students passed or failed.

Schools that fail to make AYP for two consecutive years become sites for "Targeted Assistance." Initially this means more financial and technical assistance. Later it means "restructuring," which can involve dismissal or transfer of teachers and/or principals. The state can impose an entirely new curriculum, remove the schools from the district's jurisdiction, or abolish the district altogether.

All children in Targeted Assistance schools have the option to transfer to another public school within the district, including charter schools, unless transfers to charters are forbidden by state law. The district must give top priority to "the lowest-achieving children from low-income families." The conference committee apparently did not think about where these children would go in terms of children who are already in the higher-achieving schools. Is there room in the schools? This could be a means of integrating schools by class rather than ethnicity, as favored by some reformers (for example, Kahlenberg, 2001). It could also be a logistical nightmare requiring transportation to distant schools and provoking class warfare if middle-class parents feel threatened by the arrival of poor, low-achieving students.

What staff or agency will find the time and expertise to satisfy the technical and reporting requirements of the act is not clear. It looks like a bad bill for forests, a good bill for those who want larger state and federal bureaucracies, and a great jobs bill for test publishers and lawyers.

It will be some time before the ramifications of the details hidden in the 1,184-page bill become manifest, but already some provisions are causing anxiety. For instance, any teacher hired with federal funds after the first day of the 2002–2003 school year must be fully credentialed by the state, must have earned at least a bachelor's degree and must have passed a "rigorous" state examination of knowledge of subject and teacher skills. All teachers must meet these criteria by 2005–2006. These requirements have caused eyes to roll in many places, but especially in the cities. California's cities are still recovering from the small-class mandate that created many new positions in the suburbs and further drained already depleted cities of fully credentialed teachers. Of the 3,100 teachers hired by Chicago in 2000–2001, one-fourth did not have complete credentials (Banchero and Ahmed-Ullah, 2002).

As usual, the devil is in the details and with legislation this means the rules and regulations promulgated by the U.S. Department of Education. Here there are signs that the Department will force more of an on-grade-level approach to instruction. This will reduce teachers' ability to tailor teaching to the various ability levels in their classes. In many elementary classrooms, there are as many as six grade levels represented.

There are also disturbing code words in the legislation. With regard to teaching reading, the phrase "scientifically based research" occurs more than 100 times. This is a code phrase calling for phonics instruction. As with the grade-level emphasis, mandating phonics is a big step toward a one-size-fits-all program of instruction.

There is already some evidence that the standards movement has increased, not decreased, the gap between whites and minorities and between affluent and poor schools (Lee, 2002). No Child Left Behind provides no evidence that it will ameliorate this trend and, indeed, promises to leave even more children behind.

In the months since this section was first written, it has become clear that in the No Child Left Behind Act, Bush appears to have found the perfect infernal machine to destroy public education in the United States. As Denis Doyle, a conservative school critic who favors the bill, put it, "the nation is about to be inundated in a sea of bad news" (Doyle, 2002b). The following week, Doyle was absolutely gleeful as he reported that a conference he had attended concluded that American public schools were about to get "pole-axed" by AYP (Doyle, 2002a). Indeed. In North Carolina, 51 percent of the schools that were honored for "exemplary growth" under the state's much-admired testing and account-ablity program would have failed to show AYP (Simmons, 2002). Given that over the summer, poor children tend to lose much of what they have gained during the school year (Bracey, 2002), we can expect to see many perpetually failing "schools."

One can only imagine what the privatizers will have to say when some 90 percent of the nation's schools fail to meet the AYP standards. "We warned you with 'A Nation At Risk,'" they will say. "We have given you twenty years to shape up. You didn't. You have proven Chester E. Finn's allegation that 'the public school system as we know it has proved it cannot reform itself. It is an ossified government monopoly . . .' (Finn, 1998). It's time to apply American business expertise to schools." Right. American business expertise as exemplified in Enron, Tyco, Global Crossing, WorldCom, Rite Aid, Adelphia, and the thousands of dot.coms that failed because their officers had no clue about how to run a business. It will be a stormy sea.

Summary

If we look at international studies, we find American students near the top in reading and in the middle in mathematics and science. America's best readers score higher than those of any of the thirty-one other nations in the study. The performance of American students in math and science on the TIMSS tests is an improvement over earlier international studies.

National data are mostly positive: standardized test scores are near all-time highs; in the SATs, the proportion of math high-scorers is at an all-time high and the proportion of verbal high-scorers is rising; and NAEP scores are near all-time highs.

The actual test data from U.S. schools do not give any information to sustain crisis rhetoric or the war on America's public schools. Critics cannot use these data to make parents nervous about their children's schools or to justify the creation of charter schools, school vouchers, or education management organizations. More extensive reviews of the data that bear on the condition of American education can be found in Bracey, 2000a, Bracey, 1997b, and Berliner and Biddle, 1995.

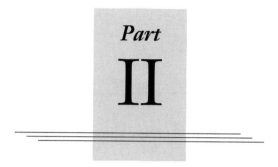

Part

II

Invasion of the
Privatizers

The data presented in Part I make one wonder how the notion that American public schools are in crisis could have become so widespread and deeply held. This is not to say that reform is not needed. In America's cities and poor rural areas, many schools really *are* in a crisis state. For instance, in the spring 2001 administration of Virginia's Standards of Learning Tests, some city schools had Algebra I pass rates of less than 10 percent. These 2001 results came from the fourth time that the tests had been administered and the 10 percent figure represented an improvement over the previous year. Some other tests in the same schools had pass rates of less than 20 percent. The passing scores on these tests were clearly set too high, but one still wonders what students are learning when only 5 percent of them can pass the standards tests.

There are other indications of distress in urban schools: For instance, of the forty-one nations participating in TIMSS, only one, South Africa, scored lower than the District of Columbia in both math and science. Among the highest-scoring states, as shown in Part 1, only six nations scored higher in math and only one in science. Although test scores do not capture many of education's outcomes, the domestic and international test results constitute the great bulk of the cross-country data that exist. These are the data that have been spun or selected, or, in the case of the international reading study, ignored, in order to "prove" that American public schools are in crisis.

In Part II we turn to an examination of the various incursions of the private sector into public schools. Public school critics have offered charter schools, school vouchers, and educational management organizations as means of improving the public schools or, as some privatizers like to say, the "government schools." Advocates of charters and privatization have claimed that such restructuring should or will increase achievement, efficiency, innovation, teacher professionalism, responsiveness, and other qualities. If one matches the claims against the results, one finds oneself humming a song written by George Gershwin for his opera, *Porgy and Bess:* "It Ain't Necessarily So."

Charter Schools

What is clear from the Arizona and Michigan experiences with charters is that without rigorous accountability, both students and taxpayers suffer.

—Thomas Toch
U.S. News & World Report, April 27, 1998

Are charter schools part of the war against public schools? Certainly charter schools have some champions who also advocate for public schools generally. In May 2000 President Clinton, a public-school advocate, announced the release of $16 million in new grants for charters and $121 million in continuation grants. His stated goal was to raise the number of charters from 1,700 to 3,000. Clinton saw charters principally as a means to provide education to children who were having difficulty in the public schools.

Just as certainly, though, the ultimate goal of some charter-school advocates is the privatization of the educational system. President Bush advocated an increase in charter schools, but his education agenda included school vouchers until both houses of Congress removed that item. Meanwhile, tuition credits, a tax break that benefits only the well-off by subsidizing private-school tuition, did pass.

Still others see charter schools as a means of fulfilling an educational vision—a means to offer education "the way it oughta be," or to provide for a particular group that is slighted by the typical public school. And still others see them as a means of making money. TesseracT, Inc., for instance, having had its school-management program drummed out of Baltimore, Hartford, and Dade

County, Florida, set up fourteen charter schools in the "Wild West" charter-friendly state of Arizona. Despite charging $8,500.00 annual tuition at its private schools, and as much as $1.95 a mile for transportation, it struggled financially and declared bankruptcy on Columbus Day, 2000 (a school holiday).

And therein lies the rub. Even ardent advocates of charter schools have had to admit that no one is watching the store. Former assistant secretary of education Chester E. Finn, Jr., and colleagues Louann Bierlein and Brunno Manno, charter fans all, acknowledged in their first Hudson Institute study that they had "yet to see a single state with a thoughtful and well-formed plan for evaluating its charter school program. Perhaps this is not surprising given the sorry condition of most state standards-assessment-accountability-evaluation systems generally. The problem, however, is apt to be particularly acute for charter schools, where the whole point is to deliver better results in return for greater freedom" (Finn, Bierlein, and Manno, 1996).

Three years later, Manno returned to say that not much progress had been made:

> Today, it's hard to know how well charter schools are actually doing. . . . There are three predominant reasons for this situation.
>
> First, the charter strategy is so new that it's difficult to measure results. There's just not much data out. Second, today's charter accountability systems remain underdeveloped, often clumsy and ill fitting and are themselves beset by dilemmas. A final reason for the death of good accountability information lies with the charter authorizers and operators. Truth be told, they are often content to leave accountability agreements nebulous and undefined. (Manno, 1999)

Manno didn't appear to realize that his final reason was in large part the cause of his first reason. There's not much data out there because people don't want to collect it. Early on in the charter movement, advocate Joe Nathan of the University of Minnesota penned what was the common charter-advocate stance on accountability: "Hundreds of charter schools have been created around this nation by educators who are willing to put their jobs on the line to say 'If we can't improve students' achievement, close down our school.' That is accountability—clear, specific, and real" (Nathan, 1996, p. xxx). It is also nonexistent. If the criterion of improved student achievement had been applied, precious few charters would still exist. As it is, only 4 percent have stopped operating and financial shortcomings, not academic failure, usually brought about their demise.

The advocates continue to advocate the idea of accountability, if not the fact of it. Finn and Manno returned to it in 2000 along with Gregg Vanourek, declaring that:

> Charter school discussions are saturated with talk about accountability. Some view it as the third rail of the charter movement, others as the Holy Grail. Staunchly leaning towards the grail side of the debate, they proposed something they called "accountability-via-transparency"—a regimen where so much is visible in each

school that its watchers and constituents (including families, staff, board members, sponsor, the press, rival schools, and others) routinely 'regulate' it through market-style mechanisms rather than command-and-control structures. (Finn, Manno, and Vanourek, 2000)

No one has been trampled in a rush by charter operators to adopt this approach. For one thing, as described by Finn and friends, the amount of information the schools would have to provide under the "transparency" scheme would create a bureaucracy at least as large and onerous as those alleged to run public schools currently. Finn calls for various kinds of test-score data and demographic data that compare the charter school to other schools, the district, or state norms or standards. To accomplish this, each school would need a separate and sizable department of testing and accountability. Most public school *districts* don't have staff equipped to handle this kind of collection and analysis of data—they are too small to afford it.

And who would oversee such a department to ensure that data were accurately collected and informatively reported? It would most likely be a monstrous state agency. The Departments of Education in each state deal with districts. In most states, they treat each charter school as a district. If that condition persists, we may see an increase from the 15,000 districts we now have nationwide to 95,000 districts.

Beyond this, a number of charter schools do not fit under the transparency rubric. The goal of some charter schools is to get dropouts off the streets and into school. They have no need for or interest in all of the information Finn proposes they collect.

Finally, Finn and his fellow advocates for charter schools ignore a fundamental fact of the human condition: Everyone wants to look good. As we shall see, some of the for-profit companies that run charter schools arrange their data to create the most positive image they can. Truth loses out to advertising.

The Genesis of Charter Schools

The idea of a charter school is not complicated. One can substitute the word "contract" with no loss of meaning. The term comes from Ray Budde, a Massachusetts schoolteacher, now retired. In the 1970s Budde based his concept for charter schools on the Charter between Henry Hudson and the Directors of the East India Company, 1609. Hudson's charter describes the purpose and vision of his trip, the risks entailed, what Hudson must do to satisfy accountability requirements, how he will be compensated, and what rewards there might be for high productivity. Would that charter schools had followed this model (the entirety of which can be placed on a single sheet of paper).

In the years that followed *A Nation At Risk*, interest in the charter idea grew slowly. Albert Shanker, then president of the American Federation of Teachers, popularized the idea in the late 1980s. Two years after Shanker delivered a speech on the topic at a Minneapolis conference on school improvement, Minnesota became the first state to enact a charter school law.

In theory, once schools are free of the stifling district and state bureaucracy, creativity flowers, energy increases, and learning soars. The word that most characterizes charter schools is "hope." Hope pervades Shanker's column: "Over time we can expect charter schools to stimulate a different and more effective school structure." Indeed, Joe Nathan titled his 1996 book *Charter Schools: Creating Hope and Opportunity for American Education.* Early paragraphs in his preface provide an excellent summary of how and why charter school advocates hold out hope:

> The charter school idea is about the creation of more accountable public schools, and the removal of the "exclusive franchise" that local school boards presently have. Charter schools are public, non-sectarian schools that do not have admissions tests but that operate under a written contract, or *charter*, from a school board or some other organization, such as a state school board. These contracts specify how the school will be held accountable for improved student achievement, in exchange for a waiver of most rules and regulations governing how they operate. Charter schools that improve achievement have their contracts renewed. Charter schools that do not improve student achievement over the contract's period are closed. . . .
>
> The charter idea is not just about the creation of new, more accountable public schools or the conversion of existing public schools. The charter idea also introduces fair, thoughtful competition into public education. (Nathan, 1996, p. xxviii)

This is, in theory, how charter schools were supposed to work, but the real world has proved messier and more complicated. In retrospect, it is clear that hopes for what charter schools would accomplish fall into the long line of proposed miracle cures and magic bullets for education's perceived ills.

In the decade since the first charter schools people have come to appreciate the complexities of accountability. Katrina Bulkley of Rutgers University describes four challenges to closing a charter school that she calls "the accountability bind":

1. Educational performance is not simple to define or measure, nor is how good is "good enough" in educational quality. In this context, authorizers sometimes turn to "proxies" to assess school quality.
2. Other aspects of a school's program, often more difficult to measure than test scores, are also important for families and authorizers.
3. Teachers, parents, and students become very invested in particular schools and destroying a community is more difficult than serving a diffuse public interest.
4. Charter schools have become a highly politicized issue on both sides and some authorizers are concerned about their decisions (to close schools) reflecting poorly on charter schools as a reform idea. (2000)

These four challenges taken together show that "accountability-via-transparency" is virtually impossible once charter schools become a central part of a community.

For their part, both Budde and Shanker were both properly skeptical and warned people not to view charters as quick fixes (Budde, 1987, 1996; Shanker 1988a, 1988b). Budde and Shanker thought charters had two great advantages over other kinds of school improvement programs: First, because a school contracted with another organization for the charter, the people at the school would feel that they owned the program; second, because the charter was for a specific time, the program was protected from the whims of a new administration that, acting as a new broom, might sweep out all previous innovations (a frequent occurrence in public schools).

Opposition to the Charter Movement

Not everyone has welcomed the charter concept. Some people have suspected all along that charter schools are just the first stage of a process that would lead eventually to vouchers and other forms of privatization. Indeed, the *Christian Science Monitor* characterized charters as a warning to public schools to shape up or get shipped out to vouchers: "Charters inject a stirring element of competition to public education. But they are still an experiment to see if the public schools will really respond. If they don't, then that argues for taking the bolder step of giving vouchers to parents to send their children to private and parochial institutions" (Weir, 2000).

Jeffrey Henig of George Washington University, one of the fairest and most dispassionate analysts of school choice, worried that it will be difficult to evaluate the "stirring element of competition" posed by charters because they show no interest in such evaluations. Henig wrote that charter schools "show few signs of interest in systematic, empirical research that is ultimately needed if we are going to be able to separate bold claim from proven performance. Premature claims of success, reliance on anecdotal and unreliable evidence are still the rule of the day" (Henig, 1994, p. 234). Eight years later, they still are.

The Popularity of Charter Schools

For whatever reasons, charters have become popular. In 1992, there were no charters; in 1995, there were 100; in 2000, 1,700; and as 2001–2002 began, there were 2,372 in thirty-four states and the District of Columbia. Still, this represents a tiny proportion of America's students, about 1 percent. Almost 25 percent of charter schools are in four states: Arizona, California, Michigan, and Texas (RPP International, 2001, p. 11).

RPP International's Fourth Year Report finds that charters differ from regular schools in some educationally important respects. For instance, the average charter school teaches 137 pupils, while the average size for public schools is about 475 students. Sixty-five percent of charters contain fewer than 200 students (p. 20). Descriptions of charters often mention the small classes, as well. The U.S. Department of Education's survey found that a major reason for creating charter schools was to provide instruction in small-class settings.

Increasingly, data indicate that small schools produce better results (for example, Gladden, 1998; Gottfredson, 1995b; Smith, 2000; Wasley et al., 2000) and the research is clear that small classes do (Finn and Achilles, 1990; Finn, 1999; Krueger, 1998, 1999, 2000; Molnar, Smith, and Zahorik, 2000). Hence, improved achievement in charter schools, if it occurs, might well derive from these factors and not from some putative effect of "charterness."

Educators and parents who start charter schools sometimes have a vision for education, but little practical experience in running a school. The vision usually encompasses only what the visionaries want to provide as instruction. They soon discover that they must cope with budgets, personnel issues, diverse opinions of parents, zoning laws, and the many state and federal laws from which the charter cannot free them.

An *Education Week* story begins with a vignette of people who started a charter school and gave up (Schnaiberg, 1997). "It was a burnout situation," said one founder of Northlane Math and Science Academy in Freeland, Michigan. The school opened in 1995 and, although quite small, had exhausted its originators by 1997. They gave the keys to Mosaica, a private for-profit Educational Management Organization (EMO).

Money and personnel are usually not included in a "vision." No doubt this is, in part, why the *Washington Post* reported that "a large number of the city's 27 charter schools have failed to comply with a wide range of regulations addressing finances, record keeping, and police background checks" (Blum, 2000). Many charters have failed to fill out and file forms, papers, and reports that public school administrators look upon as routine. Although a flawed concept for various reasons, "accountability-via-transparency" is impossible as long as charters fails to provide the most routine information.

Idyllwild

In Idyllwild, California, a mountain town described as a place "where artists and intellectuals dwell among the pines," the parents decided to operate a charter school. They had a vision of using the community's talents to enrich high school education and they also hoped to eliminate the bus trip to the nearest public school, "a 45-minute bus ride, and a world away, in cultural terms" (Brennan, 2000a).

Although a number of teachers in the town had taught at the university level, they lacked certification and were not able to get the state bureaucracy to provide emergency credentials. A computerized attendance system failed. Staff fingerprinting, routine in public schools, "baffled administrators." "School officials acknowledged that they had little experience running a school and were stumped by the obstacles they faced." Although they didn't face a hostile local school, the board revoked the charter, encouraging the school's founders to submit another proposal once the problems were solved. The charter school founders said they might be too tired to do it again (Brennan, 2000a).

The Idyllwild saga is not an isolated one and it has implications for the control of charter schools. The lack of skills and the long hours required will influence trends in who opens and runs charter schools. The U.S. Department of Education study of charters listed "to realize an alternative vision of education" as overwhelmingly the number-one reason for starting a charter. A number of seers have found their visions dimmed by the harsh realities of managing a school. As with Michigan's Northlane Academy, many other founders of "mom-and-pop" charter schools have handed control over to private managers of "cookie-cutter" charter schools. In 1996, EMOs controlled only 16 percent of the charters; in 2000, they had appropriated 71 percent. In Ohio, independent charter school operators pointed to the large education management organizations (EMOs) as having the kinds of management and financial skills that they lacked, and Ohio appears to be following Michigan's "lead."

Three Case Studies: Arizona, Michigan, and California

Three states, Arizona, California, and Michigan, have led the nation in creating charter schools. Ohio, Texas, and Florida are gaining rapidly on these three leaders. Evaluations produced in the top three states show that Joe Nathan's idealistic aims and hopes are not being realized. A series of articles in the *Akron Beacon Journal* reveals what happens when educational goals, such as those expressed by Nathan, collide with political ambitions and the desire to make money (Oplinger and Willard, 1999a, 1999b, 1999c; Willard and Oplinger, 1999a, 1999b, 1999c). Let us now examine the results to date in these three states.

Arizona

Arizona state senator Lisa Graham introduced voucher legislation, but it proved divisive and was voted down. She came back with a charter bill that elicited broad bipartisan support. The bill, passed in 1994, contains the fewest restrictions of any in the nation. "Anyone who could stand up and breathe got a charter," observed one legislator (Toch, 1998). Graham, now Lisa Graham Keegan, went from the legislature to become the fox-in-the-henhouse superintendent of public instruction and at one time was said to be George W. Bush's preferred candidate for Secretary of Education.[1]

---

1. In the summer of 2001, Keegan left Arizona to head the Education Leaders Council, a group of conservative education reformers headquartered in Washington, D.C.

Keegan entered the superintendency as very much an advocate for vouchers, and secondarily for charters. She has protected her charters from all harm. She helped form the Charter School Board, an independent entity whose function is to fend off interference from perceived opponents. When the Arizona Department of Education received many complaints and launched an investigation of the charters, Keegan withheld the report for a year, releasing it only after the state school board association's lawyer had filed a freedom-of-information-act request. Before she released the report, she had her top aide remove the evaluators' handwritten notes, as permitted under Arizona law. Then she killed the monitoring program.

The *Arizona Tribune* was not amused. In a seething editorial, the paper said, "What is especially outrageous is that Keegan killed a monitoring program with charter schools that was starting to uncover some serious problems. After some charter school owners complained, the monitoring program was scrapped and the complaints were buried in department files" (1998, p. A12). Two days later, the *Tribune* was back with another editorial essay titled "Wake up, Keegan" (1998, p. A14). It accused her of having been a tireless cheerleader for charter schools but "now that problems have surfaced, she's got all fingers pointing in other directions."

While the *Tribune* editors were outraged at Keegan for killing the monitoring program, some observers might find another episode more troubling. Paul Street, a former district administrator, was recruited to the evaluation team. "We did every school in the state," he said, and turned all of his notes in to the Department of Education. However, the department's folder marked "Street" contains a single scrap of paper.

Meeting the Standards.   Arizona state law requires only that high school students attend class four hours a day. As a consequence, some charter high schools operate in two or three four-hour shifts—not a bad strategy for increasing profit. Standards are often low. Marilynn Henley, a deputy associate superintendent and former curriculum director of the Arizona Department of Education, and a team of monitors visited more than 100 of the 241 schools then operating in Arizona. She found that many courses in these high schools lasted only a few weeks, and rarely did they assign homework.

Computer coursework at the charter high schools consisted of seventh- or eighth-grade–level drill-and-practice worksheets transferred to computers. At one school, which paid faculty bonuses for rising enrollments, thirty students sat through a course called "American Literature through Cinema." When *U.S. News & World Report* reporter Thomas Toch visited, the class was studying *The Last of the Mohicans.* They did not see Daniel Day-Lewis dashing through the woods, however. The students merely listened to the soundtrack—except, notes Toch, those who were asleep (Toch, 1998).

Henley and her team of monitors found that a majority of the schools were not living up to the terms of their charters. A *Tribune* article said that while Henley and her group "were supposed to focus on whether schools were complying with laws and charters, those with education backgrounds found it hard to ignore such things as out-of-control classrooms or the absence of instruction" (Todd, 1998a, 1998b, p. A1).

Henley's study also found many instances where the enrollments submitted to the state were considerably higher than average daily attendance. State payments to districts are based on attendance, so the bloated numbers meant that the schools were receiving more money than they were due. In addition, according to one article, "it's nearly impossible for the state to recover money in the event a charter school fails" (Donohue, 1998, p. 63). This was true even in one instance when the owner of a failed charter used school money to buy her mother an expensive home.

Keegan reassigned Henley and shut her monitoring group down. Henley later became a consultant in private practice.

Given such staggering problems, we would expect a number of Arizona charter schools to have lost their charters. In fact, after the report, only two operators had lost the privilege to operate schools. Some forty others deemed by the report as "bad enough to close," writes Toch, "were left alone on the grounds that they weren't physically endangering students or defrauding taxpayers." At the end of the 2000–2001 school year, sixteen of the now 409 sites had closed, but only three charters had been revoked, not for failing their students academically, but for mishandling money.

Keegan appeared unconcerned. Commenting on the evaluation report, she said "I would prefer that everything [the monitors saw] was wonderful. But if it wasn't, OK. In the main, I'm pleased, far and away, with the quality of the public charter schools. . . . How much monitoring do you think is going on in the traditional system?" Given the tenor of the monitors' report, one could wonder what criteria she is using to judge "quality."

Arizona's Instrument to Measure Standards (AIMS), a state testing program, was introduced on a pilot basis in the spring of 1999 with "for real" testing beginning the following spring. According to the *Tribune*, this permitted comparisons between charter schools and public schools. It didn't accomplish this, however, because it didn't take into account how the charter schools selected their students. In the first AIMS administration, 90 percent of *all* children failed the test. Charters had some of the lowest scores. However, without knowing the students' scores before they entered the charter school, or measuring their growth over time at the charter school, there is no way to determine if these low scores actually represent failure.

The quality of the AIMS test came under attack, as did the contractor, NCS (formerly National Computer Systems). In September 2001 the Arizona Department of Education decided to change contractors, to cancel the fall 2001 administration, and to delay implementation of the test as a graduation requirement until 2006 (Flannery, 2001, p. A1).

Asked by the *Tribune* what kind of society he thought the charter schools movement would lead to, then–Arizona State University School of Education Dean David Berliner replied, "Bosnia" (Van Der Werf, 1998, p. B3). Berliner's comment suggests that if thousands of schools go off in thousands of directions, each following its own "vision," it will be like dividing a country into many nations: At best there will be no unity of purpose, and at worst there will be warring factions. Our national motto, *e pluribus unum*, is usually translated as "From many, one." Schools are a force in taking the multicultural, polyglot student body and giving them a sense of communality as citizens. Berliner thought charters would destroy that force.

While Berliner used hyperbole to make a point, evaluations in California and Michigan make a similar point more quietly (Wells, 1998; Horn and Miron, 1999). Some parents clearly see charters as schools that will serve families "like them." Thus, ironically, while charters might produce more variation in the types of schools across districts, the students inside a given school might well come to look more like each other in terms of ethnicity, socioeconomic status, the values of their parents, and the curriculum received.

The Demographic Makeup of Arizona's Charter Schools.   For his doctoral dissertation at Arizona State University, Casey Cobb looked at whether Arizona charter schools were increasing ethnic segregation in the state. Even at the state level, Cobb found data suggesting a trend toward resegregation. For 1995, 1996, and 1997, Cobb found these percentages of white students in charter schools: 64.8 percent, 67.0 percent and 68.4 percent, respectively[2] (1998).

Cobb asked What is the proportion of white students in a charter school? and What is the proportion of white students in the geographically closest public school? Cobb conducted this analysis on all charters in the Metropolitan Phoenix area, which contains about 65 percent of Arizona's population.

Cobb uncovered some large differences. One charter school contained 82 percent white students, while the nearest public school had only 12 percent white students. In most school comparisons, whites constituted a minority in the public schools and a substantial majority in the charter schools—never below 50 percent and usually above 70 percent. The only places where there were more whites in public schools than in private schools were residential areas that were overwhelmingly white in the first place.

Arizona has a student database that permits the state to track students no matter what school they are in. This database permitted researchers at the Center for Market-Based Education at the Goldwater Institute in Phoenix to see how students fared over time in charters and traditional public schools (TPSs) (Solmon, Paark, and Garcia, 2001).

---

2. In 1998, the most recent year for which data are available, the proportion of white students declined in both public and charter schools. Associate Dean of Education at Arizona State University Gene V Glass reports, though, that there is reason to suspect the accuracy of this data.

Arizona administers the Stanford 9 (SAT9) achievement tests as well as its own AIMS. The Goldwater researchers claim that students who were in charter schools for two and three years gained slightly more than those who were in TPS for two or three years. However, it is extremely hard to determine from the research study how the researchers reached their conclusions. I asked several other researchers from education and economics to look at the paper and the typical comment was "It's a little hard to tell what they actually did. The descriptions of their research methods are poor."

In addition, the study also found that students who started in a TPS and then moved to a charter lost ground. Students who started in a charter and moved to a TPS after one year gained ground. The researchers offer a complex and unconvincing explanation for this. Furthermore, the loss is contradicted by other school choice experiments that typically claim improvements after a year, although those claims are suspect as well.

Finally, a norm-referenced achievement test like the SAT9 was not constructed to measure growth over time (at least, not in the way the Goldwater team did, with changes in percentile ranks), and using it in this way is not sound. Even if the results are solid, though, we must come back to the fact that charter schools are typically smaller than public schools and have smaller classes. Since both factors increase achievement, one could ask why the increases for charter school students were so small.

California

In 1992 California became the second state to pass charter legislation (Minnesota had enacted its law a year earlier). As with Arizona, it is relatively easy for an individual or group to start a charter school. Chartering authorities are local boards of education with the charter applicant having the right to appeal to a county board and then to the state board of education. Initially, the number of charters was capped at 100. The cap rose to 250 in 1998–1999 with an additional 100 schools permitted every year thereafter.

Charters are supposed to enroll anyone who applies and to use a lottery in the event of too many applications. They may give preferences based on the proximity of residence and other siblings in the school. Existing public schools, start-up schools, and home schools can be chartered, but private schools cannot convert to charter school status. A charter denied by a local board can be appealed first to a county board and then the state board of education.

Evaluations of California's Charters. Evaluations of charter schools have been undertaken by Eric Rofes at the University of California at Berkeley, and by Amy Stuart Wells and colleagues at the University of California at Los Angeles (Rofes, 1998; Wells, 1998). The Wells study is of particular interest because of its thematic organization. Charter schools generally make certain claims for why they will be superior to regular public schools. Wells and her team evaluated them in the light of these claims, stated briefly below:

1. *Accountability:* Because charter schools are more accountable for student outcomes, charters will work harder to meet their stated goals.
2. *Efficiency:* Freed from the shackles of bureaucracy, charter schools will be more efficient and/or will be able to do more with fewer resources.
3. *Competition:* By creating competition for the other schools in the district, charters will force change in the public schools.
4. *Innovation:* Charters will create new models of schooling and serve as laboratories of innovation from which public schools can learn and adopt.
5. *Choice:* Because charter schools will be developing new models, they will provide parents with a wider range of choices.
6. *Autonomy:* Because charter schools are freed from bureaucracy, they will be empowered to better serve students and their families.

These are the common claims of charter school advocates. What did the UCLA study find regarding them?

Accountability.   It is complicated to examine these claims in part because the "goals and outcomes are often vaguely written and ill-defined; they frequently cover a wide range of desired outcomes, such as the goal of 'enabling pupils to become self-motivated, competent, and life-long learners'" (Wells, 1998, p. 20). These are noble goals, but all but impossible to assess. Most educators, it must be said, cannot write clear goal statements any better than they can write symphonies. They also think about evaluating a program two or three years after the program has been in place when proper program evaluations should begin before the program has started.

The UCLA investigation was hampered during the study because California was revamping its assessment system; it had no state test against which the charter schools, or any public schools for that matter, could be measured. (The system currently in place, moreover, is inadequate for such evaluations; its "Academic Progress Index," the principal means of accountability, is often called the Affluent Parents Index because the correlations between the API and community wealth are enormous.) But even if an adequate system had been in place, it would not have been applicable to all charters. Some of the charter schools in the UCLA study were "back-to-basics" schools that featured basic skills, drills, memorization, and the mastery of discrete pieces of information. Such schools usually favor the use of standardized, norm-referenced tests.

On the other hand, some charter schools had project-based, thematic curricula that emphasized learning through experience and interdisciplinary study. Some charters wanted to improve student and staff attendance rates, to increase parent participation, or to offer new opportunities for professional development of teachers. Not only were such goals not directly tied to specific student achievements, but the goals sections of the chartering documents were often "extremely vague" (Wells, 1998).

We can observe again that the accountability notions of Chester Finn and Joe Nathan are simplistic when held up against the reality and complexity of charter schools. People start charter schools for many reasons and with many different aims. A single test would not be appropriate for all of them. Still, one must wonder both about why granting agencies paid so little attention to achievement outcomes or to what kind of instrument would be appropriate if a test were not. Why have so many chartering agencies let charter schools begin without planning appropriate instruments or observations to evaluate the school's goals?

The answer to this question appears to be, at least in part, that most states have short-staffed and weak granting and oversight agencies. Sometimes the states deliberately created accountability weakness in order to give charters as much leeway as possible.

Such leeway has been extended in Arizona. Michigan and Ohio are other cases in point, as is Texas. As its governor, George W. Bush "touted Texas's charter schools" (Associated Press, 2000). But between the time that Bush left the governorship and assumed the presidency, a panel of the Texas legislature called for a moratorium on charters. Noting that the state educational agency gave an "unacceptable" grade to over one-quarter of the 103 charters it evaluated, committee chairman Jim Dunnam said "I think that the expansion of any program that is suffering from such admitted and recognized lack of oversight is not responsible government, whether it is a state park or a charter school" (Associated Press, 2000). Both houses of the Texas legislature passed Dunnam's bill to curb charters, but Bush's successor, Rick Perry, opposed it. To prevent a veto, the legislature then merely capped the number of permitted charters at fifteen more than were then operating. Perry let the bill become law without signing it.

Wells found that accountability in the charter schools involved money, not achievement. The schools that lost their charters lost them because they misappropriated or misspent public tax dollars. Schools with clean books had their charters renewed even though they had not met the academic goals required by the charter contracts.

The UCLA study was sympathetic to the accountability plight of charters:

> Charter school reform in its purest sense is about community-based groups trying to respond to dissatisfaction with the public schools by creating alternatives to what they perceive to be an unresponsive public system. In many cases, the value of these alternatives will not be accurately measured by a state-imposed assessment. While a centralized, common state test causes many problems in the regular public educational system, it is particularly problematic for charter school educators, many of whom assume that their schools are anything but standardized and that they know more than politicians in Sacramento about how to serve their particular students. (1998, p. 24)

The Wells study concluded that "as long as finance, not learning, is the central focus of the accountability arrangements, the promise of student accountability may be deceptive" (1998, p. 24).

To complicate matters more, there is confusion about whom the charter is accountable to. Clearly, the market theory of charters puts the parents in charge; if the charter does not respond to their needs, the parents will "vote with their feet" and leave. Good schools will flourish and bad schools will close. Yet charters also have accountability responsibilities to the chartering agencies, state oversight agencies, and, in some states, to the public school districts in which the charters reside.

The accountability to parents has a side effect of discouraging some parents from enrolling their children. Some charters are founded with a particular vision of education. This vision is clearly communicated to parents. "This means that charter school communities—parents and educators alike—often try to send clear signals to prospective families about who is welcome and who is valued in the school. Sometimes, families who are not a good fit are encouraged to leave" (Wells, 1998, p. 27).

The accountability issue could become more important in the future. As we shall see, most of the charter schools in Michigan are run by education management organizations (EMOs). Some of these organizations reside in Michigan and some do not, but all bring with them a curriculum prepared elsewhere. This makes them unresponsive to parental input. Indeed, one evaluation of Michigan charter schools refers to them as "cookie cutter schools" (Horn and Miron, 1999).

Efficiency.   While advocates have claimed that charter schools will be more efficient, and thus require fewer funds, the UCLA study found them to require more. To survive, charter schools relied on private sources, and their ability to tap into such sources varied greatly.

The ability to tap other sources showed great variability from school to school, largely because of the great variability in the quality of leadership from school to school. "We learned that charter schools are highly dependent on another critical resource: a visionary and well-connected leader." The study did, indeed, find some charter schools functioning without heat, adequate plumbing, science labs, or any athletic facilities. "These schools did not seem efficient, just poor" (Wells, 1998, p. 60).

Competition.   Public schools failed to compete with the charters because public school officials felt that the charters had an unfair advantage. The charters could require parent contracts, could require a certain number of hours of parent involvement, could select students or limit enrollments, and had greater hiring autonomy and less paperwork. All these meant that the playing field was not level.

Charter schools did not have to accept children after the school year started. As a consequence, they had considerably more stable enrollments. They didn't have to adjust class activities to the arrival of new students, or attend to the needs of the new students. These freedoms gave the charters a considerable advantage.

Rofes's study found that some teachers and administrators saw competition as a positive development, but most did not. Districts that did respond to charters had "reform-minded leaders who seized on charters as a strategic tool to step up reforms in their districts" (Rofes, 1998, p. 18). That is, the charter school became an instrument that permitted the administrators to accomplish what they had wanted to do all along. On the other hand, one teacher responded to competition this way: "I don't do my job based on thinking I have a competitor. I do it based on knowing what the child needs to grow and have a good education to get somewhere. That's what motivates me" (p. 21).

Innovation. That charter schools will be laboratories of innovation is tightly linked to the idea that they will provide competition. Joe Nathan wrote: "The charter school movement attempts to promote widespread improvement in public education both by allowing people to create new kinds of schools and by encouraging existing school systems to improve in order to compete effectively with these new schools" (1996, p. 18).

Rofes didn't find this happening at all. In fact, he made a series of predictions about how charters would affect public schools and was a bit surprised when the predictions didn't hold. "Few superintendents, principals, and teachers in district schools were thinking of charter schools as educational laboratories or attempting to transfer pedagogical innovations from charters to the district schools; districts were still building large school facilities and were rarely creating smaller schools; the large urban districts studied rarely had responded in meaningful ways to charter laws and charter schools" (Rofes, 1998, p. 13).

Wells and her research team would find no surprise in Rofes's conclusion. They found that "there are no mechanisms in place for charter schools and regular schools to learn from each other." As a consequence, "all but two of the public school educators we interviewed reported that they had very little information about what was going on in the charter schools, and nearly all of the educators we interviewed said they saw little if any direct impact of charters schools on their schools" (1998, p. 54). Beyond that, the feeling that charters operated under better conditions led to a feeling of resentment that further inhibited cooperation. Even the charters' mere presence was taken by some as "a slap in the face" (1998, p. 55). The very existence of the charter implied to educators in public schools that they were doing something wrong.

For their part, few charter educators saw informing public school colleagues about their charter schools as part of their purpose. And even if they did, most charter school personnel lacked the time and resources to participate in meaningful collaboration.

Choice. Charter schools did offer more programmatic choices although, as the Wells report concludes, it was not often to those parents who had the fewest options to begin with. Requirements on parents and students alike allowed the schools to do some choosing of their own: For instance, few of the charter schools provided transportation. Thus, only parents with a car and a flexible schedule could send their children to those schools.

As we shall see in the Michigan charter evaluations, many charter schools there did not offer meaningful choices that would differentiate them from public schools.

Autonomy.   The UCLA study found mixed results. Administrators said that the area of autonomy that was perceived as most important was the hiring of teachers and, indeed, this was the area in which they also reported having the most autonomy. Otherwise, they often used and even depended on the bureaucracy of the school district in which they were located.

This led Wells to conclude that "It is time to rest the tired rhetoric that all bureaucracy is bad and all autonomy from bureaucracy is good. There are many charter schools in California that could not exist without the ongoing support of their local school districts. In fact, policy makers and educators have a lot to learn from charter school operators about which aspects of autonomy are most important . . . and which aspects of bureaucracy are most supportive" (1998, p. 6).

However, this last conclusion is contingent upon how the charter law is framed. In California, the charter schools are part of the school district and operate through it. In Michigan, charters receive grants directly from the charter authorities, which are mostly Michigan public universities. Wells's conclusion is no doubt true—not all bureaucracy is bad, but the Michigan system provides charters with, and requires of charters, a great deal more autonomy. Some people would conclude that these provisions and requirements have produced disastrous consequences, as described below.

In California's fall 2000 election, a little-noticed section of a public referendum had major consequences for charters and the districts in which they reside. The biggest obstacle to opening a charter is finding available space or finding capital funds to construct such a space. Proposition 39 required the public school districts to provide charters with facilities that are "reasonably equivalent" to those provided to regular public schools. All districts must be in compliance by 2003. In late 2001, some districts are reported to have made substantial progress while others remain in "deep denial" (Premack, 2001).

Michigan

The intent of Michigan's charter law is fairly typical. As summarized at the beginning of an evaluation report on Michigan charter schools, those schools should improve student achievement, stimulate innovative teaching methods, and improve student achievement for all pupils (including but not limited to educationally disadvantaged pupils), by improving learning environments, creating new professional opportunities for teachers, achieving school-site accountability, providing parents and pupils with greater choice, and determining the best way to allocate state funds.

The law does not limit the total number of charters. It does limit the number of schools chartered through state universities to 150 and no one university may have more than half of this total. An individual or any legal entity may apply for a charter and may apply through a number of authorizing agencies: local school boards, intermediate school boards, community colleges, and state public universities. The great majority of Michigan charter schools, locally called Public School Academies (PSAs) are chartered through one of the state universities—150 of 173 in 2002. Public and private schools can convert to charter status and schools can start from scratch. Home-based schools are not allowed.

Charter schools cannot have entrance requirements and in the event that too many children apply, they must select students by lottery. In those charter schools authorized by universities, all students in the state are eligible to enroll; for charters authorized by other bodies, only students in the district where the school is located may attend.

Evaluations of Michigan's Charters.   Various agencies have conducted evaluations of PSAs: Western Michigan University (Horn and Miron, 1999, 2000), Michigan State University (Arsen, Plank, and Sykes, 1999; Mintrom, 1998), Columbia University (Bettinger, 1999), the Upjohn Institute for Employment Research, and a private consulting firm, Public Sector Consultants (Khouri, Kline, White, and Cummings, 1999).

Evaluators have been struck by the similarity of charter schools to each other and to regular schools. Says Mintrom, "More striking [than the amount of innovation] is the degree of similarity that we find across all schools, be they charter or traditional. . . . While some charter schools definitely are doing some innovative things, overall Michigan's charter schools are no more remarkable than many traditional public schools in their practices" (1998, pp. iv–v). Where Mintrom did find innovation, he didn't find it spreading beyond the PSA itself largely, he thinks, because charter advocates have "often been unnecessarily harsh in their disparagement of traditional public schools" (p. v).

The Western Michigan researchers also noticed the absence of innovations in curriculum or teaching. They did not find any innovations in PSAs that did not already exist in the public schools. "In fact, the charter schools were remarkably similar to the regular public schools, with the notable exceptions of generally smaller student enrollments, the presence of additional adults in the classroom, governance, and span of contracted services" (Horn and Miron, 1999, p. 99).

Michigan State researchers found parents had somewhat of a "not-with-my-kid-you-don't" attitude toward innovation. "Insofar as this is what parents want, PSAs have little to gain and much to lose from experimentation with innovative practices (Arsen, Plank, and Sykes, 1999, p. 57).

Michigan has a long-standing testing program, the Michigan Education Assessment Program (MEAP). Although the evaluators agree that MEAP is an inappropriate evaluative tool for all Michigan charter schools, it is the one instrument available for all charters.

Only one evaluation, concentrating on the urban areas of Detroit, Flint, and Lansing, found evidence that students at PSAs were showing more achievement growth than those in regular schools. The evaluations that examined the entire state found the reverse. Western Michigan researchers found that the percentage of students passing MEAP declined in charter schools. The public schools in districts that hosted the PSAs increased their passing rate from 49 percent to 68 percent. Bettinger's evaluation concluded that "when charter schools are compared to public schools with similar characteristics, pupils in charter schools score no higher, on average, and may even be doing worse" (1999, p. 3). Eberts and Hollenbeck found that "students attending a charter school scored about 2 to 4 percent lower" than public school students on the state's fourth-grade reading and math assessments, about 4 percent lower on the science test, and about 6 percent lower on the writing tests.

The five different groups of researchers who evaluated student achievement in Michigan charter schools used different research methods. Sometimes different techniques make different assumptions about the variables and this sometimes leads to contradictory results. Not in Michigan.

The most striking differences between the charters and the regular schools were in how the schools were managed. PSAs contracted for services from profit-making and nonprofit companies. Some schools contracted for instructional services rather than hire teachers. PSAs required parents to provide transportation. People from the same family often held different, and key, management or instructional positions, a practice either avoided or forbidden in the public service sector.

On the other hand, nepotism occurs often in the private sector and is touted as a productivity multiplier—people from the same family will work harder toward a common goal, profitability, than will unrelated people. The WMU evaluators considered that in the PSAs, however, some of these practices might be undesirable. For instance, would accountability be compromised in a school where members of the same family were employed? The evaluators concluded that "there are no convincing arguments or evidence that all of these [innovations in how schools are run] are legally or ethically desirable" (Horn and Miron, 2000, p. 74).

Beyond nepotism, Horn and Miron found that the most significant innovations associated with charter schools are found in the area of school governance and management. The most important charter school innovations were not about teaching and learning, but rather about control over school operations. Of particular significance in Michigan, they thought, was the emergence of the EMO as a new and important actor in the management and governance of charter schools.

Educational Maintenance Organizations.   EMO stands for Educational Maintenance Organization, so named because some people consider them analogous to the Health Maintenance Organizations (HMOs) found in the field of health care. Given the many questions and complaints about HMOs, this analogy would give some people pause. EMOs vary greatly in the kind of services they offer: Some have a limited range and some take over an entire school, providing the curriculum and instructional program as well as food service, physical plant management, and other noninstruction-related services.

Just why EMOs should be flourishing in Michigan, in contrast to many other states, is revealing. In the first place, not all state charter laws even permit EMOs; Michigan's does. Second, PSAs get set amounts of state funding, not an amount negotiated with the school district, as in some other states. Third, Michigan offers very little in the way of start-up funding; working through an EMO allows the new schools access to private capital. In 2000–2001, some 71 percent of Michigan charters are run by some kind of for-profit organization, usually an EMO (compared to 10 percent nationally). These schools contain 75 percent of the charter students. Five years ago, only 16 percent of the schools were run by EMOs (Horn and Miron, 2000, p. vi). The figure is currently 75% (Miron, 2002).

As we will see more clearly when discussing charters in Ohio, people who have a vision but no experience in running a school often turn to EMOs to provide the resources and skills they lack. This does not appear to be a positive trend: It takes money away from public schools and out of the area and delivers a curriculum created in some remote location.

As noted earlier, Michigan's law permits private schools to convert to charter status and receive public funds. This has increased competition, but not between PSAs and public schools. The increased competition comes between the formerly private schools that convert to charter status and those that remain private. Given the amount of money that Michigan provides for each pupil, the former private schools can drop their tuition (which, by law, they must), and get by nicely on state funds while those that remain private must continue to charge tuition in order to survive.

Accountability. The charter school movement is small, even in Michigan. This is one reason that calls for accountability have been muted. In addition, in growing areas, new students replace those lost to the charters. If, however, charters come to seize a hefty chunk of the students, we could see the evolution of a system similar to those found in much of Europe. On that continent, most countries fund private as well as public schools, but hold both to the same rules for accountability. The students in private schools must study the same curriculum and take the same tests as those in public schools; the teachers must meet the same professional requirements and be paid the same, and so on. In some countries, the state even dictates the instructional techniques that private schools must use. The major difference between public and private schools in much of Europe is only that the latter are free to offer specific religious instruction. If charters become a large movement in this country, I expect taxpayers will object to giving them a free ride. Since everyone is crying for public school accountability, why should charters be let off that hook?

According to some people, some chartering agents are steering Michigan charter applicants toward EMOs rather than toward the small, idiosyncratic "mom-and-pop" charters. The agents do this partly because if all the charters were unique, they would have too many different schools to oversee well. It also helps prevent some scandalous story popping up in a newspaper describing some particularly inept or corrupt school. The EMOs are known quantities.

Teachers.   Michigan charter legislation also has a goal to provide additional professional development activities for teachers. It is not clear that schools lacking true innovations can attain this goal. It might be, however, that the difference between schools provides teachers with an opportunity to gravitate to schools whose pedagogy they prefer. A charter school focused on phonics and back-to-basics math is not likely to recruit or attract teachers who wish to use whole language or the University of Chicago's "Everyday Math" program. Indeed, in one California Edison school, when teachers expressed desires to make changes, they were told "Maybe our model is not for you."

In general, the teachers in PSAs are younger, less experienced, and receive lower salaries than teachers in public schools. Eberts and Hollenbeck found that the teachers in PSAs received average salaries of just over $31,185, compared to $47,315 for public school teachers. When one remembers that PSAs are not required to make contributions to the state retirement fund, this difference becomes even greater (some PSAs do make these contributions if it is a part of their contract with the school). PSA teachers generally do not have tenure. The low salary and lack of tenure have further implications: One cannot imagine a strong union state like Michigan evolving into an all-PSA state under such conditions.

Charter administrators often deliberately recruit younger teachers, not only because they are cheaper, but also because the administrators feel they are better trained, not "set in their ways," and have more energy for the long hours that charter schools often require. Teachers not "set in their ways" would also presumably be more amenable to adapting to the canned curricula offered via EMOs. On the other hand, they have fewer opportunities to learn from or to be mentored by veterans.

The Impact on Public Schools.   Charter schools have caused some public schools to offer new services, such as before- and after-school programs, all-day kindergartens, foreign languages in elementary grades, clearer school-mission statements, and more open and receptive relationships with parents. Some districts reported large losses of students, but statewide the net impact has been nearly zero. Most charter school growth is occurring from the entry of students into kindergarten. Smaller districts and districts with stable or declining population are most heavily affected. The impact has been felt mostly as a reduction in support services.

Some districts reported that charters would hold students until "count day." Most states have a day or two when they count students to determine how much money a school district will receive from the state budget. Public schools reported that after count day, the charters would then send some students back to the public schools. The charters get the money and the public schools would get the students.

The charters provide little special education, even in the most common categories, such as learning disability. Some 12.5 percent of public school students receive special education services. Only 3.7 percent of charter school students have such classification in Michigan with about half of the charters reporting no special education students at all. A few cater only to students with disabilities.

The early advocates of charters envisioned a group of people in a community electing to start a charter school. Charter schools run by EMOs reverse this idea. They search for communities in which to place their schools. Thus, charter schools are choosing communities, not vice versa. "While charter schools emphasize that they are a new form of public schools, they are increasingly appearing and behaving like private schools" (Horn and Miron, 2000, p. iv). Employees in charters are private, not public, workers. Many facilities, including equipment and furniture, are privately owned. And, perhaps most significant, the student bodies look more and more like private schools: fewer minority and special needs students are enrolled. Requirements for parent participation, preapplication interviews, and absence of transportation all help structure or shape the student body: Only parents with cars and some free time can meet these requirements.

In their conclusions, Horn and Miron have this to say: "After nearly five years of operation in Michigan, we conclude that (i) the state's charter schools are producing few and limited innovations; (ii) few schools are implementing comprehensive accountability plans; and (iii) the extensive involvement of EMOs is creating new "pseudo" school districts in which decisions are made from great distances rather than at the school level" (p. vii).

If these conclusions are valid, then the charters in Michigan appear to be doing largely just the opposite of what Nathan, Finn, and other champions claimed they would do. The Arsen, Plank, and Sykes study, though, found that charters in Arizona and California are authorized and funded by different rules than those in Michigan. "The rules matter" and a similar summary study in Arizona or California might reach different conclusions.

Ohio and Elsewhere

The evaluations discussed so far don't depict charters as laboratories of innovation for improving the public school system overall. One growing organization in Michigan, National Heritage Academies, has an overtly Christian tenor to its operation and has occasionally been sued over First Amendment issues. At times, charters are established for ideological or political reasons and at other times for personal financial gain. We can see the latter motivation at work in Ohio.

Even before a formal evaluation of Ohio's charter schools was planned, Dennis Willard and Doug Oplinger, reporters at the *Akron Beacon Journal*, had done an excellent job in ferreting out some of the charter-school shenanigans in that state (Willard and Oplinger, 1999a, 1999b, 1999c; Oplinger and Willard, 1999a, 1999b, 1999c). These journalists bring the issues up close and personal in a way that academic evaluations such as those reported earlier for California and Michigan cannot.

The opening paragraphs from the first article in the Oplinger-Willard series paint a somewhat lurid picture of charters in Ohio:

> Ohio, already No. 1 in the 90s for putting public dollars into private schools[3] and last in the nation for placing children in safe and sanitary buildings, is on course to earn a new distinction in the next decade.
>
> The state is ready to rival Arizona, California, Florida, and Michigan for funneling state and local tax dollars to a new class of schools—charter schools—that are public in some ways and private in others. . . .
>
> Now, less than five months into the second year [of charter school funding]—as charter schools move from concept to reality—serious questions and disturbing problems are starting to arise.
>
> • Private, profit-minded companies, known as education management organizations, are making strong inroads into the state. In doing so, these EMOs are concentrating school ownership in the hands of a few and brushing aside the people who were to be given control of their local charter, or community, schools—parents, teachers, and community members.
> • The Ohio Board of Education, responsible for oversight, is rubberstamping contracts as fast as it can without thoroughly reviewing the written proposals or hearing from a single charter school representative. One reason: Most board members say they have almost no authority to reject a proposal.
> • Lawmakers did not fund an oversight office for charter schools until the program's second year and after more than 60 contracts had been approved and 15 schools had opened. The undermanned office is hard-pressed to complete routine checks for fire safety and criminal backgrounds, and is barely monitoring academic progress.
> • Children are bearing the brunt of the charter school problems. The state has allowed charter schools to open without textbooks or indoor toilets. Students have attended class in unsafe buildings that lacked sprinklers or fire alarm systems. And local police in Columbus were called 12 times in two months to one charter school to investigate disturbances, including one case of sexual assault.
> • Most charter schools are not models for reform. First-year test scores indicate students in charter schools are doing dramatically worse than public school-

---

3. This is a true statement, but it is not only because of the recent trend toward charters, vouchers, and other forms of privatization. Ohio has a long history of state support of private schools, support that is substantially larger than in any other state.

children, and the new schools are not incubators for innovation as proponents promised they would be.

- Profits are being reaped, but there is no evidence that charter schools are reducing education costs or saving Ohio taxpayers money—despite lower pay for teachers and exemptions from 191 state mandates that hike the cost of education in public schools. (Willard and Oplinger, 1999a)

Ohio looks like Michigan all over again, except that it has one additional component: The charge for charters is led by a single individual, David Brennan, one of Ohio's political powers, and a man who has been considered a serious candidate for chairman of the Republican National Committee. The *Akron Beacon Journal* series depicts Brennan using his influence with the governor and the state legislature to get favors and favorably written laws from which he benefits. At least one such favor violated Ohio's constitution.

At other times, Brennan's behavior simply looks like an entrepreneur in action. When Cleveland set up its voucher program, Brennan quickly created two new schools to receive voucher students. When the charter legislation became law, Brennan immediately converted his schools to charter status. Why? The tuition he receives for charter students is about three times the value of the voucher. It looks as though the bottom line and not scholastic achievement is the driving force in Brennan's pedagogy.

Evaluation of Ohio's Charters.   Ohio's charter schools, known as Community Schools, are relatively new and no formal evaluations have been conducted. The nonpartisan Legislative Office of Education Oversight (LOEO) has described some charter characteristics and is gentler than Willard and Oplinger (LOEO, 2000). It did find, however, that most of the charters failed to provide evidence of how they met their educational goals or how they evaluated student performance. Although required by law to provide annual reports to parents, most did not, and most school directors claimed they did not even know that they should.

The next year, the situation improved, but LOEO reported that "Although community schools' annual reports have gotten progressively better, information critical to the accountability of these schools continues to be missing" (LOEO, 2001, p. 13). Even most of the oldest schools failed to deliver reports on their educational goals or progress toward those goals. Although charter schools claim that they will be more accountable than normal public schools, they have so far failed to provide data to prove that—data that would allow parents or the state to hold them accountable.

As in Michigan, Ohio charter school teachers are younger and earn less. The Community School teachers had an average of 4.2 years of experience and received an average salary of $22,070. Teachers in the public school districts where the charters operated averaged 14.8 years of experience and were paid on average $43,162.

Class size in the charter schools averaged 18 students. In spite of these small classes, data from the Ohio Proficiency tests indicates that charter school students did not perform as well as public school students in the same districts.

The LOEO's second report contains information that some will find disturbing:

> LOEO found that community schools benefit significantly from the assistance of management companies in areas such as financial management, curriculum development, teacher inservices, and general support and guidance. Directors (of charter schools) remarked to LOEO that the management company is the first place they turn when they have questions.
>
> Community schools not operated by a management company must be responsible for all aspects of running the schools, ranging from curriculum design to staff hiring and evaluations to planning budgets. The director of one community school without a management company commented that, "Schools operated by a management company have the assistance I was looking for this year." (LOEO, 2001, p. 6)

Thus the LOEO report depicts many charter operators as in over their heads and turning to EMOs to bail them out. One can predict for Ohio that the "cookie cutter" schools will gain the same kind of ascendancy that they have in Michigan. This is not what the charter school movement was supposed to be about.

Charter Schools and Public School Funding

Advocates of charter schools contend that charters will not adversely affect the public schools because the publics can simply reduce services. This does not accurately reflect how school finances operate. Charter schools typically draw students from a wide geographical area, not merely the attendance area of a public school. They thus can affect many different schools. The twenty-two students in a charter school third grade, for instance, do not arrive as a group from the third grade of a single public school. If they did, that public school could dismiss one third-grade teacher, although that would not recoup all of the public school's loss, because the cost to operate the building, transport the students, and so on, remains. Class size in public schools from which charter pupils leave might be reduced a bit, but expenses will remain the same and resources—money—to cover the expenses will be reduced.

Going into the 2001–2002 schoolyear, it was clear that management companies that operate charter schools were siphoning off funds previously spent on public schools. That's how the management companies make money even if, as is the case, most of the companies are themselves in the red. In 1997–1998, management companies received $16.7 million in Michigan. According to one report, the city of Cincinnati lost $21 million in 2000–2001 because of the nearly 4,000 students who attended charters (Tortora, 2000). Edison, the largest EMO, has never turned a profit, but its officers pay themselves a generous $300,000 a year. If EMOs are chosen to manage the charters in many states, it will be bad financial news for public schools.

In addition to predicting that EMOs would not manage schools well, a number of critics also predicted corruption and scandals, because of the difficulties of oversight. There have been some, although the treatment of misdeeds has been light, both from the press and from those appointed to oversee charters. However, in Texas, reporter Stuart Eskenazi heard rumors about the Renaissance Charter School. State officials had touted the school as a model, but when Eskenazi visited, he found

> A decrepit, two-story gray stucco office building that sat woefully along a busy commercial street. The City of Arlington [Texas] had declared the second level of the vacant building unsuitable for habitation, so the school set up shop in two large rooms on the ground floor. The building had no heat. The classrooms had no desks, no chairs, no textbooks, no chalkboards, no trash cans, no gymnasium, no lunchroom, no vending machines, no functioning toilet. (Eskenazi, 1999)

All of this came to light after frustrated teachers instructed students to write the Texas Education Agency about the conditions of the school. Children could write only if they brought materials from home—there were no pencils or paper at the school. One letter said simply "If you name it, we don't have it."

Summary

A look at the data reflecting how well charter schools are doing indicates that, in general, they perform no better than regular public schools. Indeed, several evaluations find charters virtually indistinguishable from traditional public schools. Some individual charter schools perform at high levels, but this is not true of charter schools as a whole. In addition, the high-performing charter schools have not served as a model for innovations and improvements in public schools.

Charter schools have failed to deliver on their initial promise that they would improve achievement or go out of business. If they had been held to that promise, few would still exist.

7

Private Schools and the Private Management of Public School Programs

Public schools have long contracted with private companies for some services. Until recently, virtually all of the services provided were managerial, not instructional—food, transportation, maintenance, and so on. Starting in the early 1990s, however, various companies began offering additional services in finance and personnel and in the management of the school's entire operation.

The privatization of management services and small instructional programs might serve as the camel's nose in the tent, to be followed shortly by the whole camel. At least one theorist, Paul Hill of the University of Washington, has argued that the camel should be welcomed (Hill, 1995). Hill contends that public schools should manage education, not provide it. That should be left to private organizations working with the schools. The war against the public schools might be termed a war of attrition.

This chapter discusses the operations of some of the better-known EMOs. Three of the best known are, essentially, no more. The TesseracT Group filed for bankruptcy in 2000 and Advantage Schools, Inc., was taken over by another EMO, Mosaica Education, Inc., in July 2001. Similarly, Beacon Education merged with Chancellor Academies.

Many of these companies do not provide EMO services exclusively. Edison, for instance, manages some existing public schools and some new charter schools. Nobel, whose major line is a group of private schools, has also entered the charter market.

The TesseracT Group
(Formerly Education Alternatives, Inc.)

The TesseracT group is included here largely because its example is illustrative. All that remains of TesseracT is the bankruptcy court filing from late 2000. TesseracT's founder, John Golle, was one of two well-known proponents of the private management of schools (Edison's Chris Whittle being the other). One article credited Golle as being the man who invented for-profit schools (Mattern, 2000a). But the profits never happened.

Golle started Educational Alternatives, Inc. (EAI), in the late 1980s when he bought a system of private schools from financially troubled Control Data Corporation and merged it with his own Capital Dimension company.

Early on, Golle looked like the golden boy of the education industry and attracted a lot of attention from investment bankers watching the "education industry." Education in general and EAI in particular were considered the analogue of the previously successful Health Maintenance Organizations ("successful," defined for the moment as making profits). Industry watchers felt that ultimately EAI would overcome hurdles and offer a national low-cost/high-quality system of schools. Given that education constituted such a huge potential market, that made EAI an ideal investment for investors interested in growth.

The Rise and Fall of EAI

EAI started with schools in inner-city settings and landed contracts in Baltimore, Hartford, and Dade County, Florida—deals that are now all defunct. EAI enjoyed some apparent early financial success, in large part because its innovative bookkeeping made its pockets look deeper than they actually were. Most of the money EAI received under its contract with Baltimore City schools, for instance, had to be used to pay teachers and to cover other expenses. Although the money was already committed, EAI's books showed it as income, a rather unusual bookkeeping practice. EAI also invested substantial amounts of the money in high-risk derivatives. For a while, the profit EAI showed was actually interest on those investments. When interest rates declined, so did EAI's fortunes, both in reality and symbolically.

The interest from the company's stocks and the practice of counting obligated money as income caused EAIs stock to rise, after which Golle and other officers sold large amounts of shares at large profits. Some people became skeptical. Disputes flared. Suits followed.

EAI's Baltimore contract was for five years, beginning in the fall of 1992. In August 1993, EAI announced that students in its nine Baltimore schools had gained an average of .88 grade levels compared to a .30 gain that would be expected under similar circumstances in the public schools. Nationally, students gain 1.00 grade levels per grade, but low-income pupils show much smaller gains.[1] EAI soon had to admit that the figure was an error and blamed its partner, Computer Curriculum Corporation (CCC, now owned by Paramount, which, in turn, is owned by Viacom). CCC blamed EAI. Stock prices plummeted. Baltimore contracted with the University of Maryland, Baltimore County (UMBC) for an external evaluation.

The UMBC report, issued in the summer of 1995, concluded that there had been no improvement in test scores in the nine EAI schools since 1991–92, the year before the contract (Williams and Leak, 1995). This was true for the district as a whole. The UMBC team also found that teachers at the EAI schools spent more time teaching in small groups and a great deal more time preparing students to take the standardized test. This makes the finding of no improvement actually look negative: It is not that hard to influence test scores. Without such attention to test preparation, the scores might well have dropped below those in a matched group of public schools.

EAI abolished most paraprofessional positions, replacing the educators with low-wage interns, many of whom stayed only one year. The paraprofessionals tended to live in the school's neighborhood, but the interns did not. This action thus removed both wealth and community resources from an impoverished area. In *Giving Kids the Business,* Arizona State University professor Alex Molnar has observed that contracting with EAI to run schools in poor districts assures that money moves from minorities in the neighborhood to whites far away (Molnar, 1996).

Researchers at the Economic Policy Institute waded with great difficulty through EAI's tangled bookkeeping and concluded that the Baltimore public schools had given EAI more money per student than it spent on a matched control group in its own public schools. EPI estimated the figure at about $1,000 for each elementary school student and $650 for each middle-school student. This violates the promise of EAI and other privatizers to do more with less—a promise they dare to make with the claim that money doesn't matter (Richards, Shore, and Sawicky, 1996).

EPI also concluded that, independent of the quality of the schooling provided, "EAI has yet to show that it can make a profit by managing schools. To the extent that it does make a profit, the profit comes from interest earnings and speculation on the price of EAI stock" (Richards, Shore, and Sawicky, p. 85). This does not mean that some of the individuals in EAI and other companies did not make money, drawing healthy salaries out of the commissions paid and selling their stock holdings after stocks rose.

---

1. Some evidence indicates that low-income students gain in school but lose some of the gain over summer, while middle-class, upper-income students continue to gain over summer (Alexander, Entwisle, and Olson, 2001).

EAI's Move Westward

With the collapse of contracts in Connecticut, Maryland, and Florida, Golle abandoned the east coast and EAI's original mission and headed for the freer clime of the west, namely, Scottsdale, a toney suburb of Phoenix. In its eastern venues, EAI had worked in poverty-ridden schools. Now it had swung to the other extreme, opening private schools with tuition as high as $8,500 a year. It acquired three private schools, thirteen charter schools, twenty-two private preschools and a business college.

Golle renamed EAI, TesseracT, from Madeleine L'Engle's novel *A Wrinkle in Time*. In geometry, a tesseract is a four-dimensional equivalent of a cube, but as fictionalized by L'Engle, it is a fifth-dimensional corridor leading to destinations otherwise beyond reach. Some said Golle used the new name to hide any association with EAI's failures.

TesseracT headed for Arizona in an upbeat mood. It would not take over existing schools or open its charters in trailers or church basements—it would build the schools. The initial application to the Arizona Charter School Board proposed twelve elementary, middle, and high schools that the company would build in the state over a three-year period. The schools would enroll around 6,600 students. In short order, TesseracT also acquired Sunrise Educational Services (a group of twenty preschools) and a business college, which were both in financial trouble.

Golle had to spend a lot of TesseracT's resources to get the charters going. He now also had two financially distressed companies. Nevertheless, TesseracT's troubles seemed to burst upon an unsuspecting company and clientele alike. As late as mid-1999, Golle was still talking about expansion plans. "TesseracT Charter School Schedules Signup" was a headline in the May 1, 1999, *Arizona Republic*. "TesseracT Group Plans High School" was another on August 3, 1999. Yet at the same time sources of money were being closed off. Some of TesseracT's charter schools received as much as $1.95 per mile from the state for student transportation, but reimbursed parents only 5 cents a mile. In just three months in 1999, TesseracT collected $760,000 in such fees. Legislators closed the loophole that allowed such outrageous profit-making, by funding transportation at a flat $174 per year, per pupil. " 'We don't know what the impact is going to be,' Golle said" (Mattern, 2000a, p. A1).

TesseracT expanded too rapidly in too many directions and found itself with cash-flow problems that soon exacerbated its general condition. Unable to pay for rent and construction costs, TesseracT borrowed $5 million at 18 percent interest. In February 2000 many of its top officers resigned—no reasons were ever given (*Arizona Republic*, 2000).

The preschools had been primarily day-care operations, and were in poor physical condition and losing money. Since Golle wanted to bill them as educational institutions, not merely child care, he had to bring the buildings up to code and replace the $7.00-an-hour workers with licensed professionals. He had planned to keep the day-care management, but, armed with generous "golden handshakes," they left.

The business school had also been losing money and Golle was not able to turn that around. TesseracT's stock, which had peaked at $48.50 per share, plunged to 56 cents per share. The NASDAQ stock market dropped it from its listing. Golle said "The worst is behind us" (Mattern, 2000a). It wasn't.

By May 2000, TesseracT's debt totaled $48.9 million and it was losing money at the rate of $12 million a year (Mattern, 2000b). To stanch the flow of money, TesseracT sold several schools and its business college. The schools were bought by Nobel Learning Communities (Mattern, 2000c). (See pages 118 to 121 for a discussion of Nobel.) Parents fretted over possible closures. Some said they were willing to pay even-higher tuition. Eventually parent groups bought two of the schools.

TesseracT limped into the 2000–2001 school year having trimmed its administrative staff by 80 percent. A restructured loan proved insufficient to shore up the organization. On October 9, 2000, a school holiday (Columbus Day celebrated), TesseracT filed for Chapter 11 bankruptcy protection. Although the company had been visibly floundering financially since early 2000, Lucian Spataro, then–TesseracT CEO, described the action as a "very strategic and well-planned filing" (Creno, 2000). He said the schools would remain open and operations would not be interrupted.

In March 2001, Spataro resigned, stating that his goal of selling assets while keeping the schools open had been accomplished.

Needless to say, under the circumstances described above, nothing like a formal evaluation of TesseracT's Arizona school adventures was carried out. TesseracT is still in bankruptcy court, but no one expects it to operate again.

Edison Schools, Inc.: The Market in Theory versus the Market in Practice

The best-known proponent trying to make money off education is now Chris Whittle. In 1991 Whittle started the Edison Project, so named because Edison didn't try to build a better candle, but instead invented a new means of producing light. Edison schools, the founders explained, would develop a whole new way to educate. And no other school management project illustrates so clearly the difference between the theory of market operations and the cold water of reality in the schools. No other project, as well, contrasts the profiteering of some EMOs to their avowed desire to help American public education in so clear a light.

Whittle made his fortune early in communications, lost it, and was forced to sell his holdings. He then embarked on a series of adventures in other industries before announcing that he would make his next fortune with a nationwide system of private schools. Whittle's schools would be high-tech, using a new, rich curriculum that Whittle would develop. They would provide a longer school day and a longer schoolyear and still, Whittle promised, not cost more than public schools. Whittle scored public-relations coups by hiring some highly visible people: Benno Schmidt, a president of Yale University, became president of Edison. Chester E. Finn, Jr., former assistant secretary of education and eloquent critic of public schools, took a top spot. Whittle also signed on John Chubb of the Brookings Institution, coauthor of *Politics, Markets, and American Schools*, a book that argues for the privatization of education. Finn has since left the Edison Schools project.

At the project's inception in 1991 Whittle estimated he would have 200 for-profit schools up and running by 1996 and 1,000 by 2000. By the 2000–2001 schoolyear, he had opened 113 by his way of counting, or 90 or 88 by more conventional counting methods. Going into 2001–2002 Edison operated, by its tally, 136 schools. Not everyone has been impressed. *New York Observer* business writer Christopher Byron had this to say about the Whittle enterprises:

> Possessed by his own sense of visionary infallibility—and the baloney-spouting skills of a Harold Hill—Mr. Whittle soon had individuals ranging from Yale University President Benno Schmidt to President Jimmy Carter's top White House aide, Hamilton Jordan, to *Fortune* magazine editor William Rukeyser coming to work for him.
>
> Suitably adorned with such names all around him, Mr. Whittle thereafter went on to start up one wacky venture after the next. They ranged from a scheme for publishing books with ads in them, to piping advertiser-supported medical news into doctors' offices via cable TV, to the same basic idea for ad-supported news for kids in the classroom. The latter clunker, dubbed Channel One, was eventually sold to a Henry Kravis brainstorm called KIII Communications Corporation that is now spewing losses in all directions under the name Primedia, Inc. (Byron, 2000)

Whittle's count of 113 schools in 2000–2001 requires some explanation: Edison can count three schools where a public district could count only one, because it considers grades K–5, 6–8, and 9–12 as separate schools even if all grades are housed in one building. By the more usual reckoning, Edison had 90 buildings employing 88 principals (Wyatt, 2001).

So far, the best that can be said for Edison Schools is that the loss per student fell from $3,927 in 1996 to $603 in 1998–1999, to $389 in 1999–2000. In 1998–1999, Edison had revenues of $132.8 million and lost $51 million. According to one article, since its inception, the project has lost $1.36 for every dollar it has made, and has suffered a total loss going into 2001 of $197 million (Wyatt, 2001). Another estimate in late November 2001 put the loss figure at $220 million (Greenberg, 2001)

Although the company's "net losses are rising and show no sign of relenting let alone reversing course" (Greenberg, 2001), Whittle himself is doing quite well. His base salary since at least 1998–1999 through 2001–2002 was about $300,000, the same as his CEO Schmidt received. This was approximately three times the average salary of a superintendent of a school district with as many students at Edison (38,000 in 1999–2000; 57,000 in 2000–2001; 75,000 in 2001–2002). Whittle has now accepted a salary of $1 per year plus stock options. This is precisely the kind of deal many were recommending *against* after the Enron collapse. As Steven Pearlstein put it in the *Washington Post*, "They reward corporate leaders for all the wrong things" (Pearlstein, 2002). Namely, they drive executives to manage for the short term, sacrificing the long-term interests of shareholders and employees.

Papers filed with the Securities and Exchange Commission indicate that Edison has a "management agreement" with WSI, Inc. of Knoxville, Tennessee. Between 1995 and 1998, WSI received $1,848,742 and as of 2001, WSI also owned 3,098,403 shares of Edison Inc. The president and sole employee of WSI, Inc. is Chris Whittle. Whittle has also received more than $1 million from Edison for "professional services" and a loan of $5.6 million, which he could use to buy 1.45 million shares of the company at $1.50 a share, tax free (the company covers the IRS's levy). Whittle has other holdings in Edison. After the public offering, the *New York Post* declared that Whittle's share of the company was worth $205 million (Miner, 2000).

For his part, Schmidt received a low-interest loan of $1.8 million. If he loses his job as president, he receives $2.5 million and two-years' salary. Other Edison officers have stock options but have lost out for the time being because the stock has plummeted to below $1 a share as of July 2002, and might soon be delisted from the NASDAQ (it has been as high as $39 and Edison officers sold some of their holdings near this price).

These cozy arrangements led *Business Week* financial writer Diane Brady to declare that "Chris Whittle's IPO deserves a D–" (Brady, 1999). Actually, that grade represents leniency on the part of the headline writer, because in the text Brady actually wrote, "this deal deserves to flunk." Brady also observed that in addition to making lots of money while the company loses lots of money, Whittle has pledged a large segment of his holdings in Edison to Morgan Guaranty Trust Co. If Whittle doesn't deliver, bankers will control about 15 percent of the company (Edison Schools, Inc., 2000).

Meanwhile, not only are the Edison schools far fewer than the initial optimistic projections, but the schools hardly constitute a new way to educate. They are mostly existing schools that have contracted for management services from Whittle. Some are new charter schools. Much of the curriculum was previously developed by "ordinary" educators: Success for All in reading and Everyday Math for mathematics. The former was developed at Johns Hopkins University and the latter at the University of Chicago.

Free-market principles hold that for markets to work properly, consumers have to have access to good information about the product. We have seen that in the case of EAI/TesseracT, such information was not forthcoming. Accurate information can be obtained about Edison only with great difficulty. Let us look at information about some specific schools, and then draw some generalizations from what we find there.

Washington Elementary School, Sherman, Texas

Consider, first, Washington Elementary School in Sherman, Texas, the first school Edison ever signed up, in 1995. Edison's *Second Annual Report on School Performance*, issued in March 1999, gives Washington its highest rating, five stars, for "strongly positive" achievement gains (a *Third Annual Report*, dated August 2000 but posted only in November 2000, contains even *less* specific information than does the *Second Annual Report*). A report on Edison schools from the American Federation of Teachers, however, rates Washington's performance among the worst of Edison's efforts. At the end of the 1999–2000 school year, the contract expired and Washington did not renew it.

How could one school generate such disparate rankings and perceptions? Take the Edison report first. Edison provides six charts on test scores. Two show the percent of students attaining minimum expectations on the Texas Assessment of Academic Skills (TAAS) for three years in grades 3 and 4. These charts show mixed results, with percentages both rising and falling. Most readers not trained in statistics would find the charts confusing.

The next two charts show the percentage of students meeting minimum expectations for the same cohort—the same students in grades 3 and 4 for 1995 to 1997, and for 1996 to 1998. These charts are organized differently than the previous charts and would likely cause most readers even more confusion. The way the report arranges some bar charts has readers' eyes jumping from one set to another to find out what is happening from year to year. When one succeeds in this somewhat daunting task, one finds test scores falling.

It is not the job of advertising to tell the whole story and the Second Annual Report is at best an "infomercial." For instance, without giving the reader information about how the Texas Education Agency calculates its "Texas Learning Index," Edison reports that "In 1998 Washington [elementary school] had the highest gains among the 40 most similar to it statewide." This is true. But in 1996, 1997, and 1999, Washington was in the bottom quartile.

When Sherman Independent School District, which contains Washington School, terminated its relationship with Edison at the same time that Dallas was initiating one, *Dallas Observer* reporter Jonathan Fox looked for reasons why, and what the implications would be for Dallas (Fox, 2000). Fox found some Edison supporters as well as detractors, and some of the dispute is a he-said-she-said affair. For instance, Sherman contends that the Edison experience cost taxpayers $4 million while Edison claims that their involvement in Sherman cost Edison $6 million. Other facts seem objective: Sherman administrators said that there had been some growth in test scores at Washington, but that scores had "soared" in the rest of the district.

Edison officials also seemed somewhat insensitive to the Washington neighborhood. Fox wrote that Washington Elementary School was 28 percent Hispanic, 24 percent black, and "in a part of the city where nearly every house needs a paint job, roofs sag, and the occasional worn sofa rests on a porch" (2000). On one trip, Edison officials arrived from the Dallas–Fort Worth airport in chauffeured Lincoln town cars. (A similar gaffe occurred in Minneapolis where parents rejected Edison, in part, because Edison officers were perceived as "behind this shield of Armani suits and gold jewelry" [Carter, 1999].)

Edison's claims of reduced costs are also challenged both in Sherman and Dallas. One Dallas school trustee who opposed the contract wants to reduce the per-pupil stipend because DISD (Dallas Independent School District) must still pay for transportation, food service, security, and other costs. Even DISD super-intendent Bill Rojas, an Edison advocate, said, "I know it's going to cost more money." (Rojas is a believer in Edison's pedagogy, not its business sense: He is also quoted as saying "that stock is not going to be in my portfolio" [Fox, 2000]. The Dallas School Board terminated Rojas in May 2000 for reasons that appear to be unrelated to his Edison advocacy; he joined an Edison competitor, Advantage Schools.) In Sherman, the district surrendered the Edison schools' share of administrative costs, but didn't cut central office staff accordingly, thus retaining duplicate managers.

According to Sherman officials, Edison tried to save money by cutting corners on maintenance and by challenging bills. Sherman administrators ordered district staff to do maintenance work at Washington that Edison had failed to do, even though contractually obligated to, simply because "This building belongs to SISD taxpayers. We can't afford for it to go downhill" (Fox, 2000). One might have thought that Edison would have learned something from EAI, which bought a fair amount of community goodwill by painting its schools and making them attractive places.

On the other hand, Edison appeared to have community support for accomplishments outside of the academic arena. Mary Doclar, a reporter for the *Fort Worth Star-Telegram*, observed that even first-graders showed discipline as they moved from their classroom to a computer lab. When the teacher said "Would you please show everybody what Edison Excellence is?", a straggly line became "ruler-straight" and children folded their hands behind their backs. Edison also pleased parents by teaching what one parent called "core values": respect and honesty. These teachings apparently caused a substantial reduction in discipline problems (Doclar, 2000).

By selecting data and using internal testing data, the Edison *First Annual Report* claimed that the seventeen schools opened between 1995 and 1997 generated "a total of 143 trends of one, two, or three years' duration" (p. 10). Edison then weighted these "trends" by their duration. "After weighting, for example, a positive trend that is three years long counts three times as much as a positive trend that is one year long" (p. 13). With this statistical sleight of hand, totally without any scientific merit, Edison then claimed that the 143 total trends yielded 176 weighted trends and that 136, or 77 percent, of those were positive.

Edison further claims that the average annual gains on norm-referenced tests are five percentile points and that Edison students gain on average six percentile points on criterion-referenced tests (the prospectus issued to potential investors in 1999 puts the NRT gains at four "percentage points"—a meaningless phrase). The Annual Report then contrasts these gains to "Achievement Gains in U.S. Public Schools." These are much smaller, –1 percent for nine- and thirteen-year-olds in reading and zero for nine- and thirteen-year-olds in math" (p. 13).

On close examination, one sees that the metrics used for national trends are not the same as those used to measure Edison students; in fact, it is not at all clear what these numbers represent. The legend on the chart says that they are the "Average Percentage Point Gain, National Assessment of Educational Progress, U.S. 9- and 13-year-olds, 1994–1996." The fine print, though, states that "Gains are for percentages of 9-year-olds reaching level 200 and 13-year-olds reaching level 250—minimum levels expected." The report only vaguely specifies what the numbers refer to. Beyond that, there are certain fundamental problems with these data: They don't exist. There was no NAEP reading assessment in 1996 and no NAEP mathematics assessment in 1994. Thus these statistics, whatever they might be, refer to data that have never been collected.

Even if one granted Edison the "5 percentile rank" gains it claims, one could consider this an admission of failure. After all, the Edison day is one-third longer than the typical school day (8 hours vs. 6) and the Edison school year, even after being trimmed, is still 11 percent longer than the usual year (200 days vs. 180). Taken together, this means that students sit in Edison classrooms fully 50 percent more hours per year than they do in regular schools (1600 [200 × 8] vs. 1080 [180 × 6]). By the time Edison first-graders finish sixth grade, they have spent as much time in school as rising sophomores in a regular public school. In addition to more time in school, Edison schools test students every month. Under these circumstances, one would certainly expect these schools to show some test score advantage.

The Thomas Edison Academy, San Francisco

The longer day and longer year aspects of Edison took their toll in the incidentally-named Thomas Edison Academy in San Francisco, leading to one of Edison's nastiest encounters. Reporter Tali Woodward, in the July 19, 2000, *San Francisco Bay Guardian*, stated that over half of the teachers were quitting. In fact, 70 percent did not return. "Frustrated by long hours, a rigid curriculum that emphasizes testing, and what they describe as a Big Brother atmosphere, teachers at Edison are abandoning what they initially saw as a welcome experiment. Even those who accepted the concept of a corporate schoolhouse now say ESI's cookie-cutter, bottom-line mentality harms everything from teacher morale to student development and diversity" (Woodward, 2000a).

The scripted curriculum also turned off a number of teachers who felt they had lost all semblance of professionalism. "They literally give you a script with what you're supposed to say," said one teacher. "Every few months somebody from Edison would come in with a clipboard to make sure you had specific things hanging up in your classroom." According to Woodward, teachers who raised issues and proposed changes received a standard response: "Maybe our design is not for you." Teachers wondered about a company that invited them to leave rather than participate in the process of change.

Comments such as "Maybe our design is not for you" evoke memories of the post-Sputnik days when curriculum development projects tried to create materials that would "speak directly to the child" without the intervention of the teacher. The materials were referred to as "teacher proof," and they were a disaster. In fact, any program that slights the teachers' roles in schools is likely doomed to fail, at least in the sense that it is likely to drive out professional teachers and leave only those who need a script.

Teachers accused the administrators at the school, all brought in by Edison, of instilling fear in teachers by telling them that if the teachers did not cooperate and get test scores up, the school would cease to exist. This threat was simply untrue: Under those circumstances, the school would have reverted to the control of the San Francisco school board.

There were also questions about the legality of the academy's charter in the first place and the validity of the teachers' signatures requesting that Edison be brought in. School board rules forbid it to deal with a for-profit company and a nonprofit entity had been established as a go-between. Some alleged that teachers' signatures had been coerced in some instances and forged in others.

Discussions of vouchers, charters, privatization, and so on, are usually cast in words that carry the ring of idealism: doing right for the children, improving the system, or giving poor children a chance. The above accounts from Texas and California reporters describe what actually happens in the political trenches.

Class Size and Special Education

Edison classes contain twenty-eight students, compared to a national average of about twenty-four for elementary schools and thirty-one for high schools (National Center for Education Statistics, 1998, table 70). This large class size argues against high achievement as does teacher turnover, which is higher in Edison schools than the national average. Edison officials in Texas balked when told that they could put only twenty-two students in a class and gave in only when shown that it was Texas *law* that caps class size at twenty-two. Edison is able to operate in similarly mandated California only because Gap founder Don Fisher used his Fisher Family Foundation (now the D2F2 Foundation) to supply $25 million to cover the additional costs of the smaller classes. Edison's resistance to small classes in the Texas instance and the need for additional subsidy in California call into question Edison's claim that their schools will not cost more than the typical public school.

The *San Francisco Chronicle* editors sided with Edison, accusing the school board of being in an ideological frenzy and "undeterred by evidence of Edison's success . . . ." The *Chronicle* accepted Edison's claims of increases and achievement. It argued that the board was driven by a political and ideological agenda, not by education concerns (*San Francisco Chronicle*, 2001). The school board voted to terminate its relationship with Edison. Edison now operates the academy through a relationship with the State Board of Education.

During the school board versus Edison conflict, opponents alleged that Edison was reducing the number of special education students, sending poor students to other schools, and recruiting students that would score higher. This, opponents said, was why scores were rising. Edison staunchly denied this accusation. Yet, in its *Fourth Annual Report on School Performance*, it admitted that "Schools often change their enrollments dramatically after Edison is introduced. . . . Edison schools are generally schools of choice, and enrollments change as families opt into or out of this new program. If enrollments change, comparisons of test scores before and after Edison become potentially misleading comparisons of different students" (Edison, 2001, p. 16).

Of course, low test scores are a principal reason, sometimes the *only* reason, that Edison is sought out. And the enrollments do change. Edison's reports show that in 1999–2000, Thomas Edison Academy listed 6.8 percent students in special education classes, well below the national average of 12.5 percent (Edison typically has a much smaller proportion of special education students and the problems of these students are less severe than some found in public schools). A year later the percentage plunged to 2 percent. From 1999–2000 to 2000–2001, the proportion of economically disadvantaged students dropped from 79 percent to 55 percent. And English-as-a-second-language learners plummeted from 32 percent to a remarkable zero (Edison, 2000; Edison, 2001).

In spite of these changes, in fall 2001 the state's school rating system, the Academic Performance Index (API), for Thomas Edison Academy fell sharply: It is now 75th—dead last—among San Francisco elementary public schools, with an API of 504 (the API runs from 200 to 1,000). The average San Francisco public school had an API of 698, and the highest, 878 (Colvin, 2001; Parents Advocating School Accountability, 2001).

Test Scores

Let us return to Edison's disclaimer on before-and-after test scores: If we can't use these as measures of performance, what can we use? The logical alternative is to follow the same students over time and see how they perform. Edison says it doesn't do this kind of analysis because, over time, there are fewer and fewer of the same students in the later grades. Instead, for example, it compares this year's fourth grade with last year's. But if, as Edison admits and Thomas Edison Academy certainly shows, the demographic characteristics of schools are changing, we can't know if we're measuring the Edison program's impact or these demographic changes.

Another possible way to evaluate progress in Edison schools is to compare those schools with similar public schools. Edison discounts this comparison because it says that the Edison schools are not independent of the public schools—that is, it claims that Edison schools also help other schools progress, although evidence of this is nil. Finally, Edison claims that its schools have no capacity to make these kinds of comparisons. It thus appears that Edison can provide a "reason" why it doesn't raise achievement no matter what kind of comparison is made. How convenient.

Edison's Contracts, 2001–2002

Edison has enjoyed some success at expanding its contracts during 2001 and 2002, but this year has also brought it spectacular failures and dubious publicity. The failures were especially sensational because they happened in big markets, New York and Philadelphia, and played out in those cities' media. They were even more breathtaking because the proposed contracts appeared to be rigged, by Mayor Rudy Giuliani and School Chancellor Harold Levy in New York, and by Pennsylvania governor Tom Ridge and his successor Mark Schweiker in Philadelphia.

In New York, Chancellor Levy shepherded a proposal from Edison to take over five low-scoring New York schools (Wyatt, 2000; Goodnough, 2001). The proposal process placed constraints on bidders that eliminated community-based potential bidders: the bidders were limited to those with prior management of schools with at least 450 students and a cash reserve of at least $1,000,000.

Edison arrived in New York with an "If You Can Make It There, You Can Make It Anywhere" attitude. Whittle said that "If we do a great job in these schools, we believe there will be more schools headed our way" (Wyatt, 2001a).

For Edison to get the contract, a vote had to be taken among the parents in the schools' enrollment areas. Initially, Edison was given a fox-in-the-henhouse privilege of conducting the vote itself. Outraged community activists, especially ACORN (Association for Community Organization for Reform Now), insisted that they be allowed to send out literature opposing Edison.

Levy had decreed that for Edison to win the contract, 50 percent of the parents of children attending the five schools would have to vote for the deal. To everyone's stunned surprise, 80 percent of the parents voted "no." Even at the school considered most likely to accept Edison, only 34 percent voted "yes" (Goodnough, 2001). Postmortems found that parents had felt blindsided about their schools being on the auction block and resented that community-based groups were being shut out. They said Levy did not even campaign vigorously for his own plan (Campanile, 2001).

Perhaps it was a coincidence, but shortly before the vote, Edison made a public offering of 6.7 million shares in the company, raising $81 million. Half of the shares were sold by officers of the company. Whittle personally pocketed $16 million (Wyatt, 2001b). After losing the New York contract, Whittle put on a brave face, noting that Edison had signed new agreements in Chester, Pennsylvania, Las Vegas, and Miami-Dade.

In the summer of 2001 Edison received another too-good-to-be-true-but-it-is sweetheart deal from the state of Pennsylvania. The state's governor, Tom Ridge, wanted to consider the privatizing of some or all of Philadelphia's public schools. He awarded Edison a $2.7 million no-bid contract to study the district and make recommendations for improving both finances and achievement. Alex Molnar of Arizona State University and expert on commercialization efforts in education said "Edison has no discernible skills for performing the analysis and is a self-interest. This stinks of conflict of interest from the top to the bottom" (Woodall, 2001).

Edison refused to reveal to the state how much of the $2.7 million it spent on subcontractors or even to name them. Rejecting inquiries from state legislators and the *Philadelphia Daily News*, Edison spokesman Adam Tucker said, "As a matter of policy in this project, we won't release dollar amounts." The *News* was incredulous: "Well, we've got a flash for the state. You just paid these guys $2.7 million [from our tax dollars] and they anticipate billing the state another $300 million for work they expect to do here. So you might try this tack: Provide the information or forget about the $300 million" (*Philadelphia Daily News*, 2001).

In testimony before Philadelphia City Council, Edison claimed that more than four-fifths of their schools showed positive test gains. By this point, readers should be skeptical. It was quickly pointed out that the figure was based on only 74 of the 113 schools that Edison operated and that 7 of the 62 that Edison reported as positive had been cited by their respective state departments of education for failure to improve (Socolar, 2001).

The Edison battle pitted Governor Mark Schweiker against Philadelphia's mayor, John Street. We're coming in, said the governor; No, you're not, said the mayor. In testimony, "a long line of parents, union leaders, college professors, and community organizers used a hearing at City Hall to pummel the governor's plan to privatize the Philadelphia public schools" (O'Neill, 2001). Philadelphia's representative to Congress, Chakah Fattah, also joined the fray, challenging Edison's version of its successes (Mezzacappa, 2001a).

The *Wall Street Journal* looked upon the donnybrook and called Philadelphia the "City of Brotherly Thugs" (2001). As the deadline for a reconciliation between Schweiker and Street approached, it looked as though it would be another *Rocky* finish, although it wasn't clear who was playing the title role. Street was reported to have a secret plan to sabotage Edison (Polaneczky, 2001). But on December 21, deadline day, Schweiker and Street hugged their way through a press conference, although some reported that their smiles looked "plastered" on and weren't convinced by their "empty-sounding assurances that all is peachy. . . ." (Polaneczky, 2001). At this point it appeared that Edison would take over much of the district much as Ridge and later Schweiker had envisioned.

Suits were filed to keep Edison out. Reporters were thrown out of a city council meeting (Davies, 2002). The *Philadelphia Daily News* claimed that Edison had paid $85,000 in "consulting fees" to gain access to the city insiders. Edison refused to comment on the amount but said that the fees had been paid out of "general corporate sources," not the $2.7 million state grant, and that, therefore, the company had no obligation to disclose the sum (Warner and Daughen, 2002).

It was all too much for the CEO of Philadelphia's school system. He quit, effective the day of the announcement, saying that "he was disgusted with the takeover process and the role that for-profit Edison Schools, Inc., is to play" (Dean and Davies, 2001).

Under the original plan, Edison would have removed the top 55 administrators in the system and replaced them with appointees of Edison's choosing. Although it was widely reported that the compromise granted Edison forty-five schools but no administrative control, the reports proved untrue.

The governor appointed a School Reform Commission (SRC) headed by James Nevels, a Philadelphia businessman. This appointment appeared to favor Edison because Nevels had also served on a board that installed Edison to manage almost all of the Chester-Upland schools. However, the SRC sent out a request for proposals and Nevels stated that the competition would be open. Some thirty-one companies announced they would respond, and twenty-two companies actually did, including the universities, community groups, and other national EMOs.

Representative Chaka Fattah wrote a long letter to the SRC that detailed flaws in Edison's report on what the city's schools needed, provided a list of places where Edison had failed to deliver, and pointed out the conflict of interest that would ensue were Edison given administrative authority to evaluate its own performance in the schools. "Edison's record creates ample reason to be concerned about Edison's ability to perform" in both the central administration and in school buildings (PR Newswire, 2002).

On March 26, 2002, the SRC named Edison as the "lead consultant" for the takeover, and three weeks later awarded Edison twenty schools, not the forty-five it had asked for. Edison's longstanding charm with investors evaporated overnight. Edison's stock had fallen from $20 a share at the start of 2002 to $14 shortly after the New York fiasco. Now it spiraled down toward $1 and potential delisting from the NASDAQ exchange.

The failure to get forty-five schools was not the only bad news that battered Edison. Indeed, during the month of May 2002, Whittle must have felt that not only his carriage but the whole world was turning into a pumpkin. The SEC investigated Edison's accounting practices and found that Edison had counted as income money that had actually been paid by districts to teachers, about 40 percent of its total. Edison agreed to change its accounting techniques, but *Education Week* declared that Edison had caught a case of "Enron-itis" (Walsh, 2002).

News of the SEC investigation was exacerbated by the fact that it had been going on for three months, but Edison had kept it under wraps. Several law firms filed class-action suits, claiming Edison had misled investors (PR Newswire, 2002b).

Results from the Chester-Upland district, a neighbor of Philadelphia where Edison managed nine schools, looked bad (Hardy, 2002). Clarke County, Nevada (Las Vegas), announced it was withholding a $3 million payment because of unfulfilled promises (Bach, 2002). Boston Renaissance School, one of Edison's oldest and largest contracts, terminated its relationship with Edison (Vaishnav, 2002).

Edison had touted its Wichita schools as models for the rest of the district, but Wichita canceled two of the four contracts because of falling test scores, high student and teacher turnover, and allegations of cheating (Funk, 2002a). Teachers claimed they had brought testing irregularities to Edison's attention; Edison denied it (Funk, 2002b). An Edison showplace, Wintergreen Magnet School in Connecticut, also announced that it was ending its relationship with Edison (Baker, 2002). And it looked as though Edison's schools in Inkster, Michigan, would be taken over by the state (Walsh-Sarnecki, 2002b).

Pennsylvania Senator Arlen Specter, and Philadelphia Congressman, Chakah Fattah, ordered Edison to compare Philadelphia's performance with other large urban districts, something which it had not actually done in its report to Schweiker (Snyder, 2002). Edison tried to counter by announcing twelve "expansions" (more grades in the same school) and two new contracts (PR Newswire, 2002c). It also brought a parent from another district to a Philadelphia get-acquainted session to try to calm parental fears.

June was better for Edison than May only because it brought less bad news. Mt. Clemens, Michigan, one of the first four districts to sign with Edison, declared it would end its contract a year before it expired (Walsh-Sarnecki, 2002a). The Texas Education Agency dropped its ratings of two of Edison's seven Dallas schools from "acceptable" to "low achieving," causing the Dallas School Board to re-evaluate its contract (Shah and Hobbs, 2002; Tomsho, 2002). A report by Dallas associate superintendent and evaluation expert, William Webster, said that the seven Edison schools had not made as much progress as demographically similar regular schools (Hobbs, 2002). The Baltimore city school board "in stinging comments" voted to "quash" a proposed Edison expansion in that city (Bowie, 2002).

Questions arose over Edison's ability to raise the money to run even twenty schools in Philadelphia. However, its perennial champion, Merrill Lynch, and a little-known investment company, Chelsea Capital, each came up with $20 million. The infusion was enough, it appeared, to let Edison open in Philly (Woodall, 2002; Steinberg and Henriques, 2002), and momentarily pushed Edison's stock from $1 to $1.60, but it then drifted back to the unit mark. Editors at the *New York Times* made the startling observation that education is labor intensive. This led them to the equally startling conclusion that it "may never be profitable on the scale that the stock market requires" (*New York Times*, 2002a). Do tell.

Evaluations of Edison Schools

Late in 2000, some evaluation data more reliable than Edison's own reports indicated that the results from Edison schools were, at best, mixed. The American Federation of Teachers researcher F. Howard Nelson wrote that "Five years into the Edison experiment, ample data now exist for the public to use in making more informed judgments about progress in Edison schools. At this point, Edison schools mostly do as well as or worse than comparable public schools; occasionally they do better. This mediocre record has not been evident to many observers of Edison schools for several reasons" (Nelson, 2000). Perhaps the record has not been evident because Edison has attempted to obscure it.

Two months after the AFT's report, researchers at Western Michigan University reached similar conclusions: "Our findings suggest that Edison students do not perform as well as Edison claims in its annual reports on student performance" (Miron and Applegate, 2000). Taking a sample of ten schools the researchers noted that Edison reported the achievement trends as "strongly positive" in five schools, "positive" in three and "mixed" in two. The researchers found no strongly positive trends. They found positive trends in three, mixed trends in four, negative trends in two, and strongly negative trends in one.

Even though the researchers used one of the common ambiguous research words, "suggest," Edison was not amused. In a press release titled "Union-Sponsored Study Provides Predictably Biased Evaluation of Schools," Edison's Chief Education Officer, John Chubb—and others—derided it. Chubb claimed that "the report is stunningly irresponsible. . . . The Western Michigan report is literally a scam. . . . It is shocking that social scientists would attempt to pass off such work as an objective evaluation" (PR News, February 22, 2001).

Certainly it is hardly as shocking as the hyperbolic funny-numbers conclusions in the various Edison *Annual Reports*. That Whittle and Chubb can publish such misleading numbers and then take umbrage at figures generated by legitimate researchers is the height of hypocrisy. Whittle's tactics are sometimes reminiscent of the flimflam artist of *The Music Man*, warning the people in song: "You've got trouble. Right here in River City."

For its part, Edison is acting as if it is here to stay. On December 18, 2001, New York's Economic Development Corporation approved a $2 million low-interest loan to mid-town–based Edison to build new headquarters in Harlem for the 300 central office employees. In addition to moving its headquarters to Bill Clinton's neighborhood, Edison's new building will house an elementary charter school and provide a 60,000-square-foot home for the Museum of African Art, currently in downtown's SoHo district. In return for the loan, Edison promised to keep the headquarters jobs in New York for at least twenty-four years (*New York Daily News*, 2001).

Summary

An examination of the operations of the most prominent corporations that manage public schools for profit finds that they have yet to demonstrate that they increase achievement or make a profit. Indeed, one must ask why, if Edison Schools has a single model of pedagogy, and it does, the achievement results vary so wildly among the schools that it operates. One might conclude it is because schools are more complex than the privatizers have acknowledged, and influenced by many more variables than the privatizers have taken into account.

Edison in particular has a remarkable track record. Reports indicate it doesn't raise achievement for most schools and it has yet to turn a profit. A December 2001 report from Flint, Michigan, revealed that Flint spends at least $600 a year more on the Edison schools than on its regular public schools, but that Edison still loses money. Edison's ability to get ever more contracts borders on the amazing.

Beacon Education Management (Formerly Alternative Public Schools)

Beacon Education Management was begun in 1992 by business-school graduates John Eason and William DeLoache. According to Eason, both founders had been involved in programs to aid inner-city children and their interests began to focus on education as their own children entered school. They first bid on a contract in Tennessee and, although they lost it, this appears to have given them connections with former Tennessee governor and former secretary of education Lamar Alexander.

Currently, Beacon provides a range of services from consulting to total school management. It has schools in Arizona, Massachusetts, North Carolina, South Carolina, Illinois, and Michigan. It recently bought a 50 percent interest in Pontiac-based JCR, Inc., a charter school management firm. (Charter schools in Michigan are public entities, but can contract with private firms for various management services; by early 1999 about 70 percent of Michigan charter schools contracted for such services and the numbers have increased slightly since then.) It also acquired ABS, Inc., which provides a variety of services to seventy-five charter schools in Arizona.

Under its former name, Alternative Public Schools (APS), Beacon acquired a lot of publicity, mostly negative, after being invited to take over a low-scoring school in Wilkinsburg, Pennsylvania. The town of 20,000 had seen its fortunes sink with the losses of the steel industry. At the time, APS had not managed any other schools and it walked into a situation rife with hostility aroused by a combination of teacher strikes, teacher protection laws, tax increases, low test scores, and charges of teacher complacency and incompetence. This incendiary mix flared when APS replaced all teachers. A succession of suits followed. APS's contract ended in 1997 when Judge R. Stanton Wettich ruled that Pennsylvania law made it illegal to turn a public school over to a for-profit company.

Beacon has since branched out into charter schools. It currently manages twenty-nine charter schools containing some 10,000 students. When I asked for information from Beacon as part of an earlier research study, I received a letter from a Beacon official, Jeff LaPlante, saying "Our company is a private company and we don't participate in these research studies" (personal communication, 2000). When I followed up and asked LaPlante to identify his position in the organization, I received no response.

Some information on Beacon schools can be found on the websites of states that require charter schools to take the state tests, such as Michigan and Massachusetts. In Michigan the test results are less than awesome and one statistic stands out: few students are eligible for free or reduced-price lunches. One also notices that Beacon teachers receive just over half what a Michigan public schoolteacher earns.

In the summer of 2001, Beacon announced it would go public. However, its initial public offering did not draw the flurry of attention that Beacon wanted and the IPO was yanked at the last minute. "It was a very soft market," said CEO Michael B. Ronan. Perhaps it was also because Beacon has yet to make money and doesn't have Edison's image. Beacon lost $2.7 million in 2000 and in the first nine months of fiscal 2001 it lost $4.6 million. Like Edison, in the past Beacon has claimed to be profitable at the school level, but not at the organizational level.

Beacon's website at one time stated "George Bush Visits Newest Beacon School." The implication was that then–presidential candidate George W. Bush had singled out the school for praise. However, the Bush in attendance was George Prescott Bush, teen-heartthrob nephew of George W. Bush. The item has since been removed. Ironically, the St. Louis school that the young Bush visited was named the Thurgood Marshall School. Thurgood Marshall was an African American lawyer who argued *Brown vs. The Board of Education* before the Supreme Court, the landmark case that ended legal segregation in public schools. Marshall was later named to the Supreme Court.

In 2001, Beacon merged with a relative newcomer, Florida-based Chancellor Academies, Inc. Started by former Miami-Dade superintendent Octavio Visiedo, Chancellor-Beacon now claims to be the second-largest educational management organization in the country with services to 19,000 students in both public charter schools and private schools.

Unlike most EMOs, Chancellor was organized largely by educators. Visiedo brought a number of Miami-Dade administrators into the organization as well as several people with experience as private-school officials.

Nobel Learning Communities, Inc.

Nobel Learning Communities, formerly Nobel Educational Dynamics, formerly Rocking Horse Child Care Centers of America in 1984, has been called McSchool because it builds most of its schools to similar specifications. Bennigan's or TGIFriday would be more appropriate analogues than McDonald's for Nobel schools. Nobel aims only for rapidly growing, upwardly mobile suburbs. It is, for the time being anyway, a niche operator. It pitches its schools at those who look longingly at private schools but cannot afford the $12,000-and-up tuition. Noel's tuition is around $8,000–$9,000 a year, depending on grade. In 2000 the average tuition for schools belonging to the National Association of Independent Schools ranged from $8,015 for preschool to $12,834 for secondary school (McGovern, 2000). Thus, until a voucher plan comes along to provide sufficient tuition money to lower-income families, Nobel will largely appeal to and be available to yuppies. Indeed, its CEO, A. J. "Jack" Clegg, says that the Nobel school is for the two-working-parents' family that needs a place to drop the children off on the way to work and pick them up on the way home (most Nobel schools stay open until six or seven o'clock).

Clegg initially avoided charter schools because there was too much variation in state legislation. Now that many state laws are virtually identical, Nobel has entered the charter field. Nobel intends to either take over or develop about seven charters each year. Nobel's income from its own schools comes from tuition. In the charter realm, it charges a percentage of its income to the school. In developing a charter school, Nobel works with the group proposing the charter and then acts as the agency that manages the school's business affairs. If the charter application is rejected, Nobel realizes no income.

In articles about Nobel (named for the inventor of TNT, not the computer company; it is supposed to convey the notion of being the best), one senses an aura of mystery about how Nobel can operate with an average class size of seventeen and turn a profit, which it has done in most years, 1997 being the lone exception. One way it manages is with low salaries. While Clegg collected a $240,000 salary in 1998 (later data not available), the average teacher makes about one-tenth of that, around $26,000 with the highest paid teachers receiving up to $35,000. The average for public schoolteachers is around $39,000, and salaries are substantially more in the affluent suburbs where Nobel builds its schools.

According to Clegg, teachers will work for such low salaries because the schools are located in relatively affluent areas and the teachers can teach and don't have to serve, in addition, as policemen, counselors, and social workers. Nobel hires only certified teachers and the organization was considered for admission to the National Association of Independent Schools. After deliberations, NAIS decided to stick with its policy of admitting only nonprofits. Nobel's claims were shown to be somewhat porous when California mandated small classes: Some Nobel teachers defected to newly available, better-paying positions in suburban public schools.

Nobel also economizes through "clustering." It will establish a cluster of preschools in an area and then add one elementary school with the preschools serving as feeders. The schools generally have only a principal and an assistant principal. Other administrative support is "regionalized" to serve the whole cluster.

As with its central offices, the Nobel libraries are "regionalized," with one library serving a number of schools, saving on both capital outlay and book acquisitions. One interviewee called the library she had seen "pathetic," about the size of a typical white-collar worker's office. The one that I visited, in an attractive facility, was about twice that size with eight computers, but the books occupied only one wall.

Nobel also saves money by minimizing capital outlays: Most of its schools are leased. In some instances it has bought schools, but typically when it builds a new school, it sells the building to a real estate investment trust and then leases the building back for fifteen to twenty years. Thus, if Nobel's market changes in a particular community, it can move out of that locale without having to dispose of the building. In addition, the buildings are designed so that they need not be forever single-function structures. A school built in what was at the time an isolated part of Loudoun County, Virginia, is now surrounded by shopping malls and boutiques—the building could be easily adapted to be a retail establishment.

A final source of savings comes from transportation. There isn't any.

Nobel is a publicly traded company on the NASDAQ. Over a four-year period its stock has ranged from a low of $4.50 to a high of $10.50. In July 2002, it was drawing about $5.50.

Nobel adapted a curriculum from the company's Merryhill schools in California, which are 50 years old. In addition, the curriculum standards of various professional education groups have been used to determine if the Nobel curriculum accomplishes what the organizations recommend. In the preschools, the standards for kindergartners have been "back mapped" to determine what would be necessary at ages three and four to prepare students for the standards that first appear in kindergarten. The preschools also seek to have a "developmentally appropriate" curriculum, as recommended by the National Association for the Education of Young Children.

In addition to appealing to middle-class families, the small class size also appears to appeal to families with very bright children. One Nobel officer claimed that some kindergarten children are reading at fourth- and fifth-grade levels.

As might be expected in a press release from a for-profit corporation, the presentation of test data put the company in the best possible light. Nobel's data are presented in grade equivalents. Grade equivalents that are better than average are more impressive than, say, percentile ranks, because they appear to represent whole years of time. In addition, many, or perhaps most, people draw the wrong conclusion about what a grade equivalent means.

For instance, a grade equivalent of, for example, 11.5 for an eighth-grader, does not mean that the eighth-grader can read material usually not seen until the middle of the junior year of high school. It refers to the score that the average eleventh-grader would make *on eighth-grade material.* Moreover, the 11.5 grade equivalent is a pure statistical abstraction: no eleventh- or twelfth-graders actually took the eighth-grade test. To test children three or four years higher (or lower) than the stated grade level of the test would be prohibitively expensive for the test publishers. The 11.5 grade-level figure in an eighth-grade test is an extrapolation, likely from students taking the test, or part of the test, in only three grades: seventh, eighth, and ninth.

Given that Nobel is a for-profit, public company (NLCI on the NASDAQ), it, like Edison, presents information in the best possible light and without sufficient detail to permit a proper evaluation. For instance, it presents grade equivalent scores for its schools nationally and by state. It does not say when it tests. For its national averages, the first-grade math score is 2.6. This will be a more impressive number if the test were given in the fall than in the spring. In the fall, 1.2 would be the national average, but in the spring, 1.8.

Perhaps more important, test publishers generate national averages with representative samples of students. Parents who pay $8,000–$9,000 a year in addition to their regular property taxes, which in large part go to public schools, are raising children who are anything but representative. In Virginia, Nobel reports its Stanford 9 fourth-grade reading score as 6.3 and math as 7.4. In Loudoun County, which contains most of Nobel's Virginia schools, the fourth-grade Stanford 9 scores range from the sixty-sixth percentile in reading to the eightieth percentile in science.

Given its targeted clientele, it's not surprising that Nobel makes no provision for special education services. In addition, should Nobel's operation expand, it will be skimming bright students from public schools.

In late September 2000 Nobel signed a partnership agreement with South Ocean Development Corporation, linking the largest provider of private non-sectarian education in the United States with the largest provider of education in the People's Republic of China. According to a press release, they plan to establish a model "international school" in Beijing. They will market the model elsewhere in China and develop "education-based" preschools, as well.

Advantage Schools, Inc.

Advantage Schools, Inc., is no more, but serves as an illustration of the rising and falling fortunes of for-profit education. The school year 1997–98 was its first year of operating schools, in Rocky Mount, North Carolina, and Phoenix. In 1998–99 it opened six new schools in Jersey City, New Jersey; Malden and Worcester, Massachusetts; San Antonio, Texas; Chicago, Illinois; and Kalamazoo, Michigan. It never attained contracts with thirty other schools, a number it claimed would bring profitability. In August 2001, Advantage was taken over by Mosaica Education.

The corporation was started by William Edgerly, chairman of the board, Steven Willson, president, and Theodor Rebarber, vice president. Edgerly was chairman of the State Street Bank in Boston and had a long-standing interest in education reform. He created "CEOs for Fundamental Change," a group of 300 Massachusetts CEOs who lobbied for education reform.

Wilson worked for a while at the right-wing Pioneer Institute in Boston and wrote a book on reforming Boston's schools. He later worked as a special assistant to Massachusetts governor, William Weld, and helped write Massachusetts's charter legislation. Rebarber worked for the Edison Project for a time and later, with Congress, he helped write the Washington, D.C., charter law.

Advantage was supported by Fidelity Ventures, part of Fidelity Investments; Bessemer Ventures; U.S. Trust out of New York; and Kliner, Perkins,

Coffield, and Byers, a Menlo Park, California, venture capital firm. The company extracted a flat fee, a fixed percentage of the school's budget. If the school operated in a deficit, Advantage had to come up with the cash to cover it.

Advantage typically operated K–5 elementary schools, retrofitting buildings that were originally not built as schools. The schools typically ranged in size from 500 to 550 pupils. It utilized the Bereiter-Engelmann DISTAR curriculum (Direct Instruction Strategies for Teaching Arithmetic and Reading). This curriculum, developed initially in the late 1960s has been expanded to include natural sciences, spelling, and cursive writing. Advantage has this to say about the DISTAR approach and how it compares with others:

> In a typical reading program, the teacher is given guidelines on how to present the material. For example, when teaching reading comprehension the teacher might be told, "discuss the concept of main idea." Guidelines such as this leave tremendous latitude concerning what the teacher actually says and does. It is very easy for teachers to knowingly change the wording used to teach essential skills or concepts, making it especially difficult for students to learn. . . . In a DI lesson, what the teacher says is actually printed out on the page. The students' responses are also printed out on the page. Teacher wording is thereby controlled, making it easier for students to learn.
>
> Q: Doesn't Just Reading What Is on a Page Get Boring for the Students— Or, for the Teacher?
>
> . . . In fact, one of the things teachers must learn how to do is to present material in a lively manner. In order to achieve this delivery goal, lessons that are about to be delivered must be studied, especially when they contain unfamiliar formats. . . . DI lessons are designed to limit the amount of teacher talk and to give students many opportunities to respond, and, in order to achieve relatively high rates of pacing, teachers must be fluent in the script.

In DISTAR, students make as many as 360 responses in a half-hour lesson. The intellectual depth of such responses is necessarily low. In addition, such lessons will teach students that each question has only one right answer.

New York Times reporter Michael Winerip visited an Advantage School and came away less than thrilled with the approach. His host, a corporate spokesman who had flown down to North Carolina, told Winerip that "All the kindergarten kids read, you know." Winerip's natural journalistic suspicions came to the fore when he found the receptionist teaching a top fifth-grade math group. She told him, "All you have to remember is you can't go off the script."

Winerip, however, did go off the script. He brought his own books. Confronted with a story that began "I am a ghostie," a kindergartner was unable to cope with "I." Another fared no better trying to read a story that began "Drip, drip, drop." Given repeated hints about the story from pictures showing raindrops, the boy finally said "Rain drops . . . no, I don't know." A girl managed to sound out a few of these words "in agonizingly slow fashion" (Winerip, 1998).

It is worth noting that although Mosaica has subsumed Advantage, the Advantage schools continue to function as described above. This is worth noting because the Advantage curriculum seems directly contradicted by Mosaica's approach. Indeed, the two approaches seem almost like matter and antimatter.

In the mornings, Mosaica schools teach reading, mathematics, and science. While reading includes explicit phonics it also includes "classical and multi-cultural literature for reading and writing instruction." In the afternoons, Mosaica offers children its proprietary "Paragon Curriculum," created by Mosaica's founder, Dawn Eidelman. This curriculum is an "Interdisciplinary, multi-media program that engages students in the hands-on study of great ideas in world history and generates connections across the curriculum." In addition the Paragon Curriculum fosters "cultural literacy that encompasses the disciplines of social science, history, drama, music, art, geography, literature, philosophy, ethics, economics and scientific innovation" (*www.mosaicaeducation.com/curriculum.html*).

Mosaica took over Advantage in hopes that the combined operations would provide economies of scale to permit a profit. At the time, neither company was in the black. One would think that Mosaica might have engineered a shift to its worldview, but according to people in individual Advantage schools, no one has communicated anything to them about a change. It appears that profit triumphs over curricular and pedagogical consistency ("appears" because neither the New York nor the California headquarters of Mosaica ever answers phones other than by voicemail. Neither office has ever provided requested information).

The "Education Industry": Wall Street Takes Notice

Some people view education as simply another service, a commercial exchange among people. While it is not clear who the "customer" actually is in the educational system, a number of bankers, brokers, and venture capitalists think that the $700 billion that America spends annually for all levels of education is a good place for investors to make money. This section takes a quick look at some who think that, and why.

On the cover of Michael Moe and R. Keith Gay's *The Emerging Investment Opportunity in Education*, Rodin's *The Thinker* sits, not atop the *Gates of Hell* as in the original sculpture, but on what looks to be a petrified tree, contemplating in his hand a lap-top computer displaying one word—"knowledge" (Moe and Gay, 1996). "The Dawn of the Age of Knowledge," reads a superscript at the top of the cover. This 120-page document builds the case that spending on public schools is horrifically high and the performance of the schools is horrifically low. Therefore, given that the United States spends $340 billion a year on primary and secondary education and another $320 billion at the college level, privatized education, which can do the same job for less, ought to be able to turn a terrific profit and is therefore a great investment opportunity. In other words, as discussed in Chapter 3, money doesn't matter.

As usual in such arguments, Moe and Gay spin the data. For example, a chart on worldwide spending on education has the United States ranked third among twelve nations in the Organization for Economic Cooperation and Development (OECD). Although all of the performance data concern grade-school students, and although Moe and Gay don't mention it, the figures given include spending on higher education, an arena where the United States is outranked only by Switzerland (which, conveniently, is not included in the list; U.S. spending on college-level education has since surpassed Switzerland's).

As noted earlier, there are many ways of calculating how much nations spend on their schools and the United States looks like a big spender on some and a miser on others. A variant of the GDP indicators, *per capita* GDP, is probably the best single measure. This eliminates differences caused by the varying sizes of nations' GDPs: for example, America's GNP is huge, but Liechtenstein's GNP is tiny. On this measure, the United States' rank in education spending remains unchanged at ninth.

Moe and Gay indict American public schools with data from the Second International Assessment of Educational Progress (IAEP-2). They do not mention Warwick P. Elley's *How in the World Do Students Read?* which appeared in July 1992, just five months after the publication of IAEP-2, and which found American students to be reading better than students in most countries. As we saw earlier, only Finnish students scored higher than American students in reading. Moe and Gay discuss the National Assessment of Educational Progress in terms of proficiency levels, not commenting that these levels have been rejected by psychometricians as well as by a GAO study.

Moe and Gay pose the question "Will More Money Help?" (p. 64) and then present the master myth (Chapter 3), using state rankings on the SAT along with state spending levels. As with William Bennett's study, described in Chapter 3, they do not mention that in the twenty top-ranked states, only 10 percent of the seniors—a small elite—take the SAT. These states instead use the ACT college admissions battery. In the lower-ranked states, two-thirds to four-fifths of the seniors huddle in angst on Saturday mornings to "bubble in" the answer sheets. One might have thought Moe and Gay would have entertained suspicions about this data upon noticing that Mississippi ranked twelfth, while Massachusetts, acknowledged as an education leader in the nation for over 150 years, ranked thirty-fifth. In fact, one study found that 83 percent of the differences among states can be traced to the differences in participation rates (Powell and Steelman, 1996).

The document concludes that the schools are in crisis and "from an investment perspective, this crisis has created an enormous opportunity and powerful momentum for those companies with solutions to our educational problems, whether through better management of traditional resources or the innovative application of technology (p. 3, boldfaced in the original for emphasis).

SSPs (special services providers) for at-risk youth are presented as especially exciting opportunities:

> The children of the baby boomers are about to become teenagers, indicating that the juvenile crime problem is going to get much worse before it gets better. Seventy percent of all juvenile delinquents come from single-family homes. Our juvenile population is exploding and more of them are home alone than at any other time in our history. SSPs that can provide the same or better programs [for at-risk youth] are positioned to ride a tidal wave of privatization that we believe will occur in this sector. We expect an explosion in this market similar to the tremendous growth that has occurred among the adult corrections companies such as Corrections Corporation and Wakenhut. (pp. 36–37)

The misery index is rising. What a time to get rich.

The Education Industry Report

Even though most of the new companies are not making any money yet, the Education Index, compiled by John McLaughlin in the monthly newsletter *Education Industry Report* until early 2000, outperformed the Wall Street indices. (In 2000, McLaughlin sold the report to Edventures, which now reports only individual stocks [www.edventures.com].) McLaughlin ran a private school, and then became a professor of educational administration at St. Cloud State in Minnesota, but left to work full time with his Education Industry Group, located in Sioux Falls, South Dakota.

The Education Index consists of thirty-five publicly traded companies categorized as Education Management Organizations (for example, Nobel), Education Products, Educational Service Organizations, At-Risk Youth, Post-Secondary Schools, and Training and Development. Each *Education Industry Report* contains several feature articles, including a profile of an organization and a profile of some personality, usually a player in the industry, but occasionally important "outsiders" such as Bob Chase, president of the NEA, or Alex Molnar, an antiprivatization author, or Paul Hill. Hill left the RAND Corporation for the University of Washington, founding the Center for Reinventing Education (not to be confused with John Goodlad's Center for Educational Renewal at the same institution). Hill advocates contracting out services such that a school system becomes an education contractor, not an education provider.

McLaughlin worried that the industry, chastened by such debacles as EAI-TesseracT and Beacon Education Management (in its earlier incarnation as APS) will take on charters as a safety move. "This is too bad," McLaughlin wrote, "for the industry, which has proven its value for children, families, and investors on either side of the K–12 spectrum, is faltering in stepping up to the area of greatest need in the country" (McLaughlin, 1998, p. 2).

Others in the investment community have taken notice of education as a place to make money. In February 1996, Lehman Brothers hosted a conference on the industry, and while it was noted that there have always been commercial companies providing textbooks and supplies, none of these were present. The conference featured the likes of Edison's Chris Whittle and Beacon APS's John Eason. Other presenters came from Nobel, the Princeton Review and Kaplan Educational Centers (two test "coaching" organizations), KinderCare Learning Centers, Inc., and TRO Learning, Inc., a provider of remedial software. According to an article in *Education Week*, attendees were especially impressed with Sylvan Learning Systems, Inc. (Walsh, 1996).

Commentary on the education industry in the press that monitors the industry is itself interestingly varied. Carl Horowitz, the lead education reporter for *Investor's Business Daily*, has commented that he thinks the criticisms of American public schools are misguided and dangerous. "I happen to take exception to the idea that our country is getting dumber and dumber. Given the rise in test scores since 1980, it is clear that we have a pretty smart and ready work force. The bottom line is that our schools are doing a decent job, but at the same time, there is room for improvement."

Asked by John McLaughlin why IBD has had such an interest in education, Horowitz replied "The owner of the paper had a conversation with [former secretary of education] Bill Bennett, and Bill emphasized that he thought that our paper could be instrumental in hammering out an education agenda." Michael Moe's *The Emerging Investment Opportunity in Education* lists fourteen articles for that publication in 1995 and 1996, most of them either assailing schools or reporting positive results from private operations. McLaughlin in 1998 puts an undated list at "more than thirty-one cover stories" (1998, p. 1).

McLaughlin also talked to former *Washington Post* education writer Rene Sanchez, *Education Week's* principal writer on charters and privatization Mark Walsh, and then–*New York Times* education reporter Peter Applebome. Sanchez was inclined to see charters as a flash in the pan, while Applebome thought them a more important trend, and Walsh thought that the privatization efforts had reached a critical mass. All agreed that more experimentation was inevitable and that the growth of Edison was critical to the industry—another pressure mitigating against any objective evaluation of Edison outcomes.

For his part, McLaughlin comes to profit-making schooling naturally: He founded and ran a school in Nashville for ten years before returning to graduate school, where he wrote his dissertation on private industry's role in education reform. He then joined the faculty of St. Cloud State University in Minnesota, where he spent another decade.

McLaughlin apparently views education from only one of the two perspectives described by Henig: the education service deliverer. He noted in conversation that private and for-profit education on either side of K–12 has been both successful and accepted. He considers it hypocritical in the extreme to claim that it is not appropriate for K–12, that, in fact, "we have sacrificed the good of the children to stakeholders"—those who run the schools.

McLaughlin believes we need to establish choice as a plank in the education platform equal in importance to three other planks: equity, access, and performance. Education in the future will be more research and development–driven as the private sector investigates further what works, and under what conditions.

McLaughlin is high on free-market reforms, but he also said that education should not have the purposes of preventing revolutionaries, keeping kids out of the markets until they're nearly twenty-two, or turning them into cogs that fit into the capitalist system (he observed that this statement causes a number of eyebrows to rise in business circles).

In early 2000 McLaughlin sold his share of the *Education Industry Report* back to Eduventures and started a new group. He sits on the boards of Bright Horizons and a Michigan, Christian-oriented charter group, National Heritage Academies. He is also consulting with national education organizations about charter schools, out-sourcing, online curriculum, and purchasing and other matters that involve "the education industry." He declined to name the organizations.

EduVentures, Inc.

Boston-based EduVentures, Inc., provides consulting services to private companies that are engaged in education enterprises. Its founder, John Sandler, started the company in 1993. He is also co-founder, with John McLaughlin, of the *Education Investor* (now the *Education Industry Report*) which EduVentures has owned outright since early 2000. He was at one time an assistant to David Kearns, former CEO of Xerox, former deputy secretary of education and, at the time, CEO of the New American Schools Development Corporation, the George H.W. Bush–sponsored private initiative to build "break-the-mold" schools.

EduVentures represented Virtual Learning (VL) in negotiations, which led to VL's obtaining $2 million in capital from Sylvan Learning Systems. Other EduVentures clients have included Corporate Family Solutions and Wall Street Institute, the latter a part of Sylvan Learning Systems. Outside of education, clients include IBM, McGraw-Hill, and other companies with an interest in the development of the education industry. For these organizations, EduVentures provides "competitive intelligence" about education corporations.

Sandler distinguishes EduVentures from other brokers such as Lehman Brothers and Merrill Lynch by pointing out that those organizations, while capable, often represent the companies that they conduct research on, and thus have a vested interested in presenting the companies in a favorable light. Edu-Ventures, says Sandler, is the only independent source of such information and has the largest database in the nation on private education companies.

Some of this database can be viewed at EduVenture's online newsletter, the *Education Economy* (www.eduventures.com/news/education_economy). This weekly publication is free. EduVentures uses it to draw readers towards their services (the *Education Industry Report*, by contrast, costs $400 a year). The *Education Economy* lists news items including two or more articles on current issues in specific companies, and offers hotlinks to the original sources of the information. Other news services from EduVentures include "Latest headlines," "Stock

Quotes," "IPO Watch," and "Notable Hires." For the clients it serves, EduVentures provides strategic planning, business-plan writing, access to capital, and the identification of acquisition targets, merger partners, and joint-venture partners.

Two Comprehensive Systems: Knowledge Universe and Sylvan Learning Systems

Milken's Knowledge Universe (KU): Its Own Private Galaxy

> *To call Kalinske's operation low-profile is a laughable understatement, and the folks at KU [Knowledge Universe] get the joke. Kalinske's assistant, Mary Biondi, responds to a request for directions with a quip: "You'll have to wait by the side of the highway for one of our people to pick you up, blindfold you, and bring you here."*
>
> —Jon Revelos, Director, Allen Academy of Multimedia
> August 31, 1998, www.epss.com

The Kalinske in this quote is Thomas Kalinske, the marketing whiz president of Knowledge Universe (KU) and former CEO of both Mattel, where he revived sales for Barbie dolls, and Sega of America, where he introduced Sonic the Hedgehog. Actually, Revelos has made great progress in revealing information about KU compared to a 1998 article by reporter Eric J. Savitz. Savitz's cover story in the March 2 edition of *Barron's*, about training workers via computers, contains only one paragraph about KU: "Lastly, in a category all its own, there's Knowledge Universe, the secretive two-year-old behemoth created by junk-bond king Michael Milken,[1] his brother Lowell Milken, and Larry Ellison [founder of Oracle]. The goal was to provide 'cradle-to-grave' educational services. If you haven't heard much about them, be patient. You will" (Savitz, 1998, p. 31).

Maybe. Contacted in August 1998, Savitz could (or would) say only, "They're very frustrating. They don't even have a website." At the time, they didn't even have a listed telephone number. They do have a website now, but it contains less at this time than earlier: in late 2001 it named some of the fifty-plus companies that KU owns, whereas an earlier version named them all. Income from the companies exceeds $1.5 billion annually. KU is 120th in the Fortune 500, a pretty rapid ascent for a company that's less than a decade old.

KU's telephone numbers were publicly listed in May 1999. Some of the secrecy makes good business sense: KU's preferred method is taking over companies. If companies thought they were the objects of KU takeovers, they'd raise

---

1. Milken is often credited with saying "Greed is good." That statement was actually made by Milken's coconspirator, Ivan Boesky.

the price. In addition, the KU people see themselves as leaders in areas where others will follow and, despite their role in education, they have no interest in educating competitors.

The organization has recently divided into two smaller galaxies: the Knowledge Universe Business Group and the Knowledge Universe Learning Group. The first consists of thirty-plus companies that KU either owns or holds shares in. Its mission statement is to "improve the effectiveness and productivity of businesses and their employees, and give people tools and services to make them more productive in life" (www.knowledgeu.com, December, 2001—this home page changes every now and then). By contrast, the learning group's fourteen companies "enhance the adventure of learning from birth through graduate school. The range of products and services includes interactive education products; technology training and resources for teachers; early childhood education; and interactive learning Web sites for children, their parents, grandparents, and teachers" (www.knowledgeu.com, December, 2001).

In the "vision" section of its website, which first appeared in 1998, KU declared that:

> Knowledge Universe seeks to create, build, and acquire education-related companies, public and private, regardless of size which:
>
> • Demonstrate a passion for improving the quality of education in the marketplaces they serve;
> • Are capable of achieving a leadership position in their respective segments of the education industry;
> • Have the opportunity to grow dramatically with the availability of adequate capital; and
> • Enjoy or have the potential to develop strong brand names recognition."
>
> Knowledge Universe *has strong relationships with the world's leading entertainment, telecommunications and technology companies* (italic added for emphasis). These relationships and its financial resources provide Knowledge Universe with a significant advantage as it pursues its objective of becoming a market leader in global education and learning.

By late 2000 (and only slightly revised by late 2001), this vision had been replaced by a more philosophical, less materialistic view:

> Knowledge Universe (KU) believes that people and organizations have an almost unlimited power to improve themselves—to realize their own potential. KU helps people and businesses do this by providing learning aids based on three principles:
>
> 1. In an information economy, physical labor is less important that knowledge, and wages depend on educational levels.
> 2. Most industrialized nations are aging, meaning that there will be fewer workers to support retirees. This in turn means that retirees will also need additional training.
> 3. "Skills that used to serve a lifetime now become obsolete in a few years."

This and other information can be found at KU's website: www.knowledgeu. com/vision.html.

Underlying this vision is another, unstated, less altruistic one: Children will attend KU preschools and play with interactive toys produced by KU companies. This starts the process of brand recognition at an early age. Children might attend KU schools and even if they don't, their schools will utilize KU-developed software. In college, they will supplement whatever they receive on campus with KU online courses from Knowledge University. Their teachers will receive professional training, especially in the use of information technology from Teacher Universe, a subsidiary of KU. Wherever they work, KU seminars and software will enhance their productivity. And after retirement, KU will be there with additional training so that retirees don't become obsolete and poor in their dotage. KU does not think small.

KU Subsidiaries.   Although there have been rumors of KU going public, its website notes that it is a private company and that this gives it flexibility. Observers do believe that the various KU companies will eventually become a parade of publicly traded corporations. KU now controls 31 percent of the shares in Nobel Learning Communities. Other educational acquisitions include Children's Discovery Centers (CDC), which operates 250 daycare centers and preschools and has revenues of $95 million. CDC is headquartered in San Rafael, California, across the Golden Gate Bridge from KU's headquarters.

They also own LeapFrog toys, a maker of educational toys that has specialized in phonics approaches to the teaching of reading and has recently expanded to include mathematics. According to LeapFrog's website (www.leapfrog.com), the system was developed by Robert Calfee of Stanford University, now dean of the school of education at the University of California, Riverside. Its LeapPad, an interactive book, has won prizes and earned lots of sales. Also in the fold is Bookman Testing Services, Inc., a specialized thirteen-year-old company that, under the brand name TeckChek, currently provides tests of students' knowledge about high-tech areas, such as computer programming languages.

Finally, among the education companies, there are Knowledge University and Knowledge Universe Interactive Studio, Inc. The university was formed in 1997 to "deliver a variety of degree, certificate, and continuing education programs to corporations, businesses, governments, and individual learners located throughout the world" (www.knowledgeu.com/companies.html). The studio "designs and develops compelling learning products utilizing state-of-the-art technologies and modes of delivery." It is listed as the parent company of MindQ Publishing, Inc.

In April 2000, KU launched KidsEdge.com, from its Knowledge Kids Network (KKN). The company focuses on reading and mathematics, "while also developing the whole child, including imagination, confidence, and character." KKN claims to do this with "graphically rich, character-driven environments that provide age-appropriate, individualized learning activities for children."

The "curriculum is based on key state standards from around the nation" (*Business Wire*, April 3, 2000). KKN's CEO Sarina Simon is a former editor at Lowell House Publishing and executive producer for a number of films at Walt Disney Company. Most recently, she was president of the Home and Family division of Phillips Electronics, which makes children's software, among other products (*Business Wire*, May 31, 2000). The distance between entertainment and education grows smaller, it would seem. ParentsEdge.com, GrandparentsEdge.com, and TeachersEdge.com complement KidsEdge.com and allow various caretakers to monitor the children's progress.

KU's business "vision" includes the buyout of troubled companies, which can be had on the cheap, and eventually, forge them together to create a dominant, integrated education provider. "Knowledge Universe is on a quest for universal domination," said Stan Lepeak, vice-president of META, a technology consulting firm. "It could easily become a Fortune 100 company" (Feldman, 1998, p. C4). Critics claim that KU appears to have no integrated purchasing strategy: It has no strong management team and has obtained little cross-fertilization or synergy from its various components.

In a 1998 article *Los Angeles Times* reporter Debora Vrana cites Milken as stating that KU wants to own a nationwide chain of private schools that will serve 2 percent of all United States children—about 1,000,000—something not seen in earlier dispatches. She also says that "Milken can make this work only if parents are willing to turn over their children to a brilliant fellow who says that he has come up with a better way to improve the educational system. That claim has yet to be proved, say skeptics." Vrana puts the worth of Milken's empire at $4 billion. She quotes several people whose opinions range from the belief that Milken wants to "save the next generation" to "He's always just making a buck" (Vrana, 1998).

According to John McLaughlin, former owner of the *Education Industry Report*, KU's strategy is to talk to virtually everyone in a field where they are interested. McLaughlin described companies as "awed" that Milken would want to talk with them. They then transact a deal in the field that no one expected, that surprises everyone, but that, in retrospect, makes perfect sense. McLaughlin contends that they have a stable of expert merger and acquisition specialists (McLaughlin, 1998).

The Milken Families Foundation. KU operated stealth-like out of Burlingame, just south of San Francisco, and then moved a bit south to Menlo Park. In contrast to covert KU, Milken Families Foundation in Santa Monica seeks publicity and is best known for its spring fling, which provides a three-day symposium on a chosen topic. In 1999 the theme was the education-job skills mismatch. Needless to say, there was no balance to the program.

The conference honors around thirty teachers who have made exemplary use of technology in their classrooms. They and most of their chief state school officers fly to foundation headquarters in Santa Monica and are put up in the

Century Plaza Hotel. The adornments of the conference are, to put it mildly, lavish, and obviously designed to build good will among the attendees. It's working. When people speak of the conference, one senses they are having trouble restraining a drool. Educators live in an economically deprived zone compared to the high fliers of finance.

Indeed, one imagines that at some time Milken will reveal Knowledge Universe with the flair he displayed as king of the junk bonds at an annual meeting of bond dealers, then known as the Predators' Ball. Milken whipped the audience into a motivational frenzy. In the middle of Milken's pitch, Frank Sinatra walked onstage. "Hey, aren't you the junk-bond guy?" Sinatra asked. "Here, make sure I've got plenty of junk bonds." At this moment, the stage curtains parted, revealing a twenty-two-piece orchestra. Sinatra sang "Start spreadin' the news"[2] (Ashworth, 1999).

No doubt Milken's flair will show again. According to one article, a then-upcoming conference would "begin and end with Milken-moderated panels of Nobel laureates; in between, Milken himself will deliver the keynote address. Fifteen hundred people are expected to attend, and through it all, Milken will stand at center stage, a smiling, benevolent visionary leading the discussion and masterminding the event. In short, even the conference's structure drives home the idea that this is Michael Milken's conference, for Michael Milken's institute, discussing Michael Milken's favorite issues" (Cohn, 2000).

Milken awes people. One senses that in the articles about him, at least two of which referred to his comeback after his jail term as "The Resurrection" (although at least a half-dozen others referred to "Milken's new empire"). Arthur Levine, president of Teachers College at Columbia University, met with Milken in 1998. "The message was, 'you guys are in trouble and we're going to eat your lunch.'" Levine characterized the message from Milken as "a predatory challenge" (Wyatt, 1999).

Some think that Milken, a survivor of prostate cancer, aims at divinity. Said Stan Lepeak, "It's a big leap of faith for Mike and Co. to come in and think they can fix America's educational system. I think it's visions of godhood. After being vilified in the 1980s, he wants to go down in history as a savior in the next decade" (Vrana, 1998). Not one to limit his activities, Milken gives millions for research on prostate cancer, lectures on the subject, and has written a cookbook designed to prevent the disease.

Others who have worked with Milken in his new venture contend that he is unchanged: a takeover junkie who is interested in buying companies. Education just happens to be the object of that interest. Journalist Russ Meyer observed that "Milken seems most successful when he is not reinventing the wheel, but

---

2. For the record, Milken was shortly thereafter indicted on ninety-eight counts, including insider trading, price manipulation, falsifying records, filing false reports, racketeering, defrauding customers, and "stock parking"—an arrangement to hide the true owners of stock. In a plea bargain, Milken pleaded guilty to six relatively minor charges, paid a $600 million fine, and served twenty-two months in prison.

buying existing businesses in hot categories" (Meyer, 1999). That approach cost him the services of one highly regarded businessman, Joseph Costello, who left KU after only three months. Costello objected to KU's lack of focus and its habit of buying firms, such as existing language-training companies, for $100 million, rather than creating a new model for such training for $10-20 million. Costello is one of those people who finds Milken unchanged from his earlier incarnation.

Milken's actions have contradicted his words on several occasions. He preaches a gospel of education as the savior of the underclass. He points to several factors that may have prevented Watts-like riots in America's cities, and claims we can experience similar urban unrest if we do not get education to all (Wiles, 2000). Yet, virtually all of the companies that make up KU presume that the client has access to information technology. Unless KU offers some kind of subsidy or grant to bridge the gap, the company will contribute to the "digital divide" between rich and poor.

Meyer was concerned by Milken's editorial control of content. When he inquired if Milken would permit KU students to do a critical assessment of the years when Milken was a junk-bond dealer, the answer from colleagues was "absolutely not." And, indeed, Meyer notes that KU's *Business Encyclopedia* "approvingly cites Milken's role in the junk-bond business without mentioning the economic and social devastation associated with it" (Meyer, 1999). This does not suggest a desire to build a stronger democracy: "In looking over the field of entrepreneurial education my worry is that marketing will dominate curriculum: Will it come down to how schools market themselves rather than how well kids learn and what they learn? Will students even be permitted, for example, to see the negative consequences of unfettered greed? In an era when even our most basic public institutions are being shaped by financial interests, defending these core principles has become increasingly important (Meyer, 1999)."

Milken's information control is also evident in his biography (www.mike milken.com/mike_bio.html). In the very short sixth (out of seven) paragraph, Milken mentions the charges against him, his $200 million fine, and twenty-two months of jail time. He doesn't mention that the judgment forbids him to work in the securities industry again and that he was later fined another $47 million for violation of this condition of parole (as a founder and part-owner of KU, he does not violate the prohibition). The end of the biography features a boxed-in statement in italics: "The Milken Family Foundation, CaP Cure, and the Milken Institute are each separate, non-profit organizations and none of them is operationally connected in any way with Knowledge University, a for-profit company." Milken works hard to keep these entities separate in the public mind. Some have accused Milken of cynically using the Family Foundation to build goodwill among educators while KU works in the background to take over the industry. From what has been written about Knowledge Universe, one gets the strong feeling that Milken not only wants to provide education and dominate the market, but also wants to control the content of education to provide a particular, business-sympathetic vision.

K12.   Perhaps an indication of Milken's drive to control and to persuade is seen in one of his latest adventures, K12, an online K–12 curriculum. In *The Educated Child*, former secretary of education William J. Bennett, John T. E. Cribb, Jr., and Chester E. Finn, Jr., wrote, "When you hear the next pitch about cyber-enriching your child's education, keep one thing in mind: so far, there is no good evidence that most uses of computers significantly improve learning" (Bennett, Finn, and Cribb, 1999, p. 619). Well, the next pitch is coming from Bennett, via Milken.

Although a number of universities and organizations are developing online educational offerings, K12 is unique (Steinberg, 2000). Milken is backing the first effort to develop a complete K–12 curriculum based heavily on Bennett's book, *The Educated Child*, influenced as well by E. D. Hirsch, Jr.'s, Core Knowledge program. John Holdren, K12's senior vice-president of content and curriculum, oversaw the development of Core Knowledge books, the "What your Xth-grader needs to know" series.

Also joining the K12 team as chief technology adviser is David Gelernter, a profession of computer science at Yale. Gelernter's name might strike some chord of recognition outside of his profession: He lost most of his right hand in 1993 when opening a package that turned out to be a bomb sent by the Unabomber, Theodore J. Kaczynski.

K12 is apparently making a serious attempt to assess outcomes, having lured psychometrician David Niemi away from the Center for Research in Evaluation, Standards, and Student Testing, coheadquartered at UCLA and the University of Colorado at Boulder. It will be interesting to see how serious this attempt is sustained once some of the KU officers not familiar with psychometrics realize the complexities involved in appropriate and valid assessment. It also will be interesting to see how Niemi, arriving from the world of academia and its free discussion of ideas, reacts to Milken's need to control content.

Given Bennett's association with the political right, some worry that the program will be more a vehicle for conservative ideology than for education (Irwin, 2000). At least one educator has expressed public skepticism. Sandra Feldman, president of the American Federation of Teachers, said, "We will have to wait and see if the quality of this particular product is as grandiose as Mr. Bennett's quotes" (Irwin, 2000).

Sylvan Learning Systems

We discuss Sylvan Learning Systems because it is a dominant player in the provision of educational services and because, to date, it is unique: Public school educators have not viewed it as a threat to their existence. To be sure, that is in part true because, for over twenty years, Sylvan's divisions have provided services to clients other than public schools. But the relationship could change, depending on circumstances.

Baltimore-based Sylvan does not present itself as a competitor to public schools. Indeed, an article about Sylvan observed that "Sylvan touts recommendations from public school clients that would make almost any principal or superintendent envious" (O'Connor, 1999). How has Sylvan accomplished this remarkable public relations coup, and can the goodwill last?

Before answering these questions, we need to track the history of this idiosyncratic organization, which got its start when Douglas Becker decided to skip college and make money. With a partner, Christopher Hoehn-Saric, Becker launched Sylvan Learning Centers, designed to provide remedial instruction in an intense setting—the pupil–teacher ratio for the centers is usually 3:1.

Sylvan's strategy over the years has been to find an area of high need and to then fill that need. When Becker sensed a need for more accessible testing, he started Sylvan Prometric in 1993, which became the world's largest provider of computer-administered tests, administering over 300 different tests, including several from ETS. In 1999, Becker felt that Prometric, while profitable and growing rapidly, was taking up too much of the organization's time and efforts. He sold the company to Thomson Corporation, a Canadian publishing house, for $775 million.

When Becker gleaned that English was becoming *the* international language, he set up the Wall Street Institute, now one of the largest providers of English-language instruction with 360 locations around the world. When Becker felt that globe-trotting executives could benefit from a distance-learning setting that updated their "global marketplace skills," he established Caliber to provide instruction, including Wharton Direct, an attempt to provide a Wharton Business School education. When he decided that European nations could not meet the burgeoning middle-class demand for tertiary education, he spent $50 million for a Spanish University and has since acquired universities Switzerland, Mexico, and, in late 2001, a Paris-based school of business and management studies.

In July 2001, Sylvan created its Online Higher Education division, composed of four smaller corporations. Canter and Associates is the largest teacher-training organization in the country, enrolling 35,000 teachers. A second part of the higher-education group is Walden University, a longtime provider of distance education, in which Sylvan bought a 43 percent interest. Sylvan Teachers Institute was formed in 1999 to address the national shortage of teachers.

OnlineLearning.net was started in 1996 and offers continuing adult education, including courses developed by UCLA for online delivery. Sylvan Learning Solutions offers two types of programs—supplementary educational programs in-school and after-school, and Career Starters, which offers remedial instruction and work skills to at-risk students, welfare recipients, and underemployed workers. The Classwell Group, formed in 2000 with Houghton Mifflin, provides teachers with teaching and learning resources.

These ventures have not always succeeded. Caliber never turned a profit and in 2001 filed for bankruptcy protection. Sylvan's own stock opened at $5 when the company went public in 1993. Later it fell from a high of $33 per share to $15 in late 2000. The reason? "Because it consisted of a number of unrelated businesses, it has been tougher for investors to understand the company's prospects and to be confident that the company was well run. That's why Sylvan Learning has been selling or spinning off its extraneous businesses. . . ." (Patalon, 2000). In mid-2002 it was trading around $19 a share.

Reacting to this perception, and armed with the income from the sale of Prometric, Sylvan made a strategic shift in emphasis. "After an appraisal that started last year while investors pounded Sylvan stock, three options occurred to Douglas Becker, the company's chairman and chief executive officer. Sylvan could commit to being a conventional, large company, putting it under endless pressure to increase earnings every year; go private, removing it from Wall Street's demands; or, make a more radical shift by selling some assets and becoming an investor itself. Sylvan chose the latter" (Somerville, 2000).

The "radical shift" commits Sylvan to a $500 million "incubator" project in which it will try to grow Internet-oriented companies. It expects to house a large number of these businesses on a single "campus" that would require 400,000 square feet of space and 1,000 to 3,000 high-tech workers (Ambrose, 2000).

Sylvan's goodwill reputation remains. Partly it comes from doing good deeds. Becker is chairman of the Children's Museum in Baltimore. He also established "Book Adventure" with partners Barnes and Noble, Houghton Mifflin, Lycos, and R. R. Bowker (www.bookadventure.org, www.bookadventure. com; the latter tells you about the former). Book Adventure encourages students to read. It provides quizzes about the 3,000 books on its list and children can win prizes, such as a trip to Orlando, if they take a lot of quizzes in a short time and get perfect scores. Maggi Gaines, executive director of Baltimore Reads, a nonprofit literacy group, had this to say about Book Adventure: "Education is big business, and we're naïve if we don't understand that. When I look at Sylvan, I see a corporation that's bottom-line-driven and philanthropy-driven. Those two things are compatible when executed properly" (Murray, 1999).

Perhaps more important than the altruism, however, is the fact that, from one public school perspective, Sylvan is free. Although Sylvan charges $1,500 per pupil, federal dollars from Title 1, not state or local funds, pay virtually all of the contract fees. It is, therefore, easy to consider Sylvan's charges as "off budget," and the teacher-pupil ratio does get results. While few school boards would spend their own money for a program with only three pupils per tutor, it's perceived as all right if federal dollars are involved.

It therefore does not appear at this time that Sylvan presents much of a threat to public schools. But if Douglas Becker ever thinks that he sees an unmet demand, that could change. Becker skipped school to make money and his company's focus is still on making money. His recent ventures into providing teacher training, teacher resources, and instruction to various student groups could be seen as a way of "surrounding" the "market" of K–12 education.

8

Vouchers, Public and Private

School vouchers are intended to provide a means of allowing families, particularly poor families, more choice in where their children go to school (middle-class and affluent families have already utilized choice by choosing where to live). Either the families receive the voucher directly and use it at any school that will accept it, or the voucher money is given to the school, depending on how many applicants for vouchers the school reports.

Vouchers have been credited with great, almost magical, changes in schools. The reality is much more mundane. Voucher students perform quite similarly to regular public school students and, if their achievement is higher, it might have nothing to do with vouchers. Students using vouchers usually attend small schools with small classes, and both factors are known to increase achievement.

The voucher is the most potentially devastating weapon in the armory of those warring against the public schools. Whenever a voucher—at least one that comes from public funds—sends money to some agency of the private sector, that money is not available for the public schools. Public school defenders fear that vouchers on any large scale would simply wreak havoc. Their concerns are not without cause.

John Stuart Mill and the Concept of Vouchers

The idea of vouchers is not new to education or to other social programs. Food stamps, Medicaid, and even some subsidized public housing, are examples of vouchers. John Stuart Mill usually receives credit for the concept of vouchers, although he did not use that word. In his 1838 essay, *On Liberty*, Mill railed that families were not required to educate their children (Mill, 1838). Even when free

137

schooling was provided, families could avail themselves of it or not. Mill argued that educating their children was among parents' "most sacred duties." Having brought a child into the world, the parents owed it to him ("hers" were not yet being educated) to provide the best possible education.

> If the government were to make up its mind to *require* for every child a good education, it might save itself the trouble of *providing* one. It might leave to parents to obtain the education where and how they pleased, and content itself with helping to pay the school fees of the poorer classes of children, and defraying the entire school expenses of those who have no one else to pay for them.

In Mill's view, the state needed educated citizens, but government, whether a dictatorship or a democracy, would only use schooling to mold children into its desired shape, not to educate them.

How would Mill decide if the schools were providing good education? Through tests. The state would administer them, beginning with reading and then extending to a "minimum competency test" of general knowledge (his actual words were a test "of a certain minimum of general knowledge"). He also proposed "voluntary examinations on all subjects." In order to keep the state from intruding where it had no business, these examinations could only test subjects of fact. In matters of politics and religion, the examination could ask only what certain authors, schools of thought, or religions *believed* to be true. It would not be permitted to present these beliefs as true. It seems not to have occurred to Mill that such examinations, even when limited to facts, could themselves mold children to a certain form.

In the late 1950s economist Milton Friedman updated Mill's ideas and elaborated on them in his 1962 book, *Freedom and Capitalism*. In 1996, Friedman and his wife, Rose, established the Friedman Foundation for School Choice in Indianapolis, with the stated goal of informing the public about the advantages of voucher programs.

Comparing Vouchers and Charters

The arguments for vouchers are similar to those for charter schools: They will increase the diversity of schools, increase innovations, allow good schools to thrive, and send poor schools into bankruptcy. Voucher supporters also make an additional claim not made necessarily for charter schools: They will empower poor people to obtain a good education for their children. Poor people cannot afford the tuition of nonsectarian private schools, which was on average $6,600 in 1994 (compared to $6,500 per pupil expenditures for public schools), or even the much-lower tuition of Catholic schools, which was around $2,000. Nor do they have the resources to move to a suburb, where, most public school critics will allow, the schools are pretty good. If the money follows the child to whatever school is chosen, this will give low-income families access to the kinds of education now enjoyed by affluent families (but could well cause taxpayers' revolts if suburban parents were *not* permitted to send their children to the local schools).

The concept of a voucher contributes nothing directly to the improvement of education. A voucher scheme is a means of paying for schools, not for improving them. It offers no innovative curriculum. It offers no new or more effective instructional strategies. Its actions are secondary and, if the market metaphor proves not to fit education well, illusory.

None of the experiments currently in progress will provide good evidence for whether vouchers would work at the system level on a large scale. The small experiments are just that, and they suffer from too many constraints to answer the hard questions about choice. In addition, the advocates of vouchers, whether politicians or entrepreneurs or philanthropists, have not shown any particular interest in asking the hard questions, much less answering them. In Milwaukee, Wisconsin, the voucher program was evaluated for each of its first five years, and the principal investigator concluded that voucher students achieved no more than a matched group of students in Milwaukee public schools. The voucher advocates proceeded to kill all funds for further evaluations of the voucher program, while at the same time expanding the program. Most voucher children in Milwaukee attend Catholic schools and the archdiocese of Milwaukee has refused to release any test scores for them.

Similarly, in Florida, children become eligible for vouchers if they attend public schools that receive an "F" grade from the state for two years in any four. The grades are determined largely by tests. The private schools that accept the vouchers do not even have to administer the tests to their own enrollees or to those coming via vouchers, much less report test scores, although the state holds public schools accountable. Once children leave the public system, the state surrenders all accountability for their further progress.

A Sample Voucher Program— Milwaukee, Wisconsin

Terry Moe of the Hoover Institute has described the conditions of research and evaluation efforts pertaining to vouchers with admirable clarity:

> Ideology aside, perhaps the most vexing problem [of voucher research] is that few researchers who carry out studies of school choice are sensitive to issues of institutional design or context. They proceed as though their case studies reveal something generic about choice or markets when, in fact—as the Milwaukee case graphically testifies—much of what they observe is due to the specific rules, restrictions, and control mechanisms that shape how choice and markets happen to operate in a particular setting. As any economist would be quick to point out, the effects of choice and markets vary, sometimes enormously, depending on the institutional

context. The empirical literature on school choice does little to shed light on these contingencies and, indeed, by portraying choice and markets as generic reforms with generic effects, often breeds more confusion than understanding. (1995, p. 20)

This is a remarkable statement from one who coauthored this rose-tinted passage five years earlier:

> We think reformers would do well to entertain the notion that choice *is* a panacea. This is our way of saying that choice is not like the other part of a reformist strategy for improving America's public schools. Choice is a self-contained reform with its own rationale and justification. It has the capacity *all by itself* to bring about the kind of transformation that, for years, reformers have been seeking to engineer in myriad other ways. (Chubb and Moe, 1990, p. 217)

Given the murkiness of the situation, it is not surprising to find different researchers taking contradictory positions on what the results of a voucher program mean. In a speech at the Cato Institute, Paul Peterson of Harvard University declared that the Milwaukee results found choice successful under "extreme duress." Hence, if choice can work under such terrible constraints, it can work anywhere and, therefore, we should "scale up" to programs for the larger system. Jeffrey Henig of George Washington University, responding to Peterson's speech, contended that there were so many unusual, even unique, features to the Milwaukee program that it had little if anything to say to that larger system (Peterson, 1997; Henig, 1997). Generalization from Milwaukee to the larger system was not possible. Oddly, Henig's position was, in fact, Peterson's just the prior year:

> Often lost in the charges and responses is the simple fact that Milwaukee's choice plan gave low-income families only a pitifully small approximation of what theorists have always regarded as essential for choice programs to succeed. Far from being a good test of the workability of a school choice program, the legislators placed it under nine restrictions [sic]. Not unlike Dante's *Inferno*, which subjected sinners to one of nine ever narrowing circles of hell, each restriction was more wrenching than the preceding. . . . The end result was a program designed to fail. (Peterson and Noyes, 1996)

Milwaukee's program forbade vouchers to children already in private schools. Peterson argued this was done merely to save the state money: If a public-school student elected to use a voucher to attend a private school, the state lost only the money already appropriated for that child. But if students already in private schools were permitted access to vouchers, the state would now have to pay for those students and incur additional costs.

In the Milwaukee program, if more students applied than a school could accommodate, it was required to accept students at random. "As a result," said Peterson, "applicants could not be assured of a school, and schools could not select the children they thought most likely to benefit from their program. . . . Still, the costs of this restriction on choice were not excessive. The number of applicants were not greatly in excess of the number of seats available. And random assignment helped the choice program avoid the accusation that they selected only the more able and more self-disciplined students."

Random assignment has a great advantage from a research and program evaluation perspective because it means that all possibility of any selection bias (based on income, education level of parents, and so on), is removed. Only chance differences will occur. Peterson's and researchers' positions inherently conflict. Schools will naturally want to try and match their programs with the children who apply and, especially, to weed out those whom they think will be problem students.[1] Researchers will want to rid their experiments as much as possible of the selection bias that this would produce. Peterson's desideratum could only be permitted in an experiment where *all* schools selected their students, but in the current condition, public schools don't get to choose.

Initially, Milwaukee's program was limited to 1 percent of the total student population, or about 900 students. In 1994, the cap was raised to 1.5 percent, and then removed. In 2000–2001, 9,638 student used vouchers to attend 103 schools at a cost to Wisconsin taxpayers of over $51 million. For 2001–2002, enrollment was up to 10,739, and the vouchers were worth $5,553 each, meaning that taxpayers paid $60 million a year to send students to private schools (45 percent comes from state aid to Milwaukee, the rest from the general fund) (Redovich, 2001).

The legislature enacted the program to be "revenue neutral," meaning that choice schools received the same amount of state aid per pupil as the Milwaukee public schools. Schools that charged a tuition higher than the voucher amount had to either waive the tuition, admit smaller numbers, or decline to participate at all. Peterson cites one private-school administrator as saying that his school "would participate further if we did not lose so much money per student accepted." This administrator's claim seems like a red herring. Unless so many students applied that schools had to hire new staff or add facilities, which has not yet happened, the added costs would be minimal—a few more books and other instructional materials, perhaps. For most private schools, students arriving with vouchers would constitute financial "gravy."

Parents were not permitted to make up any difference between the tuition and the value of the voucher. "The ostensible purpose of the ban was to keep school choice from becoming elitist, but this goal was already assured by the rule that no money could go to families with income substantially above the poverty line. . . . [This restriction] guaranteed that most choice students would attend fiscally constrained institutions with limited facilities and poorly paid teachers" (Peterson and Noyes, 1996).

---

1. This is probably not so true for Catholic schools which, from 1960 to 2000, saw their proportion of all students shrink from 12.1 percent to 4.7 percent.

Peterson here raises an issue that divides voucher advocates. He and other proponents of choice hold that parents who invest in their children's education will endeavor to see that it pays off. They will be more likely to become involved with the school and see that their children behave, complete homework, and so on. There are several private voucher programs that stipulate that parents must contribute their own funds, often as much as the value of the voucher itself. No data exist to test the hypothesis that paying parents are more involved. Studies of voucher programs do find parents more involved, but their involvement could derive from other factors. Voucher-using parents in Milwaukee and San Antonio, Texas, for instance, were more involved with school *prior* to the voucher program. In San Antonio, where the voucher covered 50 percent of tuition, parents had to come up with the rest, and they did not become more involved after the program began than they were prior to the program.

The legislation prohibited vouchers to go to religious schools. A challenge to this restriction ended with the Wisconsin Supreme Court ruling in favor of the church-affiliated schools. Both the plaintiffs and defendants wanted the U.S. Supreme Court to settle the issue, but it declined to hear the case. The Wisconsin court ruled that since the money did not go to the school, but followed the student, the program did not violate the separation of church and state clause. About one-third of all Milwaukee voucher students now attend Catholic schools and have done much to end the declining enrollments of these schools. Another 30 percent attend other religious schools.

Peterson impugned the skills and experience of the state-chosen evaluator of the Milwaukee program, University of Wisconsin political scientist John Witte, with curious acrimony, considering that Witte advocates school choice, if not necessarily vouchers. Finally, according to Peterson, the Wisconsin State Superintendent of Public Instruction, Bert Grover, did everything he could to avoid having the program in the first place, and, once the program was brought into existence, Grover did everything in his power to kill it.

I have presented this discussion of Milwaukee's voucher program to show that even small programs are extremely complex and do not permit conclusions such as "vouchers work" or "vouchers don't work." Still, these simplistic conclusions are often used by voucher proponents and sometimes by opponents.

Voucher Programs in Florida and Elsewhere

Fall 2000 produced a number of voucher developments. In October, an appeals court in Florida reversed a judge's earlier decision and declared the voucher program constitutional. This decision was immediately appealed, but the Florida Supreme Court refused to hear the case. Furthermore, the Institute for Justice asked that the judge who ruled the plan unconstitutional recuse himself. His son has since married the daughter of an official in a Florida Teacher's Union. The judge refused, but the appeals court ruled in favor of the Institute for Justice (Associated Press, 2001a).

In 2000 Florida's public schools rendered the Florida program at least temporarily moot. The state awards its schools letter grades annually and school-children become eligible for vouchers if their school receives an "F" grade in two years out of four. Two schools in the Pensacola area received their second "F" at the end of 1999 and fifty-seven[2] children from those schools used vouchers to attend private schools during 1999–2000. Another seventy-eight schools received their first "F" that year. However, when the grades arrived in the summer of 2000, all of the schools had improved to "D" or better, rendering their students ineligible for voucher assistance.

Interestingly, Florida's law makes no provision for returning the voucher children to improved public schools. The public schools that lose students to vouchers have no way to retrieve them other than to cajole them and their parents, regardless of what letter grade the schools might attain. Of the fifty-seven students who left public school for private in 1999–2000, forty-seven remained there at the start of 2001–2002.

Two months after the Florida decisions, a federal appeals court, noting that 96 percent of Cleveland, Ohio's, 4,000 voucher students attended Catholic schools, ruled that the voucher program was indeed unconstitutional (Wilgoren, 2000a). The court also said that "Practically speaking, the tuition restrictions mandated by the statute limit the ability of nonsectarian schools to participate in the program, as religious schools often have lower overhead costs, supplemental income from private donations and consequently lower tuition needs" (Cooper, 2000). In other words, the vouchers were worth much less than the tuition at most nonsectarian schools, making it financially difficult for them to participate in the vouchers program. The U.S. Supreme Court will hear the Cleveland case during its 2000–2001 session.

November 2000 saw the election of a voucher-advocating president and the overwhelming rejections of voucher referenda in both California and Michigan. The California referendum would have provided $4,000 in taxpayer money to any student who wanted to attend a private school, including the 600,000 students already in private California schools. Supporters argued that the resulting program would have given consumers "total freedom of choice." Not quite. While California private schools enroll 600,000 students, the state's public schools contain over 6,000,000. Even a rapidly expanding private school system could handle only a tiny fraction of these students. National estimates find that existing private schools could accommodate only 4 percent of existing public school students (MacInnes, 2000). In addition, many private schools have no desire to expand. One story, unconfirmed but plausible, stated that 85 percent of

2. The figure 58 is sometimes given, but one student was using a voucher under a very different plan to assist special education students.

the private schools in California had announced that they would not accept voucher students who scored below grade level.

Even if the specifics of this story are inaccurate, it indicates that private schools are not opening their doors to students bearing vouchers. Catholic schools, which have been hemorrhaging students (and faculty, who can no longer work for the low salaries) in the past decade, are more likely to accept voucher students, but to date, they have been asked to absorb only small numbers of poor and/or low-performing students (Catholic schools enrolled 12.6 percent of all American students in 1960, but only 4.7 percent in 2000 [Brimelow, 2000]).

Unlike the money-for-everyone referendum in California, the Michigan proposal would have provided up to $3,300 per year for students in "failing districts"—those which do not graduate at least two-thirds of their seniors in a four year period. Referendum proponents said it would affect about thirty districts throughout the state, but according to figures from the Michigan Department of Education, only seven districts would qualify (Sandham, 2000, p. 1).

The California proposal, although amply funded by Silicon Valley venture capitalist Timothy Draper, met resistance early on. Homeschoolers opposed the measure on the grounds that it would lead to increased government regulation of *all* schools—the state would have to monitor the operation (Duffy, 2000). Others objected to subsidizing wealthy families whose children already attended private schools. Even voucher advocate Terry Moe of the Hoover Institute opposed the measure. Said Moe, "There were plenty of voucher supporters who would have told him [Draper], if asked, not to do it this way. But he didn't ask" (Walsh, 2000b). For whatever reasons, voters soundly rejected the measure by a 70–30 margin.

When first proposed, the Michigan referendum was given a fighting chance even though a seemingly natural ally, Republican Governor John Engler, opposed it. Engler apparently favored his charter program instead. Former governor James Blanchard, a Democrat, also opposed it. A bill opposed by prominent members of both parties confused voters. Throughout September and October, polls gave the measure about even odds. Proponents outspent opponents two to one. It came as a shock, then, when it also failed by 70-30.

Mulling over the results, especially from Cleveland, a number of commentators reasoned that the voucher proposals simply did not offer enough to attract private schools other than those run by the Catholic Church. Cleveland's vouchers were worth $2,500, Michigan's $3,300, and California's $4,000. Schools that belong to the National Association of Independent Schools charge much more. In the Midwest, 1999–2000 median cost for an NAIS preschool was $8,200, while that for twelfth grade was $11,525 (McGovern, 2000; NAIS tuitions are higher in other regions of the country except the South). Thus the vouchers neither provided impoverished families with anything close to the private schools' fees, nor did they offer the schools anything close to their costs.

Until recently, advocates have paid little attention to costs. Seymour Sarason wrote about this inattention, "Of one thing I am certain. Should voucher proponents come to the realization about how much more it will cost to make it possible for parents of little or modest means to use and benefit from vouchers, the proponents will lose their enthusiasm. A realistic school voucher program will not be cheap. I seriously doubt that proponents are prepared for that eventuality" (Sarason, 2002, p. 91).

Given all of the uncertainty introduced by the courts and the ballot box returns and the recognition by some advocates that Sarason is right, voucher supporters mobilized to decide what to do next. In general, advocates seemed to be scaling back their ambitions, taking a longer view, and abandoning the word *vouchers*. Voucher proponent Paul Peterson of Harvard said, "Five percent of families will want vouchers, not 50 percent. Voucher proponents want to do something massive, and that concerns me. It's better if we crawl along." Peterson also reflects a growing tendency among voucher people in how to look at the movement. He stated that inadequate education in the inner cities "is the biggest civil rights question of our era" (Coeyman, 2000). Thus, at least among some voucher proponents there has been a shift in how they think about the concept and they see it more limited in scope as a civil rights issue.

The word *voucher* currently carries so much heavy emotional and ideological baggage that even ardent advocates are dropping it. One of the most energetic (some would say zealous) voucher supporters, Jeanne Allen of the Center for Education Reform, said, "There are fewer and fewer people who think only school vouchers are the key. There are more and more people talking about choice" (Wilgoren, 2000b). Senate majority leader Trent Lott weighed in with "I think maybe the word is part of the problem. Maybe the word should be 'scholarship'" (Wilgoren, 2000b). During his confirmation hearings, Secretary of Education Rod Paige said vouchers were no longer part of the administration's vocabulary (Schemo, 2001).

But vouchers were part of the education agenda that President Bush sent to Congress in 2001. Some felt this gesture was just a sop to conservatives—Bush knew that Congress would remove the provision and both houses did so. Bush's proposed vouchers were worth only $1,500, and were, therefore, just a transfer of wealth from taxpayers of all denominations to private institutions such as the Catholic Church. Only the heavily subsidized Catholic schools could benefit from such a paltry sum.

A relatively new organization, the Black Alliance for Educational Options (BAEO), states that it is for educational "options." BAEO's home page says that the organization will work in a variety of ways to make the "general public" aware of choice programs and of "efforts to reduce or limit educational options available to parents" (*www.baeoonline.org*). BAEO's President and source of inspiration is Howard Fuller, president of the Institute for the Transformation of Learning at Marquette University. Fuller has criticized the Milwaukee public schools and attempted to establish an all-black school district. In 1991 when the Milwaukee school board was unable to agree on a superintendent, the legislature waived the requirement that superintendents had to have at least three years of

K–12 teaching and Fuller was appointed. Fuller is husband of Deborah McGriff, former superintendent of schools in Detroit and currently a vice president with Chris Whittle's Edison Schools, Inc.

BAEO grew out of symposia Fuller sponsored in 1999 on Options for African Americans and was formally organized in late August 2000. Aside from symposia, BAEO's principal activity to date has been a multimillion-dollar advertising campaign in Washington, D.C., media and in black-owned news-papers. The campaign is supported by conservative organizations such as the Walton Family Foundation, the Lynde and Harry Bradley Foundation, and the Milton and Rose Friedman Foundation. According to one article, "The alliance endorses all forms of parental choice—charter schools, education tax credits, pri-vate scholarships, home-schooling, public school innovations as well as the much-debated tax-supported vouchers" (Mathews, 2000).

Making Vouchers Accountable

Public schools hear the constant drumbeat of "accountability, accountability, accountability," yet there is no accountability whatsoever in the schools that accept vouchers in Milwaukee, Cleveland, or Florida. The complaints are only a low grumble that the voucher programs are small. If the programs grow, though, this attitude will change. Using taxpayer money for programs that have no ac-countability to the taxpayer will eventually annoy enough people that they will call for the regulation of the private schools. Why, they will say, should the pri-vate schools get a free ride when the public schools do not? Good question.

This is something John Stuart Mill, for all his considerable genius, did not consider. He thought the state could administer tests to see if children had learned what they were supposed to have learned. It's a benign scenario. He wor-ried greatly that the "State is a mere contrivance for molding people to be just like one another." If the state wishes to mold people, will it not try to shape them no matter what educational system is in place? If there is no state education, the state will simply resort to other techniques in other settings.

John Jennings of the Center on Education Policy investigated what could happen in the United States if voucher programs funneled large sums of taxpayer dollars into the private sector. Many other nations have systems where private schools receive government funds to educate a large proportion of the students. Jennings examined how these nations regulate the private schools and found that "Often, subsidized private schools must follow the same national curriculum as public schools, although they may retain control over their teaching methods" (Center on Education Policy, 1999). These subsidized private schools in many countries must pass a government inspection before they can offer a diploma that the country will recognize. The students must pass national exams before graduation or, in some cases, moving on to the next level of schooling. Teachers in subsidized schools must have the same qualifications as those in public schools and, in some cases, be paid the same salaries. Some nations require pupil-teacher ratios in private schools to be the same as in public schools.

In this country, both state aid to and regulation of private schools is quite limited. Thirty-eight states require certification of private schools but these mostly involve judgments about minimum criteria with regard to education, health, and safety. Jennings observes that:

> [Currently], the U.S. provides only very limited kinds of assistance to private schools and regulates them far less than many other countries. But the basic impetus that has led other countries to link funding with government regulation also exists in the U.S. It is reasonable to assume that if American private schools began receiving substantially more funding through voucher and choice programs, the states or the federal government would increase the amount and scope of private school regulation beyond the current level. (p. 12)

Some observers, especially Christian fundamentalists, have predicted that vouchers would bring just the kind of government control that Jennings found in Europe:

> If such a [choice via vouchers] plan were ever adopted, powerful interests would immediately begin lobbying in support of restrictive legislation that would undercut the element of free choice in the plan as it now stands. Under pressure from special interest groups such as Shanker's United Federation of Teachers [sic], laws might be passed to require that teachers in private schools meet standardized licensing requirements and that the physical plant of private schools meet arbitrary standards established by the government. Laws could (and would) follow laws, self-proclaimed reformers would come to advocate the imposition, on private schools, of what they would term "academic standards; and, just as we now have a costly system of public education that wears the label "free," we may easily end up with a system of state education that bears the appellation "private." (Patton, 1991, pp. 24–25)

Similarly, Barrett Mosbacker, headmaster of a Christian school in North Carolina wrote, "Although vouchers ostensibly offer freedom of choice, they may actually eliminate that freedom by encumbering Christian schools with government regulations. If this happens, choice will be replaced by coercion. Unless sufficient 'court-proof' safeguards are enacted that guarantee the freedom of Christian schools, vouchers should be opposed" (Mosbacker, 1998).

In more specific terms, home educator and author, Cathy Duffy, has argued against the California voucher proposal in part on the grounds that it will lead to increased regulation. "Regulation must address questions such as how to verify information provided by private schools, how to determine that children actually exist, how to deal with the fact that illegal aliens may qualify for vouchers, and how to fund and operate the bureaucracy necessary to answer the above questions as well as to process quarterly enrollment reports, payment, and mid-year transfers and dropouts" (Duffy, 2000).

Schools that wish to retain their autonomy by refusing vouchers will find it hard to compete, says Duffy. Most parents will prefer to use vouchers rather than pay tuition, putting the voucher-refusing schools out of business. We have seen this happening already in Michigan. Private schools can convert to charter status and use public funds rather than charge their students tuition. Mosbacker has voiced the same concern.

Duffy does not emphasize a point about voucher proposals that Columbia's Henry Levin has raised: under a voucher system, the state would be dealing with *schools* not *districts*. Levin conjectured that the inherent inefficiency of the infrastructure needed to operate such a system would actually render vouchers more costly than the current public school arrangement.

Are vouchers constitutional? Martha McCarthy of Indiana University has observed that recent Supreme Court rulings might open the door for spending tax dollars not only in nonsectarian schools but in church-affiliated schools as well. "The central rationale that voucher proponents use to defend the legality of voucher plans is the *private* nature of the decisions that ultimately result in government funds flowing to religious institutions. The parents, not the state, decide where to send their children to school, and the funds simply follow the child" (McCarthy, 2000, p. 375). The Court heard the arguments in February 2002 and reached its decision on June 27, 2002 (see pages 159–160).

A Nation of Vouchers: Chile

We can get some information about the operation of vouchers by looking at the results in Chile, which has had a national voucher system for over twenty years. Stanford University researchers Patrick McEwen and Martin Carnoy studied Chile's system. Chile is not the United States, a reader might likely say. But a market is a market is a market, the free-marketeers would respond.

Influenced directly by Milton Friedman's writings, in 1980 Chile's government began a sweeping education reform effort. It transferred the management responsibility for public schools from the centralized Ministry of Education back to local municipalities. Teachers became employees of these municipalities, not civil servants of the state. By 1982, this transfer was essentially in place. Under the new system, the Ministry of Education disbursed payments each month based directly on the number of students enrolled and multiplied by the value of the voucher. Vouchers had a base value plus adjustments based on location and grade. The law specified the factor by which the base was adjusted for each grade and additional compensations were made for schools with high levels of poverty or situated in remote locations.

New private schools were founded and attracted a quickly increasing share of students. Existing private schools were eligible for vouchers if they did not charge tuition in addition. By 1987 public schools' share of the enrollment had fallen to just over 60 percent. It has inched downward only slightly since 1987, to 58 percent. By 1987 new private schools using vouchers had siphoned off just over 30 percent of the students and their enrollment has increased only slightly since 1987 to about 35 percent. All during the period, high-tuition private schools enrolled from 5 percent to 9 percent of the students, with the figure being 7 percent or 8 percent in most years.

In an analysis of fourth-grade data, McEwan and Carnoy found what they called "mixed" results. Nonreligious voucher schools had lower test scores than the public schools. However, they also cost less and when costs are figured in these schools were slightly more cost-efficient than public schools. The Catholic voucher schools were more effective in producing achievement outcomes for students similar in background characteristics, but they cost *more* and so their cost efficiency was likewise similar to the public schools. Say the researchers:

> The results are probably not satisfying for either voucher advocates or opponents. They are inconsistent with advocates' claims that privately managed voucher schools produce significantly higher achievement than public schools for pupils with similar socioeconomic backgrounds. Even so, nonreligious voucher schools are more cost-efficient than publicly run schools. Another category, Catholic voucher schools, is able to achieve higher test scores for similar students but only by spending more. (McEwan and Carnoy, 2000, p. 23)

McEwan and Carnoy feel that vouchers and for-profit schools might be a good investment for poor nations strapped for resources. For the U.S., they think the results show that "a broad caricature of private schools—either positive or negative—is misleading; in fact different categories vary widely in their effectiveness and efficiency." The for-profits, though, "successfully compete by cutting costs, rather than significantly raising achievement."

McEwan returned to the scene to analyze eighth-grade data which became available later. This data also had the advantage of reporting scores for individual students. The earlier, fourth-grade data had already been aggregated to the school level. In addition, at the eighth-grade level, parental questionnaires provided a much richer set of background information on the students.

As in the earlier study, private schools that charge high tuition and don't take vouchers achieve the best results. Religious voucher schools score slightly higher than public schools while nonreligious voucher schools scored slightly lower. However, when background characteristics were taken into account, only the private, tuition-charging schools scored better than the public schools.

If voucher schools don't score higher than other schools except for the elite private schools, what accounts for their popularity? McEwan suggests that because the voucher schools contain a larger proportion of high socioeconomic status (SES) students, these schools have a certain cachet of class that impresses parents. "The implication is that vouchers provided many middle-class Chilean families with the means to choose the 'right' peer group, rather than the 'best' school" (p. 23).

The fact that the new private voucher schools attracted students whose parents are better educated is a Chilean instance of "creaming," which the researchers consider a negative outcome. They call for a more comprehensive analysis of the effects of competition. "A curious feature of the voucher literature is that advocates and critics have a tendency to emphasize one of these effects, and ignore or downplay others. For example, advocates have emphasized the positive effects of competition, while skeptics have focused on the negative effects of sorting and cream-skimming. To adequately evaluate the impact of vouchers, we need to consider both" (pp. 24–25).

Moe, in *Private Vouchers*, contends that while "private voucher programs have their own rules" which "have a lot to do with the kinds of outcomes that get generated," they also have more to offer than the mere accretion of additional evidence. "In comparison with the public programs, private voucher programs give us a simpler, more direct indication of how choice and markets actually operate when the most burdensome trappings of bureaucracy and political control are removed" (1995, p. 20).

In both the public and private voucher programs, an observer might be disconcerted by what appears to be a most unusual set of political bedfellows: rich, white, conservative Republican parents, and poor, minority, urban, probably mostly Democratic parents. Suburban whites are either not interested or actively oppose vouchers. As any number of commentators have observed, this alliance, odd as it seems at first, makes sense. The conservative whites press market-oriented programs because they believe in markets (and, in some cases, hope to make money from the shift to market-driven schools). Urban minorities want to escape inner-city schools but are trapped by the harsh economic realities of those areas. Whites in suburbs have already exercised considerable school choice by their prior decision of where to live. As Moe views it:

> The educational establishment is solidly behind the poor when it comes to mainstream educational programs—for compensatory, bilingual, and special education, for instance. But the establishment has its own reasons for opposing vouchers, even when poor kids are the only ones to receive them. Vouchers allow children and resources to leave the public system. A fully developed voucher systems, moreover, would largely dismantle the establishment's own system of bureaucracy and political control in favor of new arrangements that decentralize power to parents and schools. From the establishment's standpoint, then, vouchers are the ultimate survival issue, and they must be defeated wherever they are proposed. (1995, p. 5)

In this statement, Moe operates partly from fact and partly from idealized theory. The "establishment" (it's not clear what Moe actually means with that loaded word), will oppose vouchers, but certainly part of the reason will be that vouchers will leave the public system with fewer resources, which would reduce the system's capabilities to provide good service. Similarly, it is not at all clear that vouchers will decentralize power and put parents in charge.

Vouchers in U.S. Cities

We now turn to a more in-depth discussion of several of the better known public and private voucher ventures.

Milwaukee

The Milwaukee school choice program involves the transfer of taxpayer dollars to private schools. Act 36, passed by the 1990 Wisconsin legislature, established a voucher program in Milwaukee permitting up to 1 percent of Milwaukee's low-income children to attend any private school that would accept the state's voucher, initially worth $2,446 and rising to $4,696 in 1997–98. The program has since been expanded to permit up to 15 percent of the students to attend. "Low-income" was defined as 175 percent or less than the official U.S. poverty rate—in 1990, about $14,000 for a family of four. The program was initially under-subscribed. One percent of Milwaukee students would be about 900 pupils. The numbers rose from 300 to 771 under the 1 percent cap and, with the further expansion of the program, to about 11,000 for the 2001–2002 school year. With each voucher worth $5,532, the cost to Wisconsin taxpayers is more than $60 million a year to support private schools.

Participating schools had to meet at least one of four criteria for continued participation:

1. At least 70 percent of the students gain at least one grade level each year;
2. Attendance must average 90 percent;
3. At least 80 percent of the students demonstrate significant academic progress; or
4. At least 70 percent of the families meet the school's criteria for parental involvement.

The Wisconsin Supreme Court upheld the law in an initial suit and later concluded that religious schools can participate. The court found the law constitutional because the children, not the schools, are the beneficiaries—the vouchers go directly to the families, who then decide where to use them. This logic has also been seen in other U.S. Supreme Court rulings on vouchers (McCarthy, 2000) and will likely be the logic used in the soon-to-be heard Cleveland case.

The Wisconsin Supreme Court's decision surprised some observers. To them, it seemed likely that this decision would be overturned because, although there is no religious intent in the voucher system itself, religious schools leave no doubt that they intend to inculcate their religion in their students. Thus Milwaukee's Gospel Lutheran School states that "children are taught to recognize God's Law and in it see their own sin. . . . Religion is taught formally in kindergarten and in all grades." St. Bernadette states that "Non-Catholic students are welcome. Because of the nature of a Catholic School, religion is taught daily as a part of the curriculum. Catholic values are incorporated into all other aspects of the curriculum." Looking at these quotes, commentator Nat Hentoff declared that "to allow parents to use public money to put children into elementary and secondary schools that are completely devoted to inculcating a particular religious faith means that there will be, in these institutions, no separation at all between church and state" (Hentoff, 1999). Although asked by both plaintiffs and defendants, the U.S. Supreme Court declined to hear the case, allowing the program to continue.

The legislature initially established the program as a five-year experiment and commissioned an annual evaluation of the program. John Witte and colleagues at the University of Wisconsin conducted the evaluations. At the end of five years, Witte concluded that there were no differences between the students choosing private schools and a control group who remained in the Milwaukee Public Schools (MPS). Paul Peterson, a political scientist at Harvard, criticized the experiment, including Witte's evaluation methods and expertise. Voucher supporters lobbied successfully not to conduct more rigorous assessments of the program, but to end the evaluations—the legislature expanded the voucher program but eliminated funds for evaluations.

MPS elementary schools received only $4,234 per student in direct aid in 1997–98. Most choice students attend private schools in the elementary grades. Public schools also receive special education funds. The rest is used by the district for capital improvements, recreation programs, alternative education, food, maintenance, and transportation. MPS also must provide transportation for choice students who require it. Thus, even without factoring in the cost of transporting the private school pupils, the amount of the vouchers in 1998, $4,696, actually exceeded what most public schools received in money for regular instruction (a suit resulted in the private schools being exempted from having to provide special education services). The private schools do not have to disclose other sources of funds and do not.

Although Milwaukee has many private schools, initially only three of them enrolled more than 80 percent of all voucher applicants. Such a concentration of students precludes any generalization of the effect of "choice," although this has not prevented people from trying. Witte concluded after five years that there were no differences between the public school and private school students (Witte, Sterr, and Christopher, 1995). Peterson and colleagues[3] concluded that

---

3. Peterson is actually the second author on many of the articles, the lead author being one of his former students, Jay P. Greene of the University of Houston. It is Peterson, however, who has attracted media attention, as indicated by the page 1 story about him in the August 5, 1998, edition of *Education Week*.

the data favored choice (Greene, Peterson, and Du, 1996). Bracey concluded that if the data favored choice, and he wasn't certain that they did, it was likely because the choice students had been in one school for four years, providing them with an academic stability rare among urban students (Bracey, 1996a). Rouse concluded that it depends on what assumptions the analyst makes and, thus, on the statistical procedure then used (Rouse, 1998). In her favored analyses, there was an effect favoring choice for math but not for reading.

Rouse also noted that disadvantaged students attending a program with extra funding and small classes outperformed both students at magnet schools and the voucher students. Nelson observed that while Rouse's paper partially replicates Peterson's analysis, it can actually be taken as a rather stinging rebuke of Peterson's approach (1998). Nelson discussed thirteen ways in which Rouse's analysis differed from Peterson's, including type of significance test used, assumptions about missing data, assumptions about family background, assumptions about student learning rates, violations of regression analysis assumptions, and comparability of samples.

In the end this is all much ado about very little because the data themselves are so flawed it is not clear that they can yield any trustworthy conclusions. Among the problems:

- Researchers could collect data only on unsuccessful voucher applicants who entered MPS. This amounted to fewer than half of those rejected. This is crucial to Peterson's analyses. He contends that those who were rejected, because they were rejected by lottery, constitute a group comparable to those admitted. Since most students were not admitted by lottery, this claim is questionable at the outset, but clearly those who were rejected and turned up in MPS could be quite different from those who were rejected and went elsewhere.
- Parents responded at low rates and different rates to a survey seeking critical background data—only 37 percent of the voucher families and 22 percent of the MPS families responded.
- The above problem meant that test scores *and* surveys were available for only 28 percent of the voucher students and 21 percent of the MPS students.
- Random selection, much emphasized by Peterson, occurred only at schools that were oversubscribed. One of the two schools admitting most of the black students admitted all students while the other had a waiting list.
- Siblings of admitted students could skip the lottery.
- There were no rules for maintaining waiting lists and no oversight of them.
- Voucher applicants with "disabilities" could be rejected but there was no oversight or supervision of the rejections. Given that most private schools have minimal expertise in special education, one wonders what they regarded as a "disability."

Finally, results from another Milwaukee experiment in which additional funds were used to reduce class size indicates that smaller classes produce much more powerful effects than whatever might occur from "choice." Indeed, the effect seen in the Milwaukee choice project might well be due to small classes. In MPS, the pupil–teacher ratio is 19.3:1. In the voucher schools it is 15.3:1.

It is important to note as an aside that pupil–teacher ratio is not the same as class size. In 1996, the pupil–teacher ratio in U.S. elementary schools was 18.8:1. The average class size was 25.2 students. Pupil–teacher ratio counts anyone in the building who has a teaching certificate and whose primary responsibility is to teach, including special education and Title 1 teachers as well as various specialists. Private schools seldom offer special education or remedial programs such as Title 1, and often do not have specialists. Thus, their pupil–teacher ratio is likely to be much closer to average class size than it is for public schools.

Rouse analyzed data for the voucher schools and the public schools with small classes (pupil–teacher ratio 17.0:1) and found that the improvements in reading were as large in the public schools as in the private schools. She also found a small gain for math in public schools and no gain at all in private schools. She suggests that *if* students in voucher schools show improvement— she still has her doubts—it is because they attend small schools with small classes (Rouse, 2000).

Small schools and small classes have emerged as important factors to explain any advantage seen in charter or voucher schools. Voucher and charter schools are often smaller than otherwise comparable public schools and have smaller classes. The effects of small classes have been known for some time as a result of Project STAR in Tennessee (Finn and Achilles, 1990; Finn, 1999). The importance of the STAR experiment comes from the fact that the three treatments—regular class, regular class with full-time teacher's aide, and small class— were randomly assigned within each school, eliminating any source of selection bias. The study's evaluators found the effects strong and sustained. A recent analysis by Princeton economist Alan Krueger controlling for factors that could have affected the randomness of assignment after the first year, for Hawthorne effects, and for John Henry effects, not only left the initial conclusions unchanged, but found that the effect was cumulative across grades (Krueger, 1998; see Bracey, 1998, for a summary of Krueger's analyses).

That Peterson's Milwaukee study will continue to be used ideologically can be seen in how it was released initially. Most such works are reviewed by peers informally, then either presented at some professional gathering or sent to some learned journal or both. The first appearance of Peterson's analysis of the Milwaukee data appeared as an Associated Press wire story (Estrin, 1996). The same day, the *Wall Street Journal* carried an op-ed essay (Greene and Peterson, 1996). The evening of that same day found presidential candidate Robert Dole addressing the Republican National Convention on education and calling for vouchers and choice. Within a couple of days, William Bennett and Lamar Alexander had wormed their way onto television talk shows touting the study and Rush Limbaugh had sent it across the airwaves.

Peterson conducted a similar analysis drawing similar conclusions for the Cleveland voucher program (Peterson, Howell, and Greene, 1999) and has been hired in several other venues as well to evaluate the programs established by the Children's Educational Opportunity Foundation (usually referred to as CEO America), now in partnership with the conservative National Center for Policy Analysis.

Most educators are likely to see voucher issues in educational and economic terms—how it affects children and public schools—and debate it on those grounds. But this is naïve and shortsighted. The issues are very much political and subject to all the depredations of the political process. Indeed, the Milwaukee situation has degenerated into what the *Wisconsin State Journal*, a conservative newspaper, has called "one of the largest political corruption cases in state history" (cited in Miner, 2000).

In a 1997 election for a seat on the Wisconsin Supreme Court, Jon Wilcox, on record as advocating the extension of the voucher program to religious schools, defeated opponent Walt Kelly. In 1998, when the extension case reached the Wisconsin Supreme Court, Wilcox voted with the majority to permit religious schools to participate. Kelly smelled a rat and encouraged an investigation into what became known as "The Case of the Mystery Postcards."

Just prior to the election, some 354,000 postcards urged citizens to vote for Wilcox. The postcards did not mention the voucher issue directly, but implied that Kelly was far too liberal for the state high court. As it turned out, the postcards were financed by wealthy supports of vouchers from all over the country. Patrick Rooney of Golden Rule Insurance, credited with the idea of private vouchers, sent $34,500. John Walton of Wal-Mart kicked in $25,000. Bare Seld, a Chicago businessman and voucher supporter sent $25,000. Another $17,500 arrived from the PMA Foundation, a Philadelphia organization that supports vouchers. Even Pierre S. Du Pont, former governor of Delaware, who advocated vouchers in his brief stint as a Republican presidential candidate, sent $1,000 (Miner, 2000).

Wisconsin State Superintendent of Schools John T. Benson said that, "It is obvious that the people who made contributions to this justice's campaign had one thing in mind, and that was to elect someone who would be an advocate for the voucher system." The Wisconsin Election Board has now sued the Wilcox campaign for accepting $200,000 in illegal campaign contributions. Given that without Wilcox's vote the extension of voucher eligibility to religious schools would still have passed, 3–2, it is unlikely that the suit will result in anything more than a fine.

Interestingly, one judge did recuse herself from the voucher vote. Observers in Wisconsin think it was because she had received money from the teachers' union, but the judge provided no reasons for her actions. And some have argued that yet another judge who voted for the extension *should* have recused herself, because her husband served on the board of a voucher school. If these recusals had occurred, the vote would have been a 2–2 tie, sending the matter back to a lower court.

In the absence of evaluation requirements, Milwaukee's program is not being adequately studied. This is too bad because there are apparently some fascinating trends. Some private schools have 90 percent or more of their students receiving vouchers. At one Catholic school, two-thirds of the teachers quit rather than cope with voucher students. And, overall, private school enrollment has *declined* in the ten years of the voucher program (Leovy, 2000). Since there are 11,000 voucher students for 2001–2002, this means that the private schools have been hemorrhaging students. This is not, according to market theorists, the way it is supposed to work.

Cleveland

In April 1995 the Ohio legislature approved the use of state funds for vouchers worth up to $2,250, which could be used to cover tuition to Cleveland private schools, including religious schools, for students in grades K–3. Proponents of the proposal had argued for vouchers in eight urban districts, but settled for Cleveland as a compromise preferable to no program at all. The $5.25 million for the program came from Cleveland public schools' share of state aid. The vouchers were available for up to 2,500 students, although only 1,900 ended up participating. Students already in private schools could claim up to 25 percent of the vouchers.

The ubiquitous Jay P. Greene and Paul Peterson, along with William Howell of Stanford, were hired by the conservative John M. Olin Foundation to evaluate the program. They found that from fall to spring, the students in the program had gained 5.5 percentile ranks in reading and 15 in math (Peterson, Howell, and Greene, 1999). No control group of any kind was established. The researchers admitted, appropriately, that their study was "just a start." Although their report was labeled an "evaluation of the Cleveland voucher program," their program evaluation had examined test scores in only two of the fifty-five participating schools. These "Hope" schools had been newly created by David Brennan, the Ohio entrepreneur and voucher advocate discussed in connection with Ohio charter schools.

It is indicative of how ideology, policy, politics, and the profit motive become intertwined in voucher programs when they involve for-profit schools. Ohio law forbids private schools from reconstituting themselves as charters, so Brennan shut down his private, voucher-using schools. He then established a nonprofit group to run two "Hope" schools, a group over which he claimed he had no direct governing authority. However, the schools' faculty and staff remained and the schools contracted with White Hat Management, Brennan's for-profit management corporation. Why would Brennan execute such a convoluted shift? Some think money plays a role. The state vouchers for private school tuition pay up to $2,250 per student. Charter schools receive $4,500 per student (Archer, 1999a).

The Ohio Department of Education commissioned a more comprehensive study by Indiana University. Researchers there tested ninety-four third-grade voucher recipients against a sample of 449 similar students who had remained in the Cleveland public schools, and found that "there are no significant differences in achievement between scholarship [voucher] students and their [public school] peers" (Walsh, 1998). Study leader Kim Metcalf said it was too early to tell if choice made a difference (Metcalf, 1999).

The American Federation of Teachers criticized the Greene et al. study because the test scores came from a fall-to-spring testing. Although fall-to-spring testing makes theoretical sense, it can create problems for interpretation. For one thing, people who know the purpose of the fall-to-spring testing can act in such ways as to depress scores in the fall and raise them in spring. In addition, students from low-income families show summer loss while middle-class students do not (if anything, they gain over the summer). This makes fall-to-fall or spring-to-spring testing more appropriate (Alexander, Entwistle, and Olson, 2001). The AFT argued that the results were an artifact of the fall-to-spring testing procedure.

Greene and his colleagues, however, returned to administer a test in the fall. The test was overseen by observers from John Carroll University. The test scores fell substantially, remaining statistically significantly higher in math (8.6 percentile rank gain) and reading (5.6 percentile gain), but not language (Peterson, Green, and Howell, 1998).

Needless to say, others found problems with the original Peterson-Howell-Greene study. The study evaluated students in only two private schools, which had been started from scratch by Akron industrialist David Brennan (who had earlier headed Ohio Governor George Voinovich's Commission on Educational Choice). Three hundred and fifty-two students entered these two schools. People who favor vouchers conducted the evaluation and a foundation, Olin, that favors vouchers funded the evaluation. Under such circumstances, a voucher-unfriendly finding seems most unlikely.

Besides the credibility problem of the test scores themselves, a number of other problems plagued the study. During a suit, Judge John C. Young told a lawyer for the voucher opponents that "It seems to me the Cleveland public school system is about to go under." Yet, most of those choosing private schools were not fleeing sinking schools. Of the 1996 students using vouchers, 834, or 34 percent were kindergartners, in school for the first time. Given that the previous year the Cleveland public schools had eliminated full-day kindergarten in all nonmagnet schools, it seems likely that the overwhelming majority of these students were delivered to the private schools by parents seeking full-day kindergarten, an option available only in private schools.

Another 496 (25 percent) of the students were already in private schools. Only 663 (34 percent) of those who used vouchers in 1996–1997 actually left public schools to attend private ones. Over time, even fewer have left. A study by Zach Schiller of the voucher student makeup in 2000–2001 found that of the 3,741 students in the voucher program, 1,234 had previously attended other private schools. Subsidizing children from private schools is a substantial expense for Cleveland. Some 1,706 students had come from elsewhere, virtually all of them enrolling from kindergarten and a few arriving from other cities. That leaves only 801, or 21 percent, who deserted Cleveland public schools for private education (Schiller, 2001).

The official cost estimate for a voucher from the Ohio Office of Management and Budget was $1,763. However, this figure did not include $629 per pupil for transportation (most of which was provided in taxis), $257 per student for administration, or $543 per pupil in state aid already directed to private schools (in a 1996 report, *The Condition of Public Education in Ohio*, I noted that Ohio gives by far more money per pupil to private schools than any other state; it actually directed more total money to private schools than the more populous states of Pennsylvania, New Jersey, and New York [Bracey, 1996b]).

An external audit by the accounting firm of Deloitte & Touche found many questionable expenditures. In the areas of residency verification, grade eligibility, guardianship, consulting services provided, transportation, and miscellaneous, the firm questioned $1,869,204, or 36 percent, of total expenditures. The first three questionable expenditures likely resulted in scholarship awards to students who were not eligible for them. For consulting services, the auditors could not establish that "the Department of Administrative Services had been involved in the procurement process" or "that the services for which the Program was billed were actually provided" (Deloitte & Touche, 1997).

In these categories, transportation ($1,882,454) and consulting services ($379,433) dominated. In a perfectly run program, not all of these costs could be recovered, of course—it would take some amount of money to transport the children, but $3.33 a day by bus compared to $15.00–18.00 by taxi.

The Ohio Department of Education also found fault with the operation of the voucher program. For instance, although the program was intended to serve low-income families, the law places no income cap on eligibility. Consequently, some thirty students whose families made more than $50,000 a year obtained vouchers. In addition, about one-third of the students did not have the same last name as the adults filing the application, but the program did not check to verify who had legal guardianship (Archer, 1999b).

An evaluation by the American Federation of Teachers observed that for the same money, Cleveland could have restored full-day kindergarten for 70 percent of the students or implemented Success For All, a well-regarded remedial program for young children, in all elementary schools, serving approximately 40,000 students (Murphy, Nelson, and Rosenberg, 2000).

The Cleveland voucher program has since been through a topsy-turvy time. The Ohio Supreme Court struck it down, not because vouchers were inherently unconstitutional, but because the voucher legislation was attached to a general budget bill, something that the Ohio constitution proscribes. The legislature quickly moved to address that problem with separate legislation signed into law by Governor Bob Taft on June 29, 1999 (Sandham, 1999). However, on August 25, 1999, U.S. District Court Judge Solomon Oliver, Jr., issued an injunction against the program on the grounds that, because the participating schools were overwhelmingly religious, the program would not survive constitutional scrutiny. The funds in the Cleveland program go to the schools, not to the parents which, as previously noted, might mean the difference between a voucher program that violates the First Amendment and one that does not.

Judge Oliver's decision was immediately appealed amid general chaos. Oliver then ruled that the students already in the program could continue, but that no new students could be admitted.

Precisely one week after the judge's decision, a second Indiana University evaluation appeared, this one covering a three-year period and analyzing variables such as attendance and parental satisfaction, as well as student achievement. The achievement analyses were conducted separately for students who had left public schools for existing private schools, those who remained in private schools, and those who left public schools to attend the two "Hope" schools created by David Brennan. Controlling for prior achievement and background characteristics, voucher students in private schools scored slightly higher in language and science but not in reading or mathematics. The students in the Hope schools scored significantly lower than both of these other groups.

Looking at parental involvement, the researchers found that the voucher parents were involved in terms of parent–teacher conferences, attending meetings, attending events, calling teachers, and serving on committees. Public school parents were more likely to visit a classroom. Interestingly, parents who had applied for a voucher but had not received one were more involved than public school parents who had not applied, often coming close to the level of the voucher parents' involvement.

The voucher parents were more educated, involved, and satisfied. Similar results were found earlier in Milwaukee. As John Witte, the evaluator of the Milwaukee program, said at the time, at one level this is precisely the kind of parent the voucher program should serve. On the other hand, this is precisely the kind of parent many would like to see staying with the public school and pushing for improvement.

On June 27, 2002, a "bitterly divided" Supreme Court ruled, with its typical 5-4 split, that the Cleveland voucher program was constitutional. Other opinion was also divided: The *Washington Post* approved of the decision, but the *New York Times* did not (*Washington Post*, 2002; *New York Times*, 2002b). In my opinion, the *Times* got it right:

> It was a bad decision on constitutional grounds and a bad one for American education. . . . Fully 96.6 percent of students end up taking their vouchers to religiously affiliated schools. Once students enroll in those schools, they are subjected to just the sort of religious training the First Amendment forbids the state to underwrite. In many cases, students are required to attend Mass or other religious services. Tax dollars go to buy Bibles, prayer books, crucifixes and other religious iconography. It is hard to think of a starker assault on the doctrine of separation of church and state than taking taxpayer dollars and using them to inculcate specific religious beliefs in young people.

Clint Bolick of the voucher-touting Institute for Justice said, "This was the Super Bowl and the kids won" (National Public Radio, 2002). Conservative pundit George Will claimed it was the most important decision since 1954's *Brown v. Board* (Will, 2002). Most commentators thought the impact would be much more modest.

The reasons for the more demure opinions varied from the legal to the practical. On the legal side, 37 states have strict prohibitions against the use of public funds for any religious purpose (Goodstein, 2002). On the practical side, existing private schools could at most find room for 4 percent of the current public school population (MacInnes, 2000). Many private schools have no interest in expanding and many will not accept low-achieving students. Moreover, only church-affiliated schools could afford to accept vouchers modeled after Cleveland's. The Cleveland vouchers are worth only $2,250, making them usable only at schools that already have subsidies from other sources and, like the Catholic schools, have classrooms full of empty chairs.

As for impact, many observers noted that where advocates had once pushed for universal voucher use on market-theory grounds, they now pushed only for poor city dwellers on civil-rights grounds. "We didn't get into this to give resources to people who already have them," said Howard Fuller, chairman of the Black Alliance for Educational Options (Zernike, 2002).

The Court had earlier declined to hear the Milwaukee case. One wonders if that was because in the Milwaukee program the money goes to the school while in Cleveland it goes to the parents, or because in Milwaukee church-affiliated schools cannot force students to participate in the religious instruction that the *Times* worried about (although they apparently do so with little being said about it). Voucher legislation is expected in states such as California and Pennsylvania, but no one is predicting large changes soon.

One wonders how large voucher programs will have to get before taxpayers notice that their money is being given to schools that are wholly unaccountable for it. None of the public-voucher programs today requires that the schools receiving the vouchers report test scores or any other evaluative data.

San Antonio

The previous sections on Milwaukee and Cleveland illustrate some of the characteristics, constraints, and foibles of choice programs operated with publicly funded vouchers that families use to attend private schools. San Antonio has one of the more long-standing and larger programs wherein private individuals and corporations provide "scholarships" for students, typically economically deprived children. Summaries of smaller private voucher experiments in Milwaukee, Indianapolis, and New York City can be found in Terry Moe's *Private Vouchers* (Moe, 1995; the Milwaukee program is not the one discussed earlier in this section).

The Children's Educational Opportunity Fund, more commonly known as CEO America, financed the San Antonio program beginning in 1992. In its first year, the foundation provided 936 scholarships in an amount up to $750. The average scholarship was for $575. This is low by the standards of other cities, but according to the researchers who evaluated the program, the average tuition in San Antonio at the time was $1,500. CEO America believes that parents who make their own investment in such a program will be more committed to it and will work harder to make it succeed. Hence, it funds up to only half the tuition. It has conducted no research to test its belief.

Half of the children receiving scholarships attended public schools at the time. Of those receiving scholarships, 60 percent enrolled in Catholic schools, 20 percent in nondenominational schools, 10 percent in Baptist schools, 1 percent in nonreligious schools, and the remainder in religious schools of various denominations (Godwin, Kemerer, and Martinez, 1997, p. 2).

During the period of the program evaluation, some 800 children, almost all of them in private schools, were on the program's waiting list. The program did not screen children for acceptability on any characterization except need. Students also had to be eligible for free or reduced-price lunches. Some schools, however, exerted admissions controls.

Researchers hired to evaluate the program found that parents who chose to leave public schools with vouchers were more educated, wealthier, more involved with their children's education both at home and at school, and had higher expectations for their children. The parents who chose private schools were more involved with their children's education *before* the program began, but participation in the program did not increase involvement. These parents also had fewer children. Parents who chose private schools were very dissatisfied with public schools, while those who stayed in public school were very satisfied there (Godwin, Frank, and Martinez, 1997).

The evaluation did not directly test the hypothesis that parents who pay part of the cost become more involved in the school. The evaluation did find that the 50 percent of the scholarship families dropped out and frequently cited lack of money and lack of transportation as reasons. It thus appears that the cost-sharing requirement caused at least some of the families to drop out of the program.

For a variety of reasons, the researchers found that "comparisons between public and private school students regarding student achievement are exceedingly difficult." The children choosing private schools had "marginal improvements in standardized reading scores and marginal declines in math." Those in the public schools, though, showed score declines every year from third grade through ninth grade.

The Condition of Vouchers and Charters According to RAND

As 2001 wound down, RAND Corporation produced a large, but not a conclusive, report on both vouchers and charters (Gill, Timpane, Ross, and Brewer, 2001). "Many of the important empirical questions about vouchers and charters have not yet been answered. Indeed, it would be fair to say that none of the important empirical questions have been answered definitively. Even the strongest evidence is based on programs that have been operating for only a short time with a small number of participants; serious questions about generalizability remain" (pp. 202–203).

The RAND report is a report for other researchers. It is cast in broad social issues such as academic achievement, access to the schools, integration, and civic socialization. It is an analysis from a distance. It does not report on corruption, mismanagement, conflict of interest, charging $1.95 a mile for transportation, using charter funds to buy your mother a nice house, or switching the schools you own from private school status to charter status to get more money per student, and so on. The report is good at laying out the conceptual dimensions of vouchers and charter schools that need to be examined, but draws no illustrations or conclusions.

At times the report's approach is downright dangerous: "Whether a system based on family choice undermines the values associated with the common school is an empirical question" (p. 201). Yes, but is that a question we want answered empirically—that is, through experimentation and comparison? What if it does undermine values we cherish? Would it be too late to restore them?

The Children's Education Opportunity Foundation (CEO America)

> *Take away their choice—take away their chance.*
>
> —Slogan on CEO America's materials.

CEO America describes its mission as to:

- Serve as the national clearinghouse for privately funded voucher program information;
- Offer and provide support services for each existing program;
- Provide matching grant money to help develop these programs;
- Coordinate the development of new programs all across America.

Its website (www.childrenfirstamerica.org) describes CEO America's raison d'être in typical alarmist rhetoric: America's education system is failing—and failing badly. To remedy this situation, CEO America has undertaken, among other things, a partnership with the National Center for Policy Analysis. This conservative Texas think tank provides a daily set of policy-related issues culled from a variety of publications, but its education-related website materials champion choice, demean public schools, and take occasional potshots at the U.S. Department of Education. The project called "Educating America" project will "employ radio, television, and syndicated newspaper columns, as well as a series of publications" with the aim "to inject free-market ideas into the school choice debate." As of March 2002, four television ads can be read at the website or watched as video clips. The text of one gives the flavor. On one screen one sees this:

America—worst education scores in twenty years.
America—lowest literacy rate of any industrialized county
America—ranked behind 15 major countries in math and science.

A voice-over intones "American education is at an all-time low. Grades are falling, schools are failing. What's the answer?" The answer is given as "choice."

The two groups sponsored a "conference" in Washington, D.C., September 23–24, 1998. Conference is in quotes because the CEO-NCPA gathering was more like a revival tent meeting complete with highly emotional testimonials from people identified as "voucher parents," one of whom turned out to work for Jeanne Allen and her arch-conservative Center for Educational Reform.

William Bennett, the author of *The Book of Virtues*, delivered the after-dinner keynote address. Having years earlier named Chicago public schools as the nation's worst, Bennett continued to hammer them with statistics that, at best, one would consider dubious. Bennett contended that 50 percent of Chicago pupils scored in the first percentile on standardized tests and later declared that one Chicago school had a 100 percent dropout rate.

Oklahoma state representative J. C. Watts led off the next morning, following the testimonial of a voucher mom from San Antonio whose child was attending a Catholic school. The voucher mom gave the game away when declaring "I so, so wanted a *religious* education for my son." Playing off this theme, Watts declared that Catholic schools "will unleash the caged eagles in the inner cities. Catholic schools are taking the worst and making them the best." Watts offered no evidence in support of his contentions.

"There is a vast left-wing conspiracy to deprive poor children of a good education," intoned former secretary of education Lamar Alexander later in the morning. "Rarely has such a grand army as our own held the high moral ground for so long and advanced so little." Alexander harkened back wistfully to 1992 when then-president George H. W. Bush has proposed a "GI Bill for children," a proposal immediately labeled the "GI Bull" by American Federation of Teachers president Albert Shanker (Shanker, 1992).

William Leininger of CEO America discussed changes that had taken place in Edgewood Independent School District, part of San Antonio, and CEO America's plans to provide $50 million in vouchers over the next five years. He touted the improved outcomes as proof that the market works. A member of the audience, however, pointed out that the information packet distributed to attendees contained a recent article from the *Wall Street Journal*, an institution presumably not part of Alexander's "vast left wing conspiracy." The article stated that the Edgewood district had improved greatly *before* CEO America had provided any dollars. "It opened magnet schools for math and technology and started its first-ever advanced placement classes. Elementary schools were rebuilt, their teaching revised. A high school for troubled youngsters was started. Edgewood still lags behind the state average, but two and a half times as many eighth graders passed their math exams last year as in 1993. Dropout rates have been cut in half. SATs are up 134 points" (Kronholz, 1998). Leininger went on to his next point.

CEO America's website (www.childrenfirstamerica.org) is replete with "research" that presents only a single point of view and much of which qualifies more as propaganda than research. For example, one section presents "Stories." Of these school choice testimonials, one of three things can possibly be said:

1. They are total fakes; or,
2. They have been heavily edited; or,
3. American public schools can be proud that they have taught low-income students—and their parents!—to write such remarkably clear, elegant, and eloquent prose. These stories are at least as literate, with large vocabularies and complex syntax, as most letters to the editor of the *New York Times* or the *Washington Post*. They can be viewed at the website; click on "Stories."

CEO America sprang from the Texas Public Policy Foundation, which approved of Indianapolis insurance magnate Patrick Rooney's idea of establishing a trust to provide vouchers that poor children could use to attend private schools. CEO America's "History" section at the website used to note that the "groundwork" for the organization was laid by a "grant from a Texas businessman" and that things began to take off in 1994 when the Texas Public Policy Foundation received a "$2 million grant." The sources of these donations are not specified.

CEO America currently has programs in seventy-three cities. Most of these programs are small (fewer than 400 students) with Milwaukee and Indianapolis being notable exceptions. Another notable exception is the CEO Horizons program recently started in the earlier-mentioned Edgewood School District of San Antonio. This is a mostly low-income, Hispanic school district. The District Snapshot from the Texas Education Agency for 1999–2000 (the most recent on the TEA website) shows 12,982 students, 94.6 percent of whom are "economically disadvantaged." Ninety-six percent of the students are Hispanic with 2 percent of the students white and 2 percent black (for the state, the percentages are 40, 43, and 14, respectively, for 1999–2000).

Into this disadvantaged setting, CEO American deposited the CEO Horizon project—$50 million to provide vouchers for any student eligible for free or reduced-price lunch programs. The vouchers are worth up to $3,600 for grades K–8, and $4,000 for grades 9–12. Scholarships for students who attend schools outside of Edgewood's defined geographic area receive 100 percent of that school's tuition. These tuitions must be less than the within-district grants, because elsewhere in a Q & A it is noted that the lesser amounts represent an attempt to keep the money concentrated in the Edgewood area. CEO America claims that once a student receives an award, it will be good for at least ten years or until such time as the state legislature provides an equivalent program. Tuition charges are paid to the schools. If parents choose a public school other than the neighborhood school, and if that school will enroll the child for a tuition charge, that school is eligible to receive the money from CEO Horizon. Transportation is not provided.

In the first year, district was unaffected because state aid is based on the previous year's attendance factors. Later years were another matter. It is difficult to know exactly how many students the district has lost: It does not keep tabs and overall enrollment reflects newcomers as well as leavers. CEO America enrolled 771 in 1998–1999 and 1655 in 2001–2002. However, some of these students came from other private and parochial schools or were previously homeschooled.

The district had earlier said it lost 600 students to the CEO program in the first year (1998–1999) and another 550 due to the closing of an Air Force base in the district. Combined, these two losses cost the district $6 million in state aid. Enrollment in the voucher program has risen from 771 in 1998–1999.

There was some temporary benefit of the closure and the vouchers in that for that one year the district had generally smaller classes with no reduction in funding. According to David Ochoa, Edgewood Director of Community and Public Relations, the district reduced staff by about one hundred through attrition and the offering of an early-retirement program (personal communication, October 18, 2000). He further commented that no programs have been canceled, but that staff is thinly spread. For instance, a teacher providing reading instruction for dyslexic students might have to spend a half day at two schools now rather than a full day at one school (personal communication, April, 2002).

Many of the students, Ochoa says, are arriving from kindergarten, as with the Cleveland program, but 112 students have returned to Edgewood thus far in 2001–2002 school year. The district, of course, receives no additional state funding for these returnees.

In fact, the improvements reported in the *Wall Street Journal* have continued. Edgewood was an "Academically Acceptable" district in 1998–1999 and is currently a "Recognized" school district, the second highest category in evaluations by the Texas Education Agency (what Texas calls its state department of education). From 1996–1997 through 1998–1999, the proportion of students passing all Texas tests grew from 55.1 percent to 74.5 percent (statewide in 2000–2001, 82 percent). SAT scores have dipped from 839 to 784, but ACT scores are up to 16.9 from 16.7. The proportion of seniors taking the tests has grown from 44 percent to 61 percent (the state does not report a combined figure; statewide, 52 percent of seniors graduating in 2000 took the SAT, 32 percent took the ACT). Normally, such increases in proportions represent a deeper dig into the talent pool and are accompanied by declining scores. Superintendent Luis Gonzales insists that the district's various gains are due to the emphasis on achievement in Texas generally, not to competition induced by CEO America's vouchers (personal communication, April, 2002).

9

Homeschooling

Although vouchers, charters, and EMOs have gotten most of the attention of late, another, older movement, homeschooling, has gotten more of the children. About 500,000 students attend charter schools and 65,000 use vouchers, but, according to the U.S. Department of Education, in 1999 there were 850,000 children being schooled at home with an 11 percent annual growth rate (Cloud and Morse, 2001; National Center for Education Statistics, 2001). Illegal in almost all states into the 1980s, homeschooling has grown to become the most popular alternative to regular public schooling, aside from traditional private schools.

That homeschooling has received so little public attention in comparison to other movements is surprising. An Ilor.com search on "Edison Schools Inc.," for example, turns up about 2,800 hits, while one on "Knowledge Universe" results in 5,300. On "homeschooling," though, one finds 140,000 citations. The difference is that most of the hits on the first two topics are articles, press releases, and business summaries in the media. Most of the material found under "homeschooling" provides advice, resources, and support from some home-schoolers to others.

Homeschooling evolved principally from the work of two men: John Holt and Ivan Illich. Holt was influenced first by Paul Goodman and later by Illich. Goodman wrote two seminal books on education, *Compulsory Miseducation* and *Growing Up Absurd*. Holt, a fifth-grade teacher in a private school, took from Goodman the idea that education was a function of the community, or should be, not a function of an institution, such as school. Holt's first books, *How Children Fail* (1964) and *How Children Learn* (1967), were popular among educators.

In 1971 Illich published his radical treatise, *Deschooling Society*. Illich claimed that the school institution "schooled the pupil to confuse teaching with learning, grade advancement with education, a diploma with competence, and fluency with the ability to say something new" (Illich, 1971, p. 1). Illich, with extraordinary prescience, proposed establishing "intellectual matches" whereby

166

"each man, at any given moment and at a minimum price, could identify himself to a computer with his address and telephone number, indicating the book, article, film, or recording on which he seeks a partner for discussion. Within days he could receive by mail the list of others who recently had taken the same initiative. This list would enable him to arrange by telephone for a meeting with persons who initially would be known exclusively by the fact that they requested a dialogue about the same subject" (p. 19). Illich then took this idea to a larger scale, describing what he called "Learning Webs," to match people who wanted to learn something with people who could teach them or to match people with common learning interests. Recall, this book was published in 1971, when even "minicomputers" still occupied most of a room, had very limited memories, and virtually no graphic capabilities.

Holt took from Illich the ideas that schools serve to maintain the social class status quo for the majority of students and that schools viewed education not as a life-long process available to anyone, but as a product which they could sell. People who had not bought enough education, such as a B.A., M.A., or a Ph.D., would be prevented from assuming certain roles, and thus advancing socially, even if they learned enough from experience to do so. Whereas Illich confronted schools, Holt opted to bypass them, writing books such as *Teach Your Own* (1981) and starting what is considered the first homeschooling periodical, *Growing Without Schooling*.

Even with the conceptual foundations established by Illich and Holt, most of the homeschoolers into the mid-1990s were "evangelicals." According to Scott Somerville of the Home School Legal Defense Association, in the early 1990s the homeschooling movement was widely perceived as a fundamentalist phenomenon (Somerville, www.hslda.org). But, in part due to the war on the public schools and signal events such as the Columbine High School slayings, more parents became interested in the homeschooling alternative.

Laws, if not attitudes, toward homeschooling have changed dramatically since 1980. The homeschooling movement conflicted with compulsory attendance laws and those who defended the laws and prosecuted homeschoolers did so in the firm belief that they were protecting children from harm. In 1980, homeschooling was illegal in most states. Over the next decade, however, all states passed laws or board of education regulations permitting homeschooling. Iowa, the last holdout, legalized homeschooling in 1991.

The website of the Home School Legal Defense Association (www.hslda. org) offers snippets indicating that homeschoolers are still the focus of harassment from public school authorities. Perhaps public school officials view vouchers and charters as somewhat abstract concepts compared to the concrete example of parents who refuse to send their children to the public school.

The reasons for homeschooling vary and they have changed over the past twenty years. In the 1980s most people who taught their children at home did so because they wished to avoid the secular curriculum of the school, or to instill a specific religion along with education, or both. According to a Department of

Education survey, though, the most-often stated reason in the new millennium is that the parents feel they can provide a better education at home (48.9 percent of respondents). Religion still plays a large role, being given by 38.4 percent of the respondents, and "poor learning environment at school" is the third most-often given reason, at 25.6 percent (numbers will not sum to 100 percent because respondents gave multiple reasons) (National Center for Education Statistics, 2001).

The U.S. Department of Education's profile of the homeschool parents finds them different from other parents on a number of counts: They are more likely to be two-parent families (80 percent vs. 66 percent for non-homeschoolers); more likely to have larger families (62 percent with three or more children vs. 44 percent); and more likely to have only one parent in the work force (52 percent vs. 19 percent). They are slightly more affluent, with 52 percent of the families making between $25,000 and $75,000 (vs. 47 percent), but much better educated. However, since many more homeschool families have only one person working, their average salary is much higher than that of public school parents (precise numbers cannot be calculated from the survey's data). Nineteen percent of homeschool parents have completed high school or less, vs. 37 percent of non-homeschoolers. A higher proportion has completed some college (34 percent vs. 30 percent), holds a bachelor's degree (25 percent vs. 16 percent), or holds an advanced degree (22 percent vs. 17 percent).

Does homeschooling work? For the nation as a whole, we cannot say, because the one study which attempted to answer this question had a sample significantly different from the comprehensive sample in the U.S. Department of Education study (Rudner, 1999). The department's survey, for instance, found the ethnic makeup of homeschoolers to be 75 percent white, 10 percent black, and 9 percent Hispanic (and 6 percent "other"). Rudner's sample, by contrast, was 94 percent white. Rudner's sample was even better educated than homeschoolers generally: Thirty-eight percent of the fathers had a bachelor's degree and fully another 28 percent had an advanced degree. Forty-seven percent of the mothers had a bachelor's degree and another 10 percent had an advanced degree.

At one level, homeschooling *should* work, at least before the student encounters the more advanced mathematics, science, and literature courses in high school. Homeschooled students often learn in a setting where the pupil–teacher ratio is 1:1, in contrast to the 25:1 ratio in public elementary schools and the 31:1 ratio in public secondary schools. Homeschoolers would also find it easier to use a variety of learning resources on an "as needed" basis than public schoolers. It takes some effort to transport a class of students to a museum, but a parent can ferry a lone homeschooler easily to the museum, public library, theatre, dance company, and other learning environments. If a homeschooled student and his tutor decide that the time is right to seek information from the Internet, that can be done immediately, presuming the tutor has the requisite hardware, software, and research skills.

Some people worry that homeschooled children will not have the social skills that children learn in public schools. This, of course, is a double-edged sword, because publicly schooled children learn some things that parents would just as soon they did not. One wonders, though, about the ability of home-schooled children to work in groups, especially now, when teamwork is considered important for later workforce success. We have no data on these issues, though, one way or another.

The number of homeschoolers probably has a natural limit. Even if shown to be effective, not all parents will be willing or able to commit what *Time* has called a "galactic" amount of time to the process. Still, because the homeschooling parents are better educated than parents in general, one can worry that the homeschooling movement is drawing away some of those children who most easily benefit from education, however it is provided. And it also may be drawing away parents who could provide considerable resources to the public schools.

10

Commercialism in the Schools

Companies like to "brand" children—they want brand-name recognition of their products to be inculcated as early as possible. The traditional technique is advertising. Schools traditionally have been commerce-free zones. Not anymore. Although some critics allege that America spends huge sums on education, many of the public schools lack even basic necessities. Traditional methods of raising money—bake sales or selling magazine subscriptions—are increasingly giving way to more commercialized ventures. Now, large corporations (Pepsi and Nike, for example) pony up sums that make the amounts raised by bake sales look paltry. Companies may sponsor stadiums or equip sports teams. In turn, they ask for exclusive contracts to sell their products in the school, the prominent display of corporate logos, testimonials, or other favors.

The activities described in this section do not involve the direct provision of either education management or instruction, although they do involve in some instances the provision of instructional materials. They are discussed briefly here in the story of Mike Cameron and other related events. Although the companies discussed are not directly operating schools, that remains a possibility. After all, an observer asks at one point, "What's next? Nike Elementary?" In any case, the presence of corporations in these commercial activities is likely to be synergistic with future private management or other takeovers.

This section was actually written in 1998. It is included here because it illustrates the nature of commercialism. Readers interested in more complete, updated information may visit the website of Commercialism in Education Research Unit, a part of the Education Policy Studies Laboratory at Arizona State University, www.educationanalysis.com, or www.asu.edu/edu/epsl, directed by ASU professor Alex Molnar.

Mike Cameron Loses His Shirt: A Tale of Our Times

On March 20, 1998, 1,230 students of Greenbrier High School in Evans, Georgia, stood in the school parking lot. The band director had arranged the seniors neatly in a giant "C." He had arrayed the juniors into an "O", sophomores shaped a "K", and freshmen modeled an "E." As some dozen-plus Coca-Cola executives looked on (Coke is headquartered in Atlanta, 130 miles to the west), photographers on a crane filmed the moment of the entire high school spelling out "COKE." As the cameras rolled, senior Mike Cameron disrobed to reveal a shirt bearing the logo of . . . Pepsi.

Principal Gloria Hamilton hustled Mike to her office, gave him a dressing down, and suspended him, telling him it was because of his disrespect and for perhaps costing the school a bundle (in Mike's words). At the time, Coca-Cola was offering $10,000 to the high school that came up with the best plan for marketing Coke-sponsored promotional discount cards. A local bottler had chipped in another $500. Mike got off lightly—a one-day suspension. Normally, said principal Hamilton, such an offense draws a six-day punishment. A Pepsi spokesman called Cameron a "trendsetter with impeccable taste in clothes" and promised that Pepsi would keep him well supplied with shirts.

There were other opportunities for "branding" that day. Some Coca-Cola executives lectured on economics; others provided technical assistance to home-economics students who were baking a Coca-Cola cake; and still others helped chemistry students analyze Coke's sugar content. If other acts of insurrection occurred, though, they went unreported. This was "Coke in Education Day" at Greenbrier, which received no money from the company for inviting the executives.

Like the first-grader who was suspended for giving a girl a kiss, Mike Cameron had his 15 minutes of fame, as did Principal Hamilton and District Superintendent Tom Dohrmann. This brief celebrity was the only upbeat aspect of the story: Newspapers around the world indignantly panned the principal and Coke. "Has American society fallen so far that teens can be punished for not following the corporate party line?" asked the Baton Rouge, Louisiana, *Advocate*. "What exactly is a school doing sponsoring a 'Coke in Education Day' anyway?" queried the *Omaha World-Herald*, "Promoting a commercial product to its captive audience of young people?" The Raleigh, North Carolina, *News and Observer* invoked Hitleresque imagery: "Without even knowing it, der furious fuhrer was imparting to the students a civics lesson in obsequiousness and greed. It is disquieting to think that a kid could be kicked out of school for refusing to regard an impersonal multinational corporation with the same reverence that the principal does."

Carl Hiaasen, a novelist and contributor to the *Miami Herald*, also saw the civic consequences of the event, saying that the incident taught students

> . . . that money is more important than freedom of choice. It taught them that silence is more desirable than dissent, that conformity is better than being different, and it taught them that there is no shame in selling out, if the price is right. . . . Forget individuality. Dismiss from your mischievous young minds any thoughts of freely expressing yourself. And God forbid you should have a sense of humor, or let it show in front of your classmates. Because it's all about money, boys and girls. For 10 grand you can darn well dress right and button those lips. . . . (Hiassen, 1998)

This is a terrible lesson, said the *Chicago Tribune*. "Schools shouldn't be in the position of selling captive students to advertisers, whatever the excuse. They are entrusted with children's minds and they have no right to sell access to them. Even a quick glance at the sales pitches made by marketing companies peddling promotion ideas to schools makes it clear the whole point is to make money for the advertisers, not to help kids" (Mills, 1997).

In London, *The Independent* ran a story asking "What's next? Some large company coughing up money and then telling the school's social studies department, 'We don't want you saying anything bad about our labor or investment practices?'" (Usborne, 1998) In a similar vein, Hong Kong's most respected paper, the *South China Morning Post*, contended that "The reason why the saga [at Greenbrier High School] strikes such a chord among students and parents alike is because of the light it sheds on the steamroller tactics of soft drinks and other corporations to turn schools into nothing more than supermarkets where children can also take lessons" (Beck, 1998).

As if crass commercialism and greed weren't enough of an indictment, Bud Kennedy in the *Fort Worth Star-Telegram* cautioned that Coca-Cola was nutritionally deficient as well: "Colas and other caffeinated soft drinks cause anxiety, irritability, and loss of concentration." Hiaasen observed, more succinctly, that soft drinks also make people fat and cause their teeth to decay. Only time will tell if the Baton Rouge *Advocate* headline writer was being prescient—the headline over its Mike Cameron story read, "So what's next, Nike Elementary?"

The stories did not say whether Coke had an exclusive "pouring rights" contract with the district. Perhaps Evans (population 13,713) is too small a market to haggle over. But there are other, larger districts. Jefferson County, Colorado, needed a new football stadium. Lebanon, Ohio, had an outdoor track that was crumbling. Keller Independent School District, a fast-growing, high-performing system outside of Fort Worth, wanted to make sure its high test scores didn't go unnoticed. Thanks to these districts, you can buy only Pepsi in Jeffco's schools, and only Coke in Lebanon and Keller's cafeterias.

So far, the soft-drink companies—the ones most active in the field of devising exclusive contracts—haven't contacted school districts in East Harlem or East St. Louis. The districts that are getting the easy money are affluent and high-scoring systems. Of course, district-level contracts are small potatoes. Don Baird, CEO of School Properties, Inc., goes for whole states. Under his guidance, Reebok signed a contract with the California Scholastic Federation, paying them $2.8 million over six years. In return, all playoffs and title games in the Golden State are called the CIF/Reebok State Championships. There are 3,800 such events each year.

The *South China Morning Post* (Hong Kong) worried that schools could become supermarkets where students could also take lessons. It did not note that some of those lessons have become tainted with commercialism themselves:

- "Educational materials" from the National Livestock and Meat Board claim that eating meat makes people taller.
- Procter and Gamble's educational materials claim that clear-cut logging— the stripping of entire hillsides of trees—is good for the environment.
- A Kellogg's cereal guide intended to help children "choose healthful foods" recommends Rice Krispies Treats as the snack to choose most often.
- Materials from the Council for Wildlife Conservation and Education (affiliated with the National Shooting Sports Foundation, which has the same address as the National Rifle Association) contend that there are no endangered species.
- A chemistry experiment offered by Prego claims that proving its spaghetti sauce is thicker than Ragu's is a legitimate classroom activity.

The worry expressed by *The Independent* of London that corporations might try to direct a curriculum through direct assertions underestimates corporate America's ability to infiltrate the curriculum through more subtle means. The Consumer Union's (CU) analysis of sponsored materials found that many of them were commercial, incomplete, biased, and error-prone. CU found a number of materials that were little more than advertisements for the sponsoring company or organization. Actual advertisements on school property are, in fact, becoming more and more common.

For $1,000, a company can put its name on a two-by-five sign in a Grapevine, Texas, gym. If the company can spring for $15,000, it gets recognition on the school's voice-mail system and rights to advertising space on a school roof seen by people flying into Dallas–Forth Worth International Airport. School buses in Colorado Springs carry a painting of the school mascot . . . and the Burger King logo. Thirty-three banners, for everything from car dealers to doctors hang on the east wall of Plant High School in Hillsborough, Florida (Cristodero, 1998).

In 1989 Steve Shulman and Michael Yanoff were twenty-five years old and hoping to earn enough money to buy carphones with their marketing idea: Most schools require students to put covers on textbooks to protect them, so why not sell advertising space on those covers? By 1994, they were an eight-person organization with sales of $4 million. It's a win-win situation, Schulman told *Chicago*

Tribune reporter, Steve Mills. "Advertisers get ads in the schools, and kids get a book cover that's trendy and free" (Mills, 1997).

"Tooned-In," produced by School Marketing Partners of San Juan Capistrano, California, charges $10,000 to $478,000 per month for corporations wishing to have their message or coupons on school menus. "Tooned-In" menus were reaching 6 million K–6 students by January 1998 (*Consumer Reports*, 1997). We haven't yet reached the point of "Nike Elementary" but it might not be far in the future: Currently, corporations are taking over the schools to manage them, and some provide a curriculum as well. The Edison Schools or Mosaica Education can do it better, they say—and for less.

More important, or at least more widespread, are company demands for tax breaks as a condition of relocating to, or remaining in, a community. In 1991, businesses gave Florida schools $32 million. They extracted $500 million from the state treasury in tax breaks. A number of people around Tuscaloosa who told me that to get the Mercedes factory, state officials "gave away the farm" (Molnar, 1996). One researcher estimates that tax breaks remove $1 billion out of the Wisconsin treasury each year. And another has calculated that the total contributions of business and industry to schools would run them for two hours (Taylor, 1992).

Few states have realized how the partnerships have been giving on the one hand and taking on the other. A recent analysis in Ohio shows how dire the situation is. In 1986, Ohio, of nine institutions with property exempt from property taxes, business was ninth, well below the eighth place federal government. It had exemptions on only about one-fifth as much property as the number-one ranked institution, school boards. By 2000, business ranked second, and if the trend has continued, by now business will be ranked number one. "Our state has been cannibalizing itself," said state senator Eric Fingerhut (Oplinger and Willard, 2002). Senator Howard Metzenbaum saw the situation quite clearly:

> In speech after speech, it is our corporate CEOs who state that an educated, literate work force is the key to American competitiveness. They pontificate on the importance of education. They point out their magnanimous corporate contributions to education in one breath, and then they pull the tax base out from under local schools in the next. Businesses criticize the jobs our schools are doing and then proceed to nail down every tax break they can get, further eroding the schools' ability to do the job. (Taylor, 1992)

Since 1991, there has been increasing activity in a new form of corporate extortion from states: wages rebates. As states have come increasingly to compete for companies, companies have become increasingly skilled at getting some of their money back. Whirlpool built a stove factory in Tulsa, Oklahoma, in 1996 and for ten years will get back 4.5 cents for every dollar it pays in wages. In some states, wage rebate is the most expensive corporate lure; in others, it is the fasting growing.

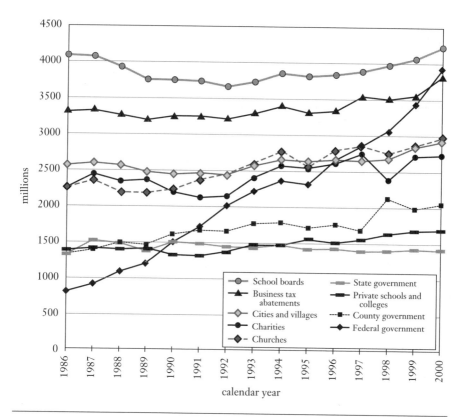

FIGURE 10.1 *Ohio Property Exempt from Real Estate Taxes—Adjusted for Inflation*
Reprinted by permission of the *Akron Beacon Journal.*

Most business complaints about schools and their graduates are not well-founded in the first place, but it appears that businessmen do not see the connection between taking money away from schools and school quality. The starvation of schools would not be permitted were it not for the widespread belief in the myth that "money doesn't matter." Common sense says money does matter. A large number of studies exist to prove that money matters, but those who write in business publications choose to cite only the ideologically driven studies of Eric Hanushek at the University of Rochester. Not only have other studies found that money does matter, but other analyses of Hanushek's own data have shown that his data contradict his rhetoric (these studies are reviewed in Chapter 3).

Sponsored materials, sponsored programs, exclusive contracts, privatization, electronic marketing, private vouchers . . . Mike Cameron, you don't know the half of it.

Conclusion

At the September 2000 meeting of the Education Leaders Council, a group consisting of various conservative chief state school officers, politicians, and reformers, Frank Brogan, lieutenant governor of Florida, said "Everyone wants the best for children"—they just differ on what "the best" means. The descriptions of some of the experiments in education reform in the previous pages indicate that Brogan's statement is not always true.

Companies that charge parents $1.95 a mile for transportation are not concerned with "the best." Companies that want to "brand" children are not concerned with "the best." Companies that tell teachers "maybe our model is not for you" are not concerned with "the best." Concerns about the bottom line, at the least, distract companies from paying full attention to curriculum and instruction.

Beyond that, there is surprisingly little innovation from the innovators. Robert Holland, former op-ed editor for the *Richmond Times-Dispatch*, penned a book titled *Not With My Child, You Don't* (Holland, 1995). Although Holland aimed his barbs specifically at outcomes-based education, his attitude probably reflects the general feeling about experimentation. As Rothstein and colleagues observed, the world after school is uncertain (Rothstein, Carnoy, and Benveniste, 1999). A school that deviates too much from what people think a school should be runs the risk of having parents worry that they might injure their children's future by sending them there.

It will be recalled that this kind of anxiety was precisely what motivated the Progressive Education Association to conduct the Eight Year Study. They collected data to prove to parents and college admissions officers that their "break-the-mold" schools provided students with an education superior to the normal high school experience.

As the 2001–2002 school year opened, the privatizers seemed to be losing interest and steam: "Just over a year ago, anyone armed with an idea for improving education and a business plan could get a lot of money from venture capitalists, or so it seemed in the supercharged economy. Now, that well has all but dried up" (Walsh 2000b). Available venture capital rose from $525 million in the third quarter of 1999 to a peak of just over $1 billion in the first quarter of 2000. It then dropped each consecutive quarter, hitting a low of less than one-quarter of its high, $247 million, in the second quarter of 2001. And that was before the terrorist attacks of September 11.

It might be just as well. Public schools provide public forums for discussing the critical issues of how we prepare our children for the future. Many of the experiments now underway remove parents from that discussion and reconvene in corporate boardrooms. This is not a good path for a democracy to take. Among the freedoms that the attacks of September 11 reminded us is how open a society we have and how precious that openness is. It would be tragic to lose that openness in the realm of education.

References

Aikin, Wilfred. (1942). *The Story of the Eight-Year Study.* New York: Harper and Brothers.

Alexander, Karl L., Entwistle, Doris R., and Olson, Linda S. (2001, Summer). "Schools Achievement and Inequality: A Seasonal Perspective." *Educational Evaluation and Policy Analysis,* pp. 171–191.

Ambrose, Eileen. (2000). "Sylvan Rethinks Venture." *Baltimore Sun,* March 31, p. 1C.

American School Boards Journal (1992). "Good News: Our 9-Year-Olds Read Well; Bad News: Our 14-Year-Olds Don't." November.

Archer, Jeff. (1999a). "Two Cleveland Voucher Schools Plan Rebirth With Charter Schools." *Education Week,* July 14, p. 20.

———. (1999b). "Policies of Cleveland Voucher Program Faulted." *Education Week,* January 20, p. 3.

Arizona Republic. (2000). "2 TesseracT Execs Quit Troubled Firm." February 3, p. D3.

Arizona Tribune. (1998). "Guinea Kids." August 25, p. A12.

———. (1998). "Wake Up, Keegan!" August 27, p. A14.

Arsen, David, Plank, David, and Sykes, Gary. (1999). *School Choice Policies in Michigan: The Rules Matter.* East Lansing: Michigan State University

Ascher, Carol, Fruchter, Norm, and Berne, Robert. (1996). *Hard Lessons: Public Schools and Privatization.* New York: Twentieth Century Fund (now Century Fund).

Ashworth, Jon. (1999). "Junk-Bond King Milken Took Over the Baton." *The Times* (London), July 24, Business Section.

Associated Press. (2001a). "School Voucher Judge Ousted." *Florida Times-Union,* September 5, 2001.

———. (2001b). "Japan Downgrades Assessment of Its Economy." August 11.

———. (2000). "Texas Charter School Moratorium Urged." *Washington Post,* December 29, p. A6.

Bach, Lisa Kim. (2002). "Edison Misses Payment of Philanthropic Funds." May 16.

Bach, Matt. (2001). "Promises Made, Promises Kept? Edison 'Dream' Schools Have Yet to Pay Off." *Flint Journal,* December 2, p. 1.

———. (2001). "Promises Made, Promises Kept? Down to Business—Critics Say Edison's Focus on Bottom Line Hurts Students." *Flint Journal,* December 3, p. 1.

———. (2001). "Edison Parent Satisfaction." *Flint Journal,* December 4, p. 1.

Baker, Keith. (1991). "Yes, Throw Money at the Schools." *Phi Delta Kappan,* April, pp. 628–630.

Baker, Rebecca. (2002). "Connecticut's Wintergreen Will Kick Out For-profit Operator." *New Haven Register,* May 31.

Banchero, Stephanie, and Ahmed-Ullah, Noreen. (2002). "Law Could Worsen Teacher Shortage." *Chicago Tribune,* March 26, p. 1

Barber, Benjamin R. (1995). "Workshops of Our Democracy." *Education Week*, April 19, p. 34.

Barry, John S., and Hederman, Rea S. (2000). *Report Card on American Education: A State-by-State Analysis, 1976–1999*. Washington, DC: American Legislative Exchange Council.

Beaton, Albert E., Mulles, Ina V.S., Martin, Michael O., Gonzalez, Eugenio J., Kelly, Dana L., and Smith, Therese. (1996a). *Mathematics Achievement in the Middle School Years*. Chestnut Hill, MA: Boston College.

———. (1996b). *Science Achievement in the Middle School Years*. Chestnut Hill, MA: Boston College.

Beck, Simon. (1998). "Enola Joke Hard to Swallow." *South China Morning Post*, March 29, America Section, p. 11.

Becker, Henry J., Nakagawa, K., and Corwin, R. G. (1996). "Parent Involvement Contracts in California's Charter Schools: Strategy for Improvement or Method of Exclusion?" *Teachers College Record*, 98(3), pp. 511–536.

Behr, Peter. (2001). "N.Y. Bank Sues over Enron Stock Trades." *Washington Post*, December 6, p. E1.

Bennett, William J. (2000a). "The State, and Future of American Education." Speech delivered to the Heritage Foundation, March 13. Accessible at www.heritage.org/leadership/lectures/bennett.html.

———. (2000b). "Critical Courses." *Washington Post*, September 4, p. A25.

———. (1993). *Report Card on American Education*. Washington, DC: American Legislative Exchange Council.

———, Finn, Chester E. Jr., and Cribb, John T. E. (1999). *The Educated Child*. New York: Free Press.

Berliner, David C., and Biddle, Bruce J. (1995). *The Manufactured Crisis*. Reading, MA: Addison-Wesley Longman.

Berry, John M. (2002). "Greenspan Declares an Expansion." *Washington Post*, March 8, p. E1.

Bestor, Arthur. (1993). *Educational Wastelands: The Retreat from Learning in Public Schools*. Champaign: University of Illinois Press.

Bettinger, Eric. (1998). *The Effect of Charter Schools on Charter Students and Public Schools*. New York: National Center for the Study of Privatization in Education, Teachers College Occasional paper #4.

Black, Edwin. (2001). *IBM and the Holocaust: The Strategic Alliance between Nazi Germany and America's Most Powerful Corporation*. New York: Crown.

Blum, Justin. (2000). "Charter Schools Break D.C. Rules." *Washington Post*, May 3, p. A1.

Blustein, Paul. (2001). "Japan Resists IMF Look at Banks." *New York Times*, September 1, p. E1.

Board of Education of the City of New York. (2000). Request for Proposal, Serial No. RFP #1B434.

Bowie, Liz. (2002). "City Board Quashed Expansion of Edison." *Baltimore Sun*, June 12.

Boyer, Ernest. (1995). *The Basic School*. San Francisco: Jossey-Bass.

Bracey, Gerald W. (2002). "What Students Do in the Summer." *Phi Delta Kappan*, March, pp. 497–498.

———. (2001). "The Eleventh Bracey Report on the Condition of Public Education." *Phi Delta Kappan*, October, pp. 157–169.

———. (2000a). *Bail Me Out: Handling Difficult Data and Tough Questions about Public Schools*. Thousand Oaks, CA: Corwin Press.

———. (2000b). "The TIMSS Final Year Study and Report: A Critique." *Educational Researcher,* May, pp. 4–10.

———. (1998a). " 'TIMSS,' " Rhymes With 'Dims' As in Witted." *Phi Delta Kappan,* May, pp. 686–687.

———. (1998b). "Tinkering with TIMSS." *Phi Delta Kappan,* September, pp. 32–45.

———. (1997a). "What Happened to America's Public Schools? Not What You May Think." *American Heritage,* November, pp. 39–52.

———. (1997b). *Setting the Record Straight: Responses to Misconceptions about Public Education in the United States.* Alexandria, VA: Association for Supervision and Curriculum Development.

———. (1996a). "The Sixth Bracey Report on the Condition of Public Education." *Phi Delta Kappan,* October, pp. 127–138.

———. (1996b). *The Condition of Public Education in Ohio.* Columbus: Ohio School Funding Cooperative (Cooperative members include the Alliance for Adequate School Funding, Buckeye Association of School Administrators, Ohio Coalition for Equity and Adequacy of School Funding, and the Ohio School Boards Association).

———. (1995a). *Final Exam: A Study of the Perpetual Scrutiny of American Education.* Bloomington, IN: Technos Press.

———. (1995b). "U.S. Students: Better Than Ever." *Washington Post,* December 22, p. A19.

———. (1993). "Filet of School Reform, Sauce Diable." *Education Week,* June 16, p. 40.

———. (1992). "Falling SATs and the Transformation of Consciousness." *Technos Quarterly,* Fall, pp. 22–29.

Brady, Diane. (1999). "Chris Whittle's New IPO Deserves A D–." *Business Week,* September 6, p. 40.

Brennan, Deborah. (2000a). "A Lesson in Hard Knocks as Charter School Closes." *Los Angeles Times,* June 25.

———. (2000b). Personal communication, October 2000.

Brimelow, Peter. (2000). "Private School Surge." *Forbes,* November 27, p. 104.

Bronner, Ethan. (1998). "U.S. Trails World in Math and Science." *New York Times,* February 25, p. 1.

Budde, Ray. (1996). *Strengthen School-Based Management by Chartering All Schools.* Andover, MA: The Regional Laboratory for Educational Improvement of the Northeast and Islands.

———. (1987). *Education by Charter within a Ten-Year Plan.* Andover, MA: The Regional Laboratory for Educational Improvement of the Northeast and Islands.

Bulkley, Katrina. (2000). "The Accountability Bind." Paper presented at the annual convention of the American Educational Research Association, New Orleans, April.

Bureau of Labor Statistics. (2000). *Occupational Outlook Handbook.* Washington, DC: Bureau of Labor Statistics.

Business Roundtable. (2001). *Assessing and Addressing the "Testing Backlash."* Washington, DC: Business Roundtable.

Business Wire, May 31, 2000.

Byron, Christopher. (2000). "Whittle and Benno Schmidt Try Another I.P.O. Fast One." *New York Observer,* October 13, 2000.

Callahan, Raymond. (1962). *Education and the Cult of Efficiency.* Chicago: University of Chicago Press.

Campanile, Carl. (2001). "Education Board Concedes Edison Mess." *New York Post,* March 28.

Carson, C. C., Huelskamp, R. M., and Woodall, T. D. (1993). "Perspectives on Education in America." *Journal of Educational Research*, May/June, pp. 259–310.

———. (1990). "Perspectives on Education in America." Unpublished monograph, Sandia National Laboratories, Albuquerque, New Mexico.

Carter, Andrew. (1999). "The Wrath of Cooper." *Minneapolis/St. Paul City Pages*, December 8.

Center on Education Policy. (1999). "Lessons from Other Countries about Private School Aid." Washington, DC: Center on Education Policy.

Cerf, Chistopher, and Navasky, Victor. (1998). *The Experts Speak: The Definitive Compendium of Authoritative Misinformation.* NY: Villard.

Chandler, Clay. (2001). "Profits Fall Sharply at Banks in Japan." *Washington Post*, November 27, p. E1.

———, and Kashiwagi, Akiko. (2001). "Leader Proposes Big Budget Cuts." *Washington Post*, August 11, p. E1.

Chea, Terence. (2000). "Providian Agrees to Restitution and Fine." *Washington Post*, June 29, p. E1.

Chomsky, Noam. (2000). Assaulting Solidarity—Privatizing Solidarity. www.zmag.org/zsustainers/zdaily/2000_05/12Chomsky.htm.

Chubb, John, and Moe, Terry. (1990). *Politics, Choice, and America's Schools.* Washington, DC: The Brookings Institute.

Ciotti, Paul. (1998). *Money and School Performance.* Washington, DC: Cato Institute.

Class Size Consortium. (2000). Class Size Reduction in California: The 1998–99 Evaluation Findings. Accessible at www.classize.org.

———. (1999). Class Size Reduction in California: Early Evaluation Findings, 1996–1998. Accessible at www.classize.org.

Christodero, Damian. (1998). "Schools Find Aid in Ads, Sponsorships." *St. Petersburg Times*, p. C1.

Clinton, William, and Gore, Albert. (1995). Letter to the editor, *USA Today*, October 11.

Cloud, John, and Morse, Jodie. (2001). "Home Sweet School." *Time*, August 27.

Cobb, Casey D. (2000). *Charter Schools as Schools of Choice: Ethnic and Racial Separation in Arizona.* Unpublished manuscript.

———. (1998). *Ethnic Separation in Arizona Charter Schools.* Unpublished doctoral dissertation, College of Education, Arizona State University.

———, and Glass, Gene V. (1999). "Ethnic Segregation in Arizona Charter Schools." *Education Policy Analysis Archives*, Vol 7, No. 1. Accessible at http://olam.ed.asu.edu/v7n1.

———, Glass, Gene V., and Crockett, Carol. (2000). "The U.S. Charter School Movement and Ethnic Segregation." Paper presented at the annual meeting of the American Educational Research Association, New Orleans, April.

Coeyman, Marjorie. (2000). "Design Is Key When it Comes to Vouchers." *Christian Science Monitor*, December 12, p. A13.

Cohn, Edward. (2000). "The Resurrection of Michael Milken." *The American Prospect*, March 13.

Colvin, Richard. (2001). "A Renewed Fight over Firm's Role in School." *Los Angeles Times*, October 28.

Cookson, Peter. (1994). *School Choice: The Struggle for the Soul of American Education.* New Haven, CT: Yale University Press.

Consumer Reports. (1997). "School Lunch Special: Tuna Melt with a Side of Coupons." December.

Cooper, Claire. (2001). "Lawsuit Offers Litany of School Woes: Depositions from Pupils and Teachers Paint a Grim Picture." *Sacramento Bee,* September 21.

Cooper, Kenneth J. (2000). "Appeals Court Rejects Vouchers in Cleveland As Unconstitutional." *Washington Post,* December 12, p. A3.

Cremin, Lawrence. (1989). *Popular Education and Its Discontents.* New York: Harper & Row.

Creno, Glen. (2000). "TesseracT Group Files Chapter 11." *Arizona Republic,* October 10, p. D1.

Cubberley, Elwood P. (1919). *Public School Administration in the United States.* Boston: Houghton Mifflin.

Curti, Merle. (1961). *The Social Ideas of American Educators.* Patterson, NJ: Littlefield, Adams, and Co.

D'Amico, Ronald. (1984). "Does Employment during School Impair Academic Progress?" *Sociology of Education,* 57(3), pp. 152–164.

Davies, Dave. (2002). "Reporters Ejected from School Reform Meeting." *Philadelphia Daily News,* January 4.

Dean, Mensah M. (2001). "Hostile Takeover Is Averted." *Philadelphia Daily News,* November 21,

———, and Davies, Dave. (2001). "Goldsmith Quits amid Day of School Turmoil." *Philadelphia Daily News,* December 14.

Deloitte and Touche, LLP. (1997). "Outside Audit of the Cleveland Voucher Program." Cleveland: Deloitte and Touche, June 30.

Digest of Education Statistics. (1997). Table 82, p. 89.

Doclar, Mary. (2000). "The Edison Enigma: School Management Company Praised, Panned in Sherman." *Fort Worth Star-Telegram,* May 1, p. A1.

Donlon, Thomas F., and Angoff, William H. (1971). "The Scholastic Aptitude Test." In William H. Angoff (Ed.), *The College Board Admissions Testing Program: A Technical Report on Research and Development Activities Relating to the Scholastic Aptitude Test and Achievement Tests.* New York: The College Entrance Examination Board.

Donohue, Kim. (1998). "Beware the Charter Threat." *NEA Today,* September, p. 63.

Doyle, Denis (2002a). "AYP, Once More Once." The Doyle Report, June 13. Accessible at www.thedoylereport.com/cyber_chair.

———. (2002b). "AYP Revealed, Now What?" The Doyle Report, June 4. Accessible at www.thedoylereport.com/cyber_chair.

———. (1996). "Education." In *Issues 96: The Candidate's Briefing Book.* Washington, DC: The Heritage Foundation, pp. 261–295.

Duffy, Cathy. (2000). "Problems with the California Voucher Initiative, Proposition 38." Accessible at www.grovepublishing.com.

Eberts, Randall W., and Hollenback, Kevin M. (2001). *An Examination of Student Achievement in Michigan Charter Schools.* Kalamazoo, MI: W.E. Upjohn Institute for Employment Research.

Edison Schools, Incorporated. (2001). *Fourth Annual Report on School Performance.* New York: Edison Schools, Inc.

———. (2000). *Third Annual Report on School Performance.* New York: Edison Schools, Inc.

———. (1999). *Second Annual Report on School Performance.* New York: Edison Schools, Inc.

———. (1998). *First Annual Report on School Performance.* New York: Edison Schools, Inc.

Education Week. (1993). "Charting a Course to Reform: The Next Ten Years." Unsigned editorial essay, February 10.

Ehrenreich, Barbara. (2001). *Nickel and Dimed: On (Not) Getting By in America.* New York: Metropolitan Books.

Eichenwald, Kurt. (2001). "Why Not to Stonewall in the Midst of a Scandal." *New York Times,* July 4, p. C5.

Elam, Stanley. (1958). "The School Behind the Masters of the Moon." *Phi Delta Kappan,* September 1969, pp. 2–7.

Elley, Warwick P. (1992). *How in the World Do Students Read?* Hamburg: International Association for the Evaluation of Educational Achievement. Available in the United States through the International Reading Association.

Eskenazi, Stuart. (1999). "Learning Curves." *Houston Press,* July 22–28. Accessible at www.houstonpress.com/issues/1999-07-22/feature.html.

Estrin, Robin. (1996). "Researchers: Milwaukee School Choice Program Boosting Students' Scores." Associated Press wire story, August 14.

Feldman, Amy. (1998). "Milken's New Empire." *New York Daily News,* March 23, p. C4.

Ferguson, Ronald. (1991). "Paying for Public Education: New Evidence on How and Why Money Matters." *Harvard Journal on Legislation,* 28:2, pp. 465–498.

Finn, Chester E., Manno, Bruno V., and Vanourek, Greg. (2000). "Accountability through Transparency." *Education Week,* April 26, p. 42.

Finn, Chester E. (1998). "Why America Has the World's Dimmest Bright Kids." *Wall Street Journal,* February 25, p. A22.

———, Bierlein, Louann, and Manno, Bruno V. (1996). "Charter Schools in Action: A First Look." Indianapolis: Hudson Institute.

Finn, Jeremy, D. (1999). "Tennessee's Class Size Study: Findings, Implications, Misconceptions." *Educational Evaluation and Policy Analysis,* Summer, pp. 97–109.

———, and Achilles, Charles N. (1990). "Answers and Questions about Class Size: A State Experiment." *American Educational Research Journal,* Winter, pp. 557–577.

Finnegan, William. (1999). *Cold New World: Growing Up in a Harder Country.* New York: Modern Library.

Flannery, Pat. (2001). "AIMS Debate Brings Progress." *Arizona Republic,* September 2, p. 1.

Fleischman, Sandra. (2000). "U.S. Conducting 240 Probes of Possible Mortgage Fraud." *Washington Post,* July 1, p. E1.

Fletcher, Michael A. (2000). "Education Nominee Sails through His Senate Test." *Washington Post,* January 11, p. A4.

Fox, Jonathan. (2000). "No Class." *Dallas Observer Online,* January 27. Available at www.dallasobserver.com/issues/2000-01-27/feature.html.

Friedman, Milton, and Friedman, Rose D. (2000). "Letter from Milton and Rose D. Friedman." Accessible at www.friedmanfoundation.org/about_milton_rose.html.

Friedman, Milton. (1962). *Capitalism and Freedom.* Chicago: University of Chicago Press.

———. (2001). Personal communication, January.

Funk, Josh. (2002a). "6–0 Vote Gives Board Control of Two Edison Schools." *Wichita Eagle,* January 29.

———. (2002b). "Three Former Teachers Say They Told the Company about Testing Irregularities, but School Officials Say That Isn't So." *Wichita Eagle,* February 3.

Gallagher, James J. (2000). "Education, Alone, Is a Weak Treatment." *Education Week*, July 8, p. 60.

Gelberg, Denise. (1997). *The "Business" of Reforming American Schools.* Albany: State University of New York Press.

Gerstner, Louis V. (2000). "World-Class Tests." *Washington Post*, September 25, p. A21.

———. (1998). Speech to the "Education Summit," Armonk, NY. Accessible at www. achieve.org.

———. (1994). "Our Schools Are Failing: Do We Care?" *New York Times*, May 27, p. A27.

———, and Thompson, Tommy G. (2000). "The Problem Isn't the Kids." *New York Times*, December 8.

Gill, Brian P., Timpane, Michael, Ross, Karen E., and Brewer, Dominic J. (2001) *Rhetoric vs. Reality: What We Know and What We Need to Know about Vouchers and Charter Schools.* Washington, DC: The RAND Corporation.

Gladden, R. (1998). "The Small School Movement: A Review of the Literature." In Michelle Fine and James Somerville (Eds.), *Small Schools, Big Imaginations: A Creative Look at Urban Public Schools.* (1998). Chicago: Cross City Campaign for Urban School Reform.

Glaser, Robert. (1987). A Review of the Report by a Committee of the National Academy of Education. In Lamar Alexander and H. Thomas James (Eds.), *The Nation's Report Card: Improving the Assessment of Student Achievement.* Cambridge, MA: National Academy of Education.

Godwin, R. Kenneth, Kemerer, Frank R., and Martinez, Valerie J. (1997). *Final Report: San Antonio School Choice Research Project.* Denton, Texas: Center for the Study of School Reform, School of Education, University of North Texas.

Gonderinger, Lisa. (2000). "Parents Fret about TesseracT's Future" *Arizona Republic*, March 1, p. A10.

Goodnough, Abby. (2001). "Scope of Loss for Privatizing of Schools Stuns Officials." *New York Times*, April 3.

———. (2000). Plan to Privatize 5 Schools Brings Confusion on All Sides. *New York Times*, December 22.

Goodstein, Laurie. (2002). "In States, Hurdles Loom." *New York Times*, June 30, Section 4, p. 3.

Gottfredson, Denise. (1985a). "Youth Employment, Crime, and Schooling: A Longitudinal Study of a National Sample." *Developmental Psychology*, 21, pp. 419–432.

———. (1985b). *School Size and School Disorder.* Baltimore: Center for the Social Organization of Schools, Johns Hopkins University.

Greenberg, Alan. (2001). "Edison's Risk Factors." *Philadelphia Business Journal*, November 23.

Greene, Jay P., Peterson, Paul E., and Du, Jiangtao. (1996). "The Effectiveness of School Choice: The Milwaukee Experiment." Available at www.ksg.harvard.edu/pepg.

———, and Peterson, Paul E. (1996). "Choice Data Rescued from Bad Science." *Wall Street Journal*, August 14, A14.

Hanushek, Eric A. (1999). "Some Findings from an Independent Investigation of the Tennessee Class Size Experiment." *Educational Evaluation and Policy Analysis*, Summer, pp. 143–164.

———. (1997). "Assessing the Effects of School Resources on Student Performance: An Update." *Educational Evaluation and Policy Analysis*, Summer, pp. 141–164.

———. (1989). "The Differential Impact of School Expenditures on School Performance." *Educational Researcher,* April, pp. 45–51.

Hardy, Dan. (2002). "Poor Marks for Edison by Chester-Upland." *Philadelphia Inquirer,* May 15.

Henig, Jeffrey. (1997). "School Choice in Milwaukee: The Evidence for Gains. A Response to Peterson." Address at the Cato Institute, Washington, DC, February.

———. (1994). *Rethinking School Choice: Limits to the Market Metaphor.* Princeton, NJ: Princeton University Press.

Hentoff, Nat. (1999). "Church-State Tangle." *Washington Post,* December 18, p. A27.

Hewitt, Jennifer. (2000). "'Junk' Bond Sinner on a Mission of Redemption." *Sydney Morning Herald,* September 21.

Hiassen, Carl. (1998). "Be True to Your School . . . and Its Cola." *Miami Herald,* March 31, p. A4.

Hill, Paul. (1995). *Reinventing Public Education.* Santa Monica, CA: RAND Corporation.

Hobbs, Tawnell D. (2002). "Edison Fails to Outdo DISD Schools." *Dallas Morning News,* June 21, p. A1.

Holland, Robert. (1995). *Not With My Child, You Don't: A Citizen's Guide to Eradicating Outcomes-Based Education and Restoring Education.* Richmond, VA: Citizens Projects Publishing.

Holt, John C. (1964). *How Children Fail.* (Reprint 1987). New York: Pitman.

———. (1967). *How Children Learn.* (Reprint 1987). New York: Pitman.

———. (1981). *Teach Your Own.* New York: Delacorte Press.

Horn, Jerry, and Miron, Gary. (2000). *An Evaluation of the Michigan Charter School Initiative: Performance, Accountability, and Impact.* Kalamazoo: The Evaluation Center, Western Michigan University.

———. (1999). *Evaluation of the Michigan Public School Initiative, Final Report.* Kalamazoo: The Evaluation Center, Western Michigan University.

Howell, William G., Wolf, Patrick J., Peterson, Paul E., and Campbell, David E. (2000). "Test-score Effects of School Vouchers in Dayton, Ohio, New York City, and Washington, D.C.: Evidence from Randomized Field Trials." Accessible at http://data. fas.harvard.edu/pepg.

Illich, Ivan. (1971). *Deschooling Society.* New York: Harper and Row.

Irwin, Neil. (2000). "E-Schooling Firm Set to Open." *Washington Post,* December 28, p. E1.

Johnson, Eugene G. (1998). *Linking the National Assessment of Educational Progress (NAEP) and the Third International Mathematics and Science Study (TIMSS).* Washington, DC: Office of Educational Research and Improvement, U.S. Department of Education. Report No. NCES 98-500.

Judy, Stephen J., and D'Amico, Carol. (1998). *Workforce 2020.* Indianapolis, IN: The Hudson Institute.

Kahlenberg, Richard. (2001). *All Together Now: Creating Middle-Class Schools through Public School Choice.* Washington, DC: Brookings Institution Press.

Kantrowitz, Barbara, and Wingert, Pat. (1992). "An 'F' in World Competition." *Newsweek,* February 17, p. 57.

Kashiwagi, Akiko. (2001). "Moody's Downgrades Japan's Bond Rating." *Washington Post,* December 5, p. E2.

Khouri, Nick, Kleine, Robert, White, Richard, and Cummings, Laurie. (1999). *Michigan's Charter School Initiative: From Theory to Practice.* Lansing, MI: Public Sector Consultants Inc., and MAXIMUS, Inc.

Kinsley, Michael. (2002). "A Wife's Tale." *Washington Post,* March 18, p. A17.

Knight, Edgar. (1952). *Fifty Years of American Education, 1900–1950.* New York: Ronald Press.

Kolderie, Ted. (1995). *The Charter Idea: Update and Prospects, Fall, 1995, Public Services Redesign Project.* St. Paul, MN: Center for Policy Studies.

Kronholz, June. (1998). "A Poor School District in Texas Is Learning to Cope in a Test Tube." *Wall Street Journal,* September 11, p. A1.

Kozol, Jonathan. (1991). *Savage Inequalities.* New York: Crown.

Krueger, Alan B. (2000). "Economic Considerations and Class Size." Working paper 447, Industrial Relations Section, Princeton University. Accessible at www.irs.princeton. edu/pubs/working_papers.html.

———, and Whitmore, Diane M. (1999). "The Effect of Attending a Small Class in the Early Grades on College-Test Taking and Middle School Test Results: Evidence from Project STAR." Accessible at www.irs.princeton.edu/pubs/working_ papers.html.

———. (1998). "Experimental Estimates of Education Production Functions." *Quarterly Journal of Economics,* 114:2, pp. 497–532.

Labaton, Stephen. (2000). "Generic Drug Maker Agrees to Settlement in Price Fixing Case." *New York Times,* July 13.

Le, Tung. (2001). Director of Assessment, Edison Schools, Inc., personal communication, January 12.

Lee, Jaekyung. (2002). "Racial and Ethnic Achievement Gap Trends: Reversing the Progress Toward Equity?" *Educational Researcher,* January/February, pp. 3–12.

Legislative Office of Education Oversight. (2001). *Community Schools in Ohio: Second-Year Implementation Report, Volume 1: Policy Issues.* Columbus, OH: Legislative Office of Education Oversight.

———. (2000). *Community Schools in Ohio: First-Year Implementation Report.* Columbus, OH: Legislative Office of Education Oversight.

Leovy, Jill. (2000). "School Voucher Program Teaches Hard Lessons." *Los Angeles Times,* October 9.

Life. (1958). "Crisis in Education." March 24, pp. 26–35.

Lockwood, Robert, and McLean, James. (1993). "Educational Funding and Students Achievement." Paper presented at the Mid-South Educational Research Association annual conference, November.

MacInnes, Gordon. (2000). "Kids Who Pick the Wrong Parents and Other Victims of Voucher Schemes." Washington, DC: Century Fund.

Manning, Anita. (1992). "U.S. Kids Near Top of Class in Reading." *USA Today,* September 29, p. A1.

Manno, Bruno V. (1999). "Accountability: The Key to Charter Renewal." Washington, DC: Center for Educational Reform. Accessible at http://edreform.com/pub/ accountability.guide.htm.

Maraghy, Mary. (1999). "Loaded up for Learning." *Florida Times-Union,* December 16, p. A1.

Massey, Joanna. (2000). "Exodus Threatens Catholic Schools." *SouthCoast (MA) Today,* September 17, p. 104.

Mathews, Jay. (2001). "Schools Trying New Treatments for Senioritis." *Washington Post,* February 19, p. B1.

——. (2000). "Group Pushes for Vouchers." *Washington Post,* December 9, p. A26.

Mattern, Hal. (2000a). "TesseracT Crisis Watched as Bellwether for Private Schools." *Arizona Republic,* February 20, p. A1.

——. (2000b). "TesseracT Nears $50 Million Deficit Mark." *Arizona Republic,* May 23, p. D1.

——. (2000c). "Schools Changing Hands, TesseracT Trying to Stop Bleeding." *Arizona Republic,* May 24, p. D1.

Maxwell, William. (1914). "On a Certain Arrogance in Educational Theorists." *Educational Review,* February, pp. 175–176.

McCarthy, Martha. (2000). "What Is the Verdict on School Vouchers?" *Phi Delta Kappan,* March, Vol. 81, No. 5, pp. 371–378.

McEwan, Patrick J. (2000). "The Effectiveness of Public, Catholic, and Non-Religious Private Schools in Chile's Voucher System." *Education Economics,* 2001, 9(2) pp. 103–128.

——, and Carnoy, Martin. (2000a). "The Effectiveness and Efficiency of Private Schools in Chile's Voucher System." *Educational Evaluation and Policy Analysis,* Fall, pp. 213–239.

——. (2000b). "Choice between Private and Public Schools in a Voucher System: Evidence from Chile." Unpublished paper, Stanford University.

——. (1999). "The Impact of Competition on Public School Quality: Longitudinal Evidence from Chile's Voucher System." Unpublished paper, Stanford University.

McGovern, Myra. (2000). Public Information Specialist, National Association of Independent Schools, personal communication, October 4.

McKnight, Curtis C., Crosswhite, F. Joe, Dossey, John A., Kifer, Edward, Swafford, Jane O., Travers, Kenneth J., and Cooney, Thomas C. (1987). *The Underachieving Curriculum: Assessing U.S. Mathematics from an International Perspective.* Champaign, IL: Stipes.

McLaughlin, John. (1998). "Grow, Baby, Grow." *Education Industry Report,* January, p. 2.

Metcalf, Kim. (1999). *Evaluation of the Cleveland Scholarship and Tutoring Grant Program, 1996–1999.* Bloomington: Indiana Center for Evaluation, Indiana University.

Meyer, Russ. (1999). "The Education of Mike Milken: From Junk-Bond King to Master of the Knowledge Universe." *The Nation,* May 3, p. 11.

Mezzacappa, Dale. (2001a). "Fattah, Edison Clash on Results." *Philadelphia Inquirer,* December 18.

——. (2001b). "Political Tension Led to School Takeover." *Philadelphia Inquirer,* December 23.

Mill, John Stuart. (1838). "On Liberty." In *On Liberty and Other Essays.* New York: Oxford University Press, 1991, pp. 5–130.

Miller, Bill. (2000). "Group Home Ex-Chief Is Indicted." *Washington Post,* July 11, p. A1.

Miller, Julie. (1991). "Report Questioning 'Crisis' in Education Triggers an Uproar." *Education Week,* October 9.

Miller, Matthew. (2001). "Bush Must Be Bold on Vouchers." *Washington Post,* January 1, p. A23.

Mills, Steve. (1997). "Marketing Idea: Be True to Your School—with Visa." *Chicago Tribune*, August 11, p. 1.

Milwaukee Journal Sentinel. (2000). "Vouchers Not Free-for-All." November 25.

Miner, Barbara. (2000). "Voucher Backers Illegally Funnel Money: Wisconsin Supreme Court Race Tainted by Corruption Scandal." *Rethinking Schools*, Summer, p.5.

Mintron, Michael. (1998). *Michigan's Charter School Movement.* East Lansing: Michigan State University, Institute for Public Policy and Social Research, Political Institutions and Public Choice.

Miron, Gary. (2002). Personal communication, March.

Moe, Michael, and Bailey, Kathleen. (1999). *The Book of Knowledge.* San Francisco: Merrill Lynch.

———, and Gay, R. Keith. (1996). *The Emerging Investment Opportunity in Education.* San Francisco: Montgomery Securities.

Moe, Terry (Ed.) (1995). *Private Vouchers.* Stanford, CA: Hoover Institution Press.

Molnar, Alex, Smith, Philip, and Zahorik, John. (2000). "1998–99 Evaluation Results of the Student Achievement Guarantee in Education (SAGE) Program." Accessible at www.uwm.edu/Dept/CERAI/documents.

Molnar, Alex. (1996). *Giving Kids the Business.* Boulder, CO: Westview Press.

Mosbacker, Barrett. (1998). "School Vouchers: Blessing or Threat to Christian Schools?" Accessible at www.charlottechristiannews.com/mosbacker/vouchers.htm.

Murphy, Dan, Nelson, F. Howard, and Rosenberg, Bella. (2000). *The Cleveland Voucher Program: Who Chooses, Who Gets Chosen, Who Pays?* Washington, DC: American Federation of Teachers.

Murray, Shanon D. (1999). "Sylvan to Launch Free Reading Site Today on Internet." *Baltimore Sun*, April 21, p. C1.

Naisbitt, John. (1982). *Megatrends.* New York: Warner Books.

Nasar, Sylvia. (1994). "The American Economy, Back on Top." *New York Times*, February 27, Section 3, p. 1.

Nathan, Joe. (1996). *Charter Schools: Creating Hope and Opportunity for American Education.* San Francisco: Jossey-Bass.

National Center for Education Statistics. (2001). *Home Schooling in the United States, 1999.* Washington, DC: National Center for Education Statistics. Report No. NCES 2001-033.

———. (1999). *Digest of Education Statistics*, Table 70, p. 80. Washington, DC: National Center for Education Statistics. Report No. NCES 1999-036.

———. (1998). *Digest of Education Statistics.* Washington, DC: National Center for Education Statistics.

———. (1997). *Digest of Education Statistics*, Washington, DC: National Center for Education Statistics.

———. (1997). *Digest of Education Statistics*, Table 82, p. 89. Washington, DC: National Center for Education Statistics.

National Commission on Excellence in Education. (1983). *A Nation at Risk.* Washington, DC: National Commission on Excellence in Education.

National Commission on Mathematics and Science Teaching. (2001). *Before It's Too Late.* Washington, DC: National Commission on Mathematics and Science Teaching.

National Committee for Responsive Philanthropy. (1998). *Moving a Public Policy Agenda.* Washington, DC: National Committee for Responsive Philanthropy.

190 *References*

National Public Radio. "All Things Considered," June 27, 2002.

National Research Council. (1999). *Grading the Nation's Report Card: Evaluating NAEP and Transforming the Assessment of Educational Progress.* Washington, DC: National Research Council.

Nelson, Howard F. (2000). "Trends in Student Achievement for Edison Schools, Inc.: The Emerging Track Record." Washington, DC: American Federation of Teachers. Available at www.aft.org.

———. (1998). "Thirteen Ways Rouse Disagrees with GPD's Methodological Perspective." Accessible at www.aft.org/research/Vouchers/mil/13ways.htm.

New York Daily News. (2001). "Public-School Management Firm to Build Office in Harlem, New York." December 19.

New York Times. (2002a). "Public Schooling for Profit." Editorial, May 26.

———. (2002b) "The Wrong Ruling on Vouchers." June 28, p. A26.

Newman, Arthur J. (1978). *In Defense of the American Public School.* Berkeley, CA: Schenkman.

O'Connor, Phillip. (1999). "Reading Tutors Seen as Remedy: K.C. Schools Weigh Pact with Sylvan." *Kansas City Star,* February 26, p. A1.

Office of Educational Research and Improvement. (2000). *The State of Charter Schools 2000.* Washington, DC: U.S. Department of Education.

Ohanian, Susan. (2001). "News from the Test Resistance Trail." *Phi Delta Kappan,* January, pp. 363–366.

O'Neill, James M. (2001). "Edison Roundly Criticized at Forum." *Philadelphia Inquirer,* November 11.

Oplinger, Doug, and Willard, Dennis J. (2002). "Business Breaks Costing Schools," *Akron Beacon Journal,* April 10, p. 1.

———. (1999a). "In Education, Money Talks." *Akron Beacon Journal,* December 13, p. A1.

———. (1999b). "Voucher System Falls Far Short of Goals." *Akron Beacon Journal,* December 14, p. A1.

———. (1999c). "Campaign Organizer Pushes Hard for Changes." *Akron Beacon Journal,* December 15, p. A1.

Oppel, Richard A., and Schemo, Diana Jean. (2000). "Bush Is Warned Vouchers Might Hurt School Plans." *New York Times,* December 22.

Organization for Economic Cooperation and Development (OECD). (2000). *Education at a Glance.* Paris: Organization for Economic Cooperation and Development.

———. (1997). *Education at a Glance.* Paris: Organization for Economic Cooperation and Development.

Oshrat, Carmiel. (2000). "Parents and Doctors Say the Load Students Are Carrying Is Too Heavy. My Aching Back. Make that Backpack." *Philadelphia Inquirer,* May 21, p. A1.

PR Newswire. (2002a). Available at www.prnewswire.com/news/index.html.

———. (2002b). "Shareholder Class Action Filed Against Edison Schools, Inc." May 20.

———. (2002c). "Edison Schools Announce Twelve Expansions and Two New School Openings." May 23.

———. (2001). "Union-Sponsored Study Provides Predictably Biased Evaluation of Schools." February 22.

Parents Advocating School Accountability. (2001). "Controversial Edison Academy Lands Dead Last in District Academic Ratings." October 16 (Press Release).

Patalon, William III. (2000). "Sylvan Has Deal to Sell Prometric." *Baltimore Sun,* January 27, p. D1.

Patton, Robert. (1991). "The Voucher System: Trap for the Unwary." In James R. Patrick (Ed.), *Choice in Education! It Sounds Wonderful But. . . .* East Moline, Illinois: The MacArthur Institute.

Payne, Kevin, and Biddle, Bruce. (1999). "Poor School Funding, Child Poverty, and Mathematics Achievement." *Educational Researcher*, August/September, pp. 4–13.

Pearlstein, Steven. (2002). "Executive Privilege?" *Washington Post*, March 24, p. HI.

People for the American Way Foundation. (2001). "Community Voice or Captive of the Right: A Closer Look at the Black Alliance for Educational Options." Washington, DC: People for the American Way Foundation.

Peterson, Paul. (1997). "School Choice in Milwaukee: Evidence for Gains." Address given at the Cato Institute, Washington, DC, February.

———. (1990). "Monopoly and Competition in American Education." In William H. Clune and John F. Witte (Eds.), *Choice and Control in American Education*. London: Falmer Press.

———, Howell, William G., and Greene, Jay P. (1999). "An Evaluation of the Cleveland Voucher Program after Two Years." Available at www.ksg.harvard.edu/pepg.

———, and Noyes, Chad. (1996). "Under Extreme Duress, School Choice Success." Available at www.ksg.harvard.edu/pepg.

Phaedra Hise, Inc. (1995). "Delivering the Kids." July, p. 76.

Philadelphia Daily News. (2001). "Open School Books." December 11.

Polaneczky, Ronnie. (2001). "Some Truth Would Be Nice." *Philadelphia Daily News*, December 22.

Powell, Brian, and Steelman, Lala Carr. (1996). "Bewitched, Bothered, and Bewildering: The Use and Misuse of State SAT Scores." *Harvard Educational Review*, Fall, pp. 29–59.

Premack, Eric. (2001). California Charter School Development Center, personal communication, August.

Prokop, H. (2001). Personal communication, December.

RPP International. (2001). *The State of Charter Schools 2000: Fourth-Year Report*. Washington, DC: U.S. Department of Education.

Rasell, M. Edith, and Mishel, Lawrence. (1990). *Shortchanging Education: How U.S. Spending on Grades K-12 Lags behind Other Industrialized Nations*. Washington, DC: Economic Policy Institute.

Raubinger, Frederick M., Rowe, Harold G., Piper, Donald L., and West, Charles K. (1969). *The Development of Secondary Education*. Toronto: Collier Macmillan.

Redovich, Dennis. (2001). E-mail to Wisconsin Governor Scott McCallum and various Wisconsin Senators. Redovich operates the Center for the Study of Jobs and Education in Greendale, WI.

Richards, Craig E., Shore, Rima, and Sawicky, Max B. (1996). *Risky Business: Private Management of Public Schools*. Washington, DC: Economic Policy Institute.

Richmond Times-Dispatch. (2001). "Do the Math." Editorial, September 24.

Rickover, Hyman. (1959). *Education and Freedom*. New York: E.P. Dutton.

Robinson, Glenn, and Brandon, David. (1992). *Perceptions about American Education: Are They Based on Facts?* Arlington, VA: Educational Research Service.

Rofes, Eric. (1998). *How Are Districts Responding to Charter Laws and Charter Schools?* Berkeley: Policy Analysis for California Education (PACE).

Rose, Lowell C., and Gallup, Alec M. (2001). "The 33rd Annual Phi Delta Kappa/Gallup Poll of the Public's Attitudes toward Public Schools." *Phi Delta Kappan*, September, pp. 41–58.

Rothman, Robert. (1992). "U.S. Ranks High in International Study of Reading." *Education Week*, September 30, p. 1.

Rothstein, Richard, Carnoy, Martin, and Benveniste, Luis. (1999). *Can Public Schools Learn from Private Schools?* Washington, DC: Economic Policy Institute.

Rouse, Cecilia Elena. (2000). "School Reform in the 21st Century: A Look at the Effect of Class Size and School Vouchers on the Academic Achievement of Minority Students." Working paper #440, Industrial Relations Section, Princeton University, June, 2000. www.irs.princeton.edu/pubs/working_papers.htm.

———. (1998). "Private School Vouchers and Student Achievement: An Evaluation of the Milwaukee Parental Choice Program." *The Quarterly Journal of Economics*, May, pp. 553–602.

Rudner, Lawrence M. (1999). "Scholastic Achievement and Demographic Characteristics of Home-School Students." *Education Policy Analysis Archives*, available at http://epaa.asu.edu/epaa/v7n8.

Safire, William. (2001). "The Sinking Sun?" *New York Times*, March 15.

San Francisco Chronicle. (2001). "Edison's Threat of Success." March 20, p. A20.

Sandham, Jessica L. (2000). "Vouchers Facing Two Major Tests." *Education Week*, September 27, p. 1.

———. (1999). "Ohio Lawmakers Reinstate Voucher Program." *Education Week*, July 14, p. 17.

Savitz, Eric. (1998). "For Adults Only." *Barron's*, March 2, p. 31.

Schemo, Diana Jean. (2001). "Easy Approval Seen for Education Official." *New York Times*, January 11, p. A19.

Schiller, Zach. (2001). "Cleveland School Vouchers: Where the Students Come From." Cleveland: Policy Matters Ohio.

Schnaiberg, Lynn. (1997). "Firms Hoping to Turn a Profit from Charters." *Education Week*, December 10, p. 1.

Schulenberg, John, and Bachman, J. G. (1993). "Long Hours on the Job? Not So Bad for Some Adolescents in Some Types of Jobs: The Quality of Work and Substance Use, Affect, and Stress." Paper presented at the biennial meeting of the Society for Research in Child Development, New Orleans, March.

Schulte, Brigid. (2001). "In Montgomery, Enrichment vs. Inequity." *Washington Post*, December 4, p. A1.

Shah, Angela, and Hobbs, Tawnell D. (2002). "Edison Schools' Hard Knocks." *Dallas Morning News*, June 19, p. A1.

Shanker, Albert F. (1988a). Speech to the National Press Club, Washington, DC, March 31.

———. (1998b). "Convention Plots New Course—A Charter for Change." *New York Times*, July 10, Section 4, p. 7.

———. (1992). "GI Bull". *New York Times*, July 5, Section 4, p. 7.

Silberman, Charles. (1970). *Crisis in the Classroom*. New York: Random House.

Simmons, Tim. (2002). "U.S. Standards Perplex N.C. Schools." *Raleigh News & Observer*, June 2, p. A1.

Slavin, Robert. (1989). "PET and the Pendulum: Faddism in Education and How to Stop It." *Phi Delta Kappan*, June, pp. 752–758.

Smith, Gregory A. (2000). Small Public Schools: Returning Education to Families and Communities. www.asu.edu/educ/epsl/archives.

Smith, John III. (1999). "Tracking the Mathematics of Automobile Production: Are Schools Failing to Prepare Students for Work?" *American Educational Research Journal*, Winter, pp. 835–878.

Snyder, Susan. (2002). "Progress Report for Edison Is Requested." *Philadelphia Inquirer*, May 14, p. B1.

———. (2001). "Edison Hires Away Philly Official." *Philadelphia Inquirer*, September 1.

Sokolar, Paul. (2001). "Edison Fray Ignites in Philadelphia." *Philadelphia Public School Notebook*, November 9.

Solmon, Lewis, Paark, Kern, and Garcia, David. (2001) *Does Charter School Attendance Improve Test Scores? The Arizona Results.* Phoenix, AZ: The Center for Market-Based Education, The Goldwater Institute. Accessible at www.goldwaterinstitute.org.

Somerville, Scott. (undated). *The Politics of Survival: Home-Schoolers and the Law.* Available at the website of the Home School Legal Defense Association, www.hslda.org.

Somerville, Sean. (2000). "Sylvan's Choice: Bigger Isn't Better." *Baltimore Sun*, March 5, p. D1.

Steinberg, Jacques. (2000). "Skeptic Now Sees the Virtue in Teaching Children Online." *New York Times*, December 28, p. A13.

———, and Henriques, Diana B. (2002). "Edison Borrowing $40 Million for Philadelphia School Takeover." *New York Times*, June 4.

Taylor, Jay. (1992). "Desperate for Dollars." *American School Boards Journal.* September, p. 23.

Toch, Thomas. (1998). "The New Education Bazaar." *U.S. News & World Report*, April 27, p. 24.

Todd, Cece. (1998a). "Oversight Overlooked." *Arizona Tribune*, August 25, p. A1.

———. (1998b). "Nobody's Watching Charters." *Arizona Tribune*, August 24, p. A1.

Tomsho, Robert. (2002). "Dallas Schools Weigh Keeping Contract with Edison." *Wall Street Journal*, June 19.

Tortora, Andrea. (2000). "Charters Will Cost CPS $21 Million." *Cincinnati Enquirer*, November 2.

Tyack, David. (1974). *The One Best System: A History of American Urban Education.* Cambridge, MA: Harvard University Press.

———, Thomas, James Thomas, and Benavot, Aaron. (1987). *Law and the Shaping of Public Education.* Madison: University of Wisconsin Press.

Tyson-Bernstein, Harriet. (1988). *A Conspiracy of Good Intentions: America's Textbook Fiasco.* Washington, DC: Council for Basic Education.

Usborne, David. "Math and Fizzies for the Students of Dr. Pepper." (London) Independent, March 29, p. 21.

Vaishnav, Anand. (2002). "Boston Charter School Dropping Links to Edison." *Boston Globe*, May 17.

Van Der Werf, Martin. (1998). "ASU Dean: We're Losing Battle for Public Schools." *Arizona Republic*, August 26, p. B3.

Viadero, Debra. (1997). "Statistics from Cleveland Add Fuel to the Voucher Debate." *Education Week*, August 6.

Vrana, Debora. (1998). "Education's Pied Piper with a Dark Past." *Los Angeles Times*, September, 7, p. A1.

Wainer, Howard. (1993). "Does Spending Money on Education Help?" *Educational Researcher*, December, pp. 22–24.

Wall Street Journal. (2001). "City of Brotherly Thugs." December 3.

Walsh, Mark. (2002). "Still in the Red, Edison Now Hit with a Case of 'Enron-itis.'" *Education Week*, February 20, p. 8.

———. (2000a). "Campaign Cash from Voucher Backers at Issue in Wisconsin." *Education Week*, May 24, p. 21.

———. (2000b). "Seed Money Drying Up for Education-Related Businesses." *Education Week*, August 8, p. 5.

———. (2000c). "Voucher Initiatives Defeated in California, Michigan. *Education Week*, November 13, p. 14.

———. (1998). "Audit Criticizes Cleveland Voucher Program." *Education Week*, April 14, p. 9.

———. (1996). "Brokers Pitch Education as Hot Investment." *Education Week*, February 21, p. 1.

Walsh-Sarnecki, Peggy. (2002a). "Mt. Clemens, Firm to Dissolve Contract." *Detroit Free Press*, June 18.

———. (2002b). "Without a Deal, Inkster Schools Takeover Likely." *Detroit Free Press*, May 13.

Warner, Bob, and Daughen, Joseph R. (2002). "Edison Paid 85G to Gain Access." *Philadelphia Daily News*, January 8.

Washington Post. (2002). "Letting Parents Decide." June 28, p. A28.

———. (2001). "Justice Looking at Enron." December 7, p. E2.

Wasley, Patricia A., Fine, Michelle, King, Sherry P., Powell, Linda C., Holland, Nicole E., Gladden, Robert M., and Mosak, Ester. (2000). *Small Schools, Great Strides.* New York: Bank Street College of Education.

Weir, Fred. (2000). "More Charter Schools." *Christian Science Monitor*, January 31.

Wells, Amy Stuart, et al. (1998). *Beyond the Rhetoric of Charter School Reform: A Study of Ten California School Districts.* Los Angeles: UCLA.

Wells, Amy Stuart. (1993). "The Sociology of School Choice: Why Some Win and Others Lose in the Educational Marketplace." In Edith Rasell and Richard Rothstein (Eds.), *School Choice: Examining the Evidence.* Washington, DC: Economic Policy Institute, pp. 29–48.

Wenglinsky, Harold. (1998). *How Educational Expenditures Improve Student Performance and How They Don't.* Princeton, NJ: Educational Testing Service.

Wheeler, Gerry. (2001). "The High Cost of Low Standards." *Washington Post*, January 4, p. A20.

Wichita Eagle. (2002). "If Edison Knew, It Should Get Thrown Out." February 5.

Wiles, Russ. (2000). "Internet, Education Are Saviors of Underprivileged, Milken Says." *The Arizona Republic*, April 11, p. D1.

Wilgoren, Jodi. (2000a). "A Ruling Voids Use of Vouchers in Ohio Schools." *New York Times*, December 12, p. A1.

———. (2000b). "Vouchers' Fate May Hinge on Name." *New York Times*, December 20, p. A20.

Will, George F. (2002). "Implacable Enemies of Choice." *Washington Post*, June 28, p. A29.

———. (1993). "Meaningless Money Factor." *Washington Post*, September 24, p. A22.

Willard, Dennis J., and Oplinger, Doug. (1999a). "Charter Experiment Goes Awry: Schools Fail to Deliver." *Akron Beacon Journal,* December 12, p. A1.

———. (1999b). "Voucher Plan Leaves Long List of Broken Vows." *Akron Beacon Journal,* December 14, p. A1.

———. (1999c). "School Battle Eludes Voters, Takes Its Cues from Coalitions." *Akron Beacon Journal,* December 15, p. A1.

Williams, Lois C., and Leak, Lawrence. (1995). *The UMBC Evaluation of the TesseracT Program in Baltimore City.* Baltimore, MD: Center for Educational Research, University of Maryland.

Wilson, Sloan. (1958). "It's Time to Close Our Circus." *Life,* March 24, pp. 36–37.

Winerip, Michael. (1998). "Schools for Sale." *New York Times Sunday Magazine,* June 14, p. 42.

Wingert, Pat. (1996). "The Sum of Mediocrity." *Newsweek,* December 2.

Wirtz, Willard, and Howe, Harold II. (1997). *On Further Examination: Report of the Advisory Panel on the Scholastic Aptitude Test Score Decline.* New York: The College Board.

Witte, John F., Sterr, Troy D., and Thorn, Christopher A. (1995). *Fifth-Year Report: Milwaukee Choice Program.* Madison, WI: Department of Public Instruction.

Woodall, Martha. (2002). "Edison Gets Funds to Open City Schools." *Philadelphia Inquirer,* June 5.

———. (2001). "Of Philadelphia Schools or Edison, Who's Really Rescuing Whom?" *Philadelphia Inquirer,* August 19.

Woodward, Tali. (2000a). "Edison Exodus: Will a Teacher Revolt Spell an End to the School Privatization Experiment?" *SF Bay Guardian,* July 19, p. 1.

———. (2000b). "Fisher Nonprofit Nets Millions from Edison Inc. Stock Deal. *San Francisco Bay Guardian,* August 23, p. 12.

———. (2000c). "Attorney General Investigates Fisher Charity." *San Francisco Bay Guardian,* October 4, p. 25.

Wurtzel, Alan. (1993). "Training Students for Work." *Washington Post,* December 23, p. A22.

Wyatt, Edward. (2001a). "Challenges and the Possibility of Profits for Edison." *New York Times,* January 1,

———. (2001b). "Founder of Edison Schools Sells Some of His Stock in Company." *New York Times,* March 23.

———. (2000). "5 Poor New York Performers Could Be Run by Company." *New York Times,* December 21.

———. (1999) "Investors See Room for Profit in the Demand for Education." *New York Times,* November 4, p. A1.

Zehr, Mary Ann. (1999). "Vouchers, Charters, a Mystery to Most." *Education Week,* November 24, 1999, p. 1.

Zernicke, Kate. (2002). "Vouchers: A Shift, but Just How Big?" *New York Times,* June 30, Section 4, p. 3.

———. (2000). "New Doubt Is Cast on Study That Backs Voucher Efforts." *New York Times,* September 15, p. A21.

Index

200 *Index*

subsidiaries of, 130–131
vision of, 129–130, 131
Kohn, Alfie, 48
Koizumi, Prime Minster Junichiro, 42
Kozol, Jonathan, 33
Krueger, Alan, 32, 154

LaPlante, Jeff, 118
Lay, Ken, 18
LeapFrog Toys, 130
Learning disabilities, 95
Lehman Brothers, 7, 125
Leininger, William, 163
Leo, John, 54
Lepeak, Stan, 131, 132
Levine, Arthur, 132
Levy, Harold, 112
Liberals, 61
Life magazine, "Crisis in Education,"
    39–40
Limbaugh, Rush, 154
London Independent, 172, 173
Los Angeles Times, 60
Lott, Trent, 145
Luce, Henry, 40
Lynde and Harry Bradley
    Foundation, 4, 146

MacArthur Foundation, 4
Man in the Gray Flannel Suit, The
    (Wilson), 39
Manno, Brunno, 76
Marshall, Thurgood, 118
Massachusetts Department of
    Education, 48
Massachusetts, test scores, 124
Massey, Joanna, 12
Math and science tests, 53, 60
Math teaching, 47, 94, 106
    in Japan, 49–50
    in the U.S., 49
Math scores, 50–53, 60, 71
    international comparison of, 43
Maxwell, William, 37
McCarthy, Martha, 148

McEwen, Patrick, 148, 149
McLaughlin, John, 125, 126–127, 131
Media, 60–61
    bias of, 52
Megatrends (Naisbitt), 47
Merrill Lynch, 115
Meyer, Russ, 132, 133
Miami Herald, 172
Michigan. *See also* Michigan charter
    schools
    Flint, 19–20, 117
    Mt. Clemens District, 115
    voucher system in, 143, 144
Michigan charter schools, 81, 87, 88,
    90–94
    accountability of, 93–94, 95
    Edison Schools in, 115, 117
    EMOs in, 88, 92–94
    evaluations of, 91–92
    funding of, 90, 93, 98
    innovation and, 95
    management of, 92, 93
    private schools and, 93
    Public School Academies (PSAs),
        91–92
    public schools and, 94–95
    student enrollment in, 91
    in urban areas, 92
Michigan Education Assessment
    Program (MEAP), 91–92
Michigan, National Heritage
    Academies, 95, 127
Middle school, 49–50
    international comparison of, 52
    math test results, 51–52
    science test results, 52
Milken Families Foundation, 131–133
Milken, Lowell, 128
Milken, Michael, 128, 131, 132–133,
    134
Mill, John Stuart, 137–138, 148
Mills, Steve, 174
Milton and Rose Friedman Foundation,
    146
Milwaukee public schools (MPS), 152

Ohio. *See also* Ohio charter schools
kindergarten, 157, 158
school enrollment in, 157, 158
Ohio charter schools, 81, 87
class size of, 98
evaluation of, 97–98
goals of, 95–97
oversight of, 96, 97–98
public funding of, 96, 98
teachers in, 97
Ohio Legislative Office of Education
Oversight, 97–98
Oliver, Judge Solomon, Jr., 158–159
OnlineLearning.net, 135
Oplinger, Doug, 96
Orel, Steve, 48
Organization for Economic
Cooperation and Development
(OECD), 29, 57, 124

Paige, Rod, 62, 145
Paraprofessionals, 102
Pearlstein, Steven, 106
Pennsylvania, textbooks in, 49
People for the American Way, 12
Perry, Rick, 87
Peterson, Paul, 140, 142, 145, 154–155,
156, 157
Phi Delta Kappa International, 3
Philadelphia Daily News, 114
Phonics, 94
Physics, 53–54
Pioneer Institute, 121
PISA (Program for International
Student Assessment), 57–58
Powell, Brian, 24
Prince Edward County, Virginia, 22
Princeton Review, 126
Private and public schools compared,
161
Private education
as investment opportunity, 123–125,
126
openings in, 160
poor people and, 138
vouchers and, 140, 148, 155–156

Private Vouchers (Moe), 140, 160
Privatization of public education, 7,
16–17, 19–20
democracy and, 177
money and, 102
prospects for, 176
venture capital for, 177
Progressive Education Association
(PEA), 38
Eight Year Study, 176
Project SAGE (Student Achievement
Guarantee in Education), 32
Project STAR (Student Teacher
Achievement Ratio), 31–32, 33, 154
Property taxes, 174–175
Public and private schools compared,
161
Public education, 53. *See also* Public
schools
criticism of, 35, 60–62, 71
factory model of, 35–36
false attacks on, 61–62
as left-wing conspiracy, 163
negative studies of, 60–62
poverty and, 73
public opinion and, 35
Public schools. *See also* Public education
bureaucracy, 90
charter schools and, 75–80, 85
criticisms of, 29
private management of, 100–136
as scapegoat for society's failings, 45,
46

Race, 29, 66–68. *See also* African
Americans; Minorities
charter schools and, 84
testing and, 57, 58
and vouchers, 145–146
RAND Corporation, 161–162
Raspberry, William, 54
Ravitch, Diane, 59
Reading skills, 60–62, 68, 124
Reagan, Ronald, 58
Rebarber, Theodor, 121
Reich, Robert, 9